ONE LAST LOOK AROUND

BOOKS BY CLARK LEE

They Call It Pacific

One Last Look Around

ONE LAST LOOK AROUND

CLARK LEE

Duell, Sloan and Pearce · New York

Copyright, 1947, by
CLARK LEE

I

28021

Dedication

Suddenly we saw a miracle. A common GI, a lowly American soldier, wandered onto the deck of the mighty U.S.S. "Missouri" as it lay at anchor in Tokyo Bay. He looked lost and lonesome and forlorn in that galaxy of star-studded admirals and generals of many nations.

We tried to reach the young GI to ask his name, and where he came from and how he happened to be here on this morning of September 2, 1945, in the midst of these big, world-famous men who were now gathered together to write finis to the world's most terrible war. This was *their* show. *His* had been the fighting and dying. But as we stepped forward to talk to him, an admiral angrily ordered us back to our places.

So we never did find out if the GI was real flesh and blood or whether he was an apparition—a wraith representing the Unknown Soldier, Sailor, and Marine, an embodied spirit who appeared to speak for all the silent dead and to shout in silent protest to all that brass and braid, "Hey you, Admiral! You, General! All you self-important men making history here this morning! War isn't a game for people like me. We get killed in wars—even if you don't. Can't you find some other way to make history?"

This book, written for L.K.L., is dedicated to that lost and lonely GI.

Contents

Foreword

THIS FOREWORD SHOULD PROBABLY BE ADDRESSED: "To my fellow guinea pigs."

I myself have felt like a guinea pig ever since talking to a prominent English scientist on Bikini. Until then, I had thought that scientists were interested in making a better life for the people of the world. The Englishman disillusioned me.

"The role of scientists," he said, "is to have fun."

Having fun includes such things as shooting off atom bombs. If you kill or wound 320,000 persons, which is the latest toll from Hiroshima and Nagasaki, why that is purely incidental to having fun. The Englishman would kill that many—or double that many—tomorrow morning. He is all for starting an atomic war right now.

You will meet the Englishman at the end of this book, in the last three chapters, which are concerned more or less directly with the atom bomb.

The first fourteen chapters are about the occupation of Japan, with some sidelights on MacArthur and Tojo and various other people, and some things about Army and Navy Public Relations that couldn't be written during the war.

The next eight chapters tell about a visit we made to Shanghai and Hong Kong, to the countries of southeastern Asia, and to the Philippines in the days of Japan's surrender. Not wanting to claim omniscience, I have not included as predictions in these chapters the things that have happened between the time of the visit and this writing. Those developments are in a separate chapter.

Japan's surrender, of course, did not end the fighting in Asia. The Nationalist-Communist hostilities in China are on our front pages nearly every day. What is less well known is that warfare still goes on in Indo-China and the Netherlands East Indies and, more recently, civil strife has broken out in the Philippines.

In several of the places that we visited, this strife is primarily a conflict of Asiatic versus white man and a conflict that holds a grave future threat for the United States. Americans today are killing Chinese and soon—unless there is a miracle—they will be killing Filipinos. British and French and Dutch, with American backing, are killing Asiatics. All this, of course, makes it seem that the Japanese were right when they told their fellow Asiatics that their only hope of freedom lay in fighting against white domination. Seeking to weld the people of the Orient into a solid bloc against us, Japan planted deeply the seed of her idea of "Asia for the Asiatics." The blood and bones of every Asiatic killed by American or British or French arms nourishes that seed, so that today it flourishes in fertile soil even though Japan lost the war.

Here is a brief introductory picture of the state of affairs in the Orient.

In Japan itself, things have been going smoothly and the greatest revolution in history has, apparently, been set in motion in record time. With Japan under single rule, without conflicting zones of interest, the job has been relatively simple. While in the United States we fumble back toward peacetime pursuits, while the GI in the occupation Army hollers to get home, MacArthur has accomplished such seeming miracles with so little opposition that nobody worries any longer over the fact that Japan is as united in peace as it was in war, and that the Emperor system—which was the soul and body of militaristic Japan—still exists.

Japan, as a nation, is out of the "Asia for the Asiatics" picture, for the time being. But all over Asia, individual Japanese are participating in the struggle of the native peoples for their freedom, always with the theme "Asia for the Asiatics." There are thousands of Japanese in the Chinese armies—on both sides. There are an estimated 100,000 Japanese soldiers "somewhere" in the Netherlands East Indies. The weak Dutch and the inept British cannot even attempt to locate them as they mingle with their fellow Asiatics. It may seem incredible, but because of our post-war actions, the Japanese have a very strong talking point when they say that they were fighting for the freedom of Asia.

Outside of Japan, the most important result of the prolonged post-war hostilities is that the separate nationalisms of Asia are gradually being pushed toward a color-racial alliance, still undefined but nevertheless inevitable if we pursue our present course. The fact of Oriental unification is good, just as Western Hemisphere solidarity is good as a step toward world unification. The fact that it is a product of dislike and even hatred for us, is definitely bad.

Millions of Chinese, both Communists and Nationalists, dislike us because each faction regards the United States as a supporter of its enemy. Millions of Koreans think we are aimless bunglers, who have failed to give them their promised independence so that their country is simply the victim of old-fashioned imperialism—but now in Soviet and American uniforms instead of Japanese.

In Java and Sumatra and French Indo-China, as in India, American guns and tanks and planes have been killing people who wanted their freedom from distant white rule. The United States, guided by so-called statesmen whose concept of one world consisted mainly of threatening Russia, has made loud noises about Iran and Trieste, but has been deaf and blind toward the oppressed peoples of Asia, so that they are forced to turn their thoughts to Russia as their sole hope for the future.

The tragedy of this is that the people of Asia looked to us as liberators. In their hearts, they nourished a dream of American-sponsored freedom. Instead, they got American-made bullets in their backs.

In the Philippines we have tossed away, through our ineptitude, our selfishness and rudeness, many of the benefits of a half-century of good work. It may be difficult to believe, but a Filipino official said in mid-1946: "We were better off under the Japs." And this man had been imprisoned and tortured by the Japs. His wife was killed by the Japs.

Japanese military imperialism is dormant, defeated for the present. But imperialism still flourishes in Wall Street and in the ruins of the Tokyo Ginza, in the Paris Bourse, in the Queen's Palace in the Netherlands, in Churchill's Tory party in England—everywhere that men believe that the oppression and enslavement of weak people is the prerogative of the strong.

Most Americans are anti-imperialists. But the average American makes neither foreign policy nor wars. He merely fights the wars. If the average American does not want his son to go to war again, he must be vigilant against our imperialists.

The average man in Asia is determined to resist imperialism, especially white imperialism, if it costs his life. Possessing the atom bomb, we can dominate Asia for the next few decades and ram imperialism down the throats of the Oriental peoples. But such a course could only end in the disaster and defeat that every empire has met eventually. The alternative is friendship on a basis of equality with the nations of Asia, including Japan, when Japan's own imperialists are finally crushed—which has not happened as yet.

In the meantime we must remember that even though Japan lost the war, she taught the nations of Asia a lesson. Here are the words of General Carlos Romulo, the Filipino leader who is the most articulate (English-language) voice of the Orient:

"It must never be forgotten that Japan nearly accomplished her purpose in the Far East. Until this war the white man was considered a god in the Orient and often an unjust and fearsome divinity. Japan broke that fetish and revealed him as a man who could suffer humiliation and defeat. That was an Asiatic victory that will not be forgotten by races who have suffered and resented imperialism."

Japan failed, for the moment, in her effort to unite the Orient against the white man. We must be careful that we do not—after defeating Japan in the military struggle—throw away the ideological victory through our own stupidity. . . .

Having the atom bomb, we could in a few hours put an end to this world of struggle and bloodshed and oppression and tyranny. We could, in fact, put an end to the world. Period. The atom bomb, in my opinion, has by the simple fact of its existence put an end to the world as we have known it up to now—a world that, despite its wars and upheavals, has not changed in essential pattern since the beginning of man, a world of begetting, harvesting, eating, development of knowledge, of government. A world in which man has played around at destroying his own kind in successive wars with ever more destructive weapons. That world exists no longer.

When I saw from the air the brown-looking wasteland where part of Nagasaki had been before the atomic bomb exploded, and later walked through the streets of what used to be Hiroshima, I became convinced that the old world had ended. There can be no more playing around at destruction. We will never again enjoy the luxury of fighting a war in which only thirty million people are killed. There will never be another naval battle. Anti-aircraft guns mean nothing. Tanks are a cave-man's weapon. Submarines mean nothing. Big bombers are a child's toys. TNT means nothing.

Almost nothing means anything. The atomic bomb is king and we are doomed men with but a few years to live—unless . . . Unless we can lick the bomb before it licks us, and "us" means everybody on the face of the earth.

Meantime there is no use worrying, in the sense of worrying over one's safety, about the atom bomb. When they start pushing the buttons and shooting off stratospheric rockets, landing them halfway around the world, it will all be over too quickly for worry. So we might just as well go on with procedural squabbles in UN sessions, with baseball and Hollywood and Congress and other trivial matters; with worrying about the growing anti-white movement in Asia and the danger to us of a united Asiatic people. We might as well think in terms of "colonies," "aggressors," "democracy in Japan," "the Commy menace," "British perfidy"—familiar words, even reassuring words because we can understand them.

We might as well reassure ourselves as much as possible because from here on it's one last war or no war, it's everybody or nobody, all or nothing at all, one world or none.

ONE LAST LOOK AROUND

Chapter One

MacArthur Saw It Coming

I̶F̶ I TOLD THEM BACK IN WASHINGTON WHAT I believe, they would think me crazy. Some of them do now."

General of the Army Douglas MacArthur rocked back in a wicker chair on the porch of his headquarters at Tacloban, on the Island of Leyte.

"What I believe," MacArthur went on, "is that the Japs will ask for peace after they lose the Philippines. They wouldn't believe me in Washington. For years, they haven't believed me.

"I have told them for years that these Philippine Islands are the key to the western Pacific. The battle of the Pacific will be decided here!"

He gestured with his unlit pipe to emphasize his point.

"And after I wipe out the Jap in the Philippines, Tokyo will ask for peace!"

That was on Christmas Eve of 1944, a wet, muddy Christmas Eve. The soggy palms dripped a continuous stream of raindrops into the morass of a road outside the stuccoed house. But MacArthur was happy. By landing at Leyte two months earlier he had started his reconquest of the Philippines, started on the campaign which he foresaw would bring victory. His voice was hard with confidence as he made his prediction which, at that time, sounded overoptimistic not only to Washington but to many people who had become convinced in the course of three years fighting that Japan could never surrender short of nearly total annihilation. . . .

And now, eight months later, on August 24th of 1945, we were sitting on a muddy, windswept hillside on Okinawa waiting to go with the occupation troops into a country that had yielded for the

3

first time in its history of twenty centuries. Behind was a long road, a road of many branches that led from the flaming wreckage of Pearl Harbor and the green jungles of Bataan to these glistening coral runways of Okinawa, where the big transport planes were poised and waiting for MacArthur's signal that would send them into Japan.

No one knew what was at the end of the road. The war that was now ending had not been just a war for our enemies, but a holy mission. The Japanese people had been exalted by a mystical, religious fervor that had made them give their lives without question. They had shown themselves brutal, treacherous enemies, but very brave and very determined. For the Japanese to surrender was not like another nation losing a war. Another nation could shrug its shoulders and say, "Oh well, that territory probably didn't belong to us anyway, and there's no oil there." The Japanese code called for death before surrender. Yet, with seven million trained troops in the field and with all Japan an armed camp, they were going to let us walk into their country. They had announced their intention of accepting the Potsdam declaration on August 14th and the date for our occupation was set for August 30th. It was to be a peaceful occupation. Or was it? None of us could quite believe that the Japs would stand by peaceably while we took over their country. More likely they would pull the whole occupied Orient and Japan itself down on their heads in a last bloody outburst of murder, rape, and suicide, as they had done in Manila. After hearing for so long that the Japs would fight suicidally until all of them were dead—and, indeed, they had fought that way for three years—it was difficult to believe they were actually preparing to lay down their arms. On Okinawa, we were at the front door of a haunted house. We didn't believe in ghosts, but we couldn't be sure what was beyond the door.

The days crawled by. The typhoons blew themselves out to the north, and then suddenly it was occupation day minus one.

Nobody slept the night before we went into Japan.

It was a little before midnight when the troops of the 11th Airborne Division started climbing up the ladders into the big bellies of the C–54s, rifles and carbines in hand and grenades strapped to their jump suits. They were restless until the props started turning, eager to end the suspense after long days and nights of waiting, sleeping in pup tents while typhoon winds drove cold rains across the island.

The atmosphere was that of an invasion, a beachhead, an assault

4

landing. The familiar emptiness tugged at your stomach. Nobody knew what was ahead. It would be at least a week before we had sufficient troops ashore to beat off the attack the Japs were capable of making against us with the forces they had in the vicinity of Atsugi, and until then anything could happen. Kamikazes might be wheeled out of secret mountain airdromes to dive onto our ships in Tokyo Bay. The airfield might be seized and our troops there isolated. The GIs tightened their ammo belts and kept disappearing into the planes.

General Robert Eichelberger was there, watching and waiting his turn. General Bob had personally led one of the decisive battles of the war when, pistol in hand, he and his men covered the last few bloody yards into Buna and brought us around the point of New Guinea and onto the straight road to Tokyo. Eichelberger's Eighth Army was to have assaulted the Tokyo area in the fall of 1945 and captured the capital. Now, like the rest of us, he was hoping Tokyo would fall into our hands without a fight. But he wasn't counting on it too strongly.

We were in the second group of planes and it was two o'clock when our B–17, supplied by the Strategic Air Forces for a party of correspondents, took to the air, winging smoothly along at ten thousand feet. Dawn came surprisingly soon and suddenly Fuji was ahead, beautiful in the soft light above the clouds and then we were circling Atsugi, seeing with a quick catch of excitement the parked planes with the red Rising Sun on their wingtips and fuselage and our own giant transports landing and taxiing; staring through the ground mist across the plains toward the heart of Japan, the great cities of Yokohama and Tokyo.

The plane landed and taxied to a stop.

"How does it look?" I asked Frank Robertson, who had landed ahead of us.

"A pushover," he said. "They even have breakfast ready in the barracks. Better go over and get some."

We followed directions, walking gingerly across the airfield as if each step might blow up the country. Japs were scurrying here and there, doing their busy best to be helpful. The advance party had already been on the field for two days and the Japs were used to Americans, but we weren't accustomed to them yet. There were scores of new, powerful fighters. Guns had been removed from the planes and the propellers were gone from the fighters.

5

To my amazement, the first white-coated waiter in the wooden mess hall called out my name, "Ree-san! Herro, herro. So gradu you returning Japan." I recognized him as a former employee of the Imperial Hotel grill room in Tokyo, once one of the best restaurants in the world. The Japanese government, knowing that the hotel waiters spoke a few words of English, had rounded them up in the few days before the occupation and taken them to Atsugi to make the Americans feel at home. They had also found, somewhere, eggs, toasted bread, butter, sugar, and what passed for coffee. I was just sampling the noxious-smelling beverage when a hand fell on my shoulder.

"Clark Lee!" said an excited voice. I looked up into the bespectacled eyes of Mizota-san, Princeton graduate of some twenty-five years ago, master of the English language and Japan's interpreter at all the important world naval conferences since the early '20's. His mother was a resident of California and he had always seemed more American than Japanese, a man of moderation who hated the job that forced him, as frequent translator at pre-war Navy Department press conferences, to apologize in double-talk for the actions of Japan's militarists. We exchanged greetings, hesitating to shake hands.

"What's going to happen?" I asked. "Is all this really true? Is the surrender genuine or is the whole thing going to blow up?"

His first words showed that our apprehensions had not been groundless. "By gosh, Clark," he said, using his strongest expletive, "I honestly don't know. I went to Manila with the Navy people negotiating the occupation plans. We asked for a delay in the date and General MacArthur thought we were stalling. We really weren't. We didn't know how we could control the hotheads. You know enough of our recent history to get the picture, to understand the likelihood of some group or groups taking things into their own hands, proclaiming that the Emperor was forced into the surrender, and continuing to fight."

We walked back out to the airfield. "We were worried stiff when the Americans picked Atsugi for the landing," Mizota went on. "This was the home base of three hundred naval Kamikazes and we didn't know if we could handle them or not. A group of them flew over Tokyo and dropped hastily printed pamphlets saying they intended to fight to the end, regardless of propaganda to the effect that the Emperor had agreed to surrender."

The Japanese negotiators had been scheduled to take off from Atsugi for their flight to Manila, but in fear of their lives they sneaked out from another field and took a roundabout route to Ie Shima, where they transferred to American planes. On their return they found that a number of people had committed hara-kiri in Tokyo, that a group of diehards had attacked Radio Tokyo and attempted to seize the station to choke off the source of the "treacherous and lying reports" of capitulation, and that the Kamikazes at Atsugi were still adamant. In frustrated protest, a number of the Kamikazes climbed into their planes and crashed them in Tokyo Bay, to demonstrate their spirit to the people.

Mizota was chosen as one of a Naval Office party sent to Atsugi to interview the young would-be suicides, who had gone through the ceremony of death and sworn to give their lives to the Emperor by "body-crashing" their planes into our ships. The pilots were lined up in front of the hangars, facing their explosive-laden planes. An admiral addressed them, "It is the Imperial wish that Japan cease fighting and therefore you are relieved of your promise to die."

The spokesman for the Kamikazes stepped forward. "Inasmuch as we are already dead we are no longer in a position to obey this new command of His Imperial Majesty. Our lives passed out of our hands at the funeral ceremonies when we joined the Special Attack Corps. We must carry out our oath to die against the enemy." This was a typical Japanese impasse and no one could think of a way to get around it. The Navy representatives returned disconsolately to Tokyo, fearful that some of the suicide fliers would get loose and dive into our ships, thereby renewing hostilities and bringing a storm of atom bombs down on Tokyo and other parts of Japan.

"We held a conference at the Navy Office," Mizota said, "with everyone scared to death. Then, one of the officers got a brilliant inspiration, a last-ditch thought: we would send for the parents of the aviators and ask them to plead with the boys. Hastily, the addresses were looked up and special messengers were dispatched all over Japan, even to remote mountain villages, summoning mothers and fathers to Tokyo. They came in trains and special planes. The admiral talked to them, and convinced them that it was the Emperor's will that the war be brought to an end. The strange group proceeded to Atsugi."

In the barracks, the parents pleaded with their sons, begging them to listen to the Imperial command. "The clinching argument," Mizota said, "was a government-authorized promise that the Kamikazes would be given an issue of candy, sweets, and toys for their brothers and sisters if they went home. That did it. The kids packed up and left. We took the propellers off their planes, so nobody could sneak back, and removed the guns. But it was really a close call because we knew that if there was even one incident you would naturally regard it as evidence of bad faith and believe the negotiations were a trick."

I walked back to our plane, watching the C–54s come in on schedule, empty themselves of troops, and take off again for Okinawa and a new load. The field could only accommodate a couple of dozen planes at a time, which made our build-up exasperatingly and perhaps dangerously slow. There were some fifteen Japanese divisions in the Tokyo-Yokohama area, and nobody knew if they had been disarmed. We would not feel safe until we had at least two divisions on land, which would take nearly eight days. Meantime, the marines were coming ashore at the Yokosuka naval base a few miles away and Halsey's ships stood offshore ready to cut loose at the first sign of treachery. The landing was being carried out like a military operation on a hostile beachhead and as the troops landed on the field they began to spread out and form a perimeter for defense. Our orders were to stay inside the perimeter, but curiosity overcame our uncertainties.

In accordance with instructions, the Japanese had assembled a group of battered trucks and passenger cars, and we climbed into an ancient Plymouth and instructed the driver, "Yokohama, *dozo* (please)." He grinned and drove off the airfield, falling in line with a procession of shaky Jap Army vehicles which were carrying the vanguard of our occupation troops. Of course, trucks don't tiptoe, but those trucks seemed to be doing just that, reflecting the grim apprehension of the soldiers who fingered their M–1s and carbines as they stared from the narrow rural road at a deserted countryside we all believed to be hostile. It was as if each turn of a wheel brought us nearer to contact with a detonating wire connected to a giant booby trap. A half-mile from the airfield, the trucks turned right at the direction of a black-uniformed policeman, but we noticed a Yokohama sign pointing straight ahead and told the driver to follow that road.

From then on, we traveled in hiccoughs. Every few miles the Plymouth broke down and the driver got out to attempt to fix the carburetor. Frequently we ran out of water, and the little Jap would grab a pail and rush off to replenish his supply. Around the airport we saw only sentries, their stiff backs turned to us and their rifles pointing into the rice paddies. They were not showing us disrespect, but guarding the route. The occupation plan had not called for us to use this road, and as we neared Yokohama we caught some people by surprise, out of doors. Seeing us, the women covered their faces and turned their backs, the children scattered in terror and the men stood stonily. Ten hours later, when we drove back down that same road to Atsugi, a few of the kids were shouting "Heroro" and giving a tentative "V" signal with their fingers, and the farm women were smiling. All over Japan the change was as quick as that, from desperate fear of an unknown invader to welcome reassurance that there would be no mass rape or bayoneting of small children.

The first reaction of the GIs, when they saw the ruins of Yokohama and later of Tokyo and other cities, was "My God! And these people had the nerve to go to war with us." Probably ninety per cent of the residential sections of Yokohama had been destroyed by fire bombs, and the survivors were living in corrugated-tin shanties built where their homes and shops had once been. Before the war you never saw a beggar in Japan, but now a good proportion of the people looked like scavengers in their patched and dirty clothing—this in a country whose cleanliness and neatness had been world famous. Seeing Japan after the visits of the B–29s, seeing the miserable way of life among the survivors, it was impossible for the GIs to realize how Japan had ever been able to build an air force or a navy. A lot of our troops, forgetting how well the Japanese had performed in battle, said, "We've been fighting babies." That sympathetic reaction contributed greatly to the quick disappearance of animosity between the occupation forces and the Japanese.

The first of the airborne troops were just arriving at the New Grand Hotel in Yokohama when we pulled up at the door. We went upstairs to the dining room and, just to see what would happen, ordered a bottle of beer. We got a bottle of beer. A waiter in a clean white coat served it, accepted our occupation money without question, and brought change in Bank of Japan notes. From the windows of the New Grand, overlooking the undamaged waterfront buildings which hid the wasteland behind it and the squatters' huts, the city looked intact—as if there had never been a war. That was the way the Japs acted.

9

"Let's get going for Tokyo," somebody urged. "Let's take a chance."

As soon as we turned onto the paved road leading to Tokyo, still as bumpy and rutted as when I last rode it four years before, we began to feel lonesome. Just past the railroad station, our car surrendered once more with a series of choking gasps. The nimble chauffeur leaped out and signaled to a passing Jap Army truck loaded with unarmed Jap troops. We waited in suspense. Here was the first test: How would these soldiers react?

The truck swung around promptly, the soldiers jumped out and walked over. A brief explanation from the chauffeur, and they joined in giving us a mighty push. The car coughed into motion and we bounced on toward Tokyo, waving our thanks. Tokyo and Yokohama were really one continuous city divided by a river, with factories of all sizes built up along the railroad tracks for a twelve-mile stretch. *Were* is right. Now this whole area, for mile after mile, was a wilderness of charred ruins, with only an occasional steel and concrete industrial plant standing more or less intact.

A few people were walking along or waiting for street cars, in contrast to the pushing throngs that had once milled along this main road. Some tried studiously to avoid seeing us, others glanced cautiously, and still others broke into smiles. At the river bridge we stopped at a barricade guarded by sentries standing in the familiar swayback Jap Army slouch, rifles with long bayonets cradled on one hip.

"*Shimbun-kisha,*" we explained. "*Domei no tsushin-sha yukitai desu.*"

An interpreter in civilian clothes sprang out of a recently constructed wooden shack and we repeated, "American newspapermen. We want to go to Domei News Agency."

"Ah, so, so," he said, looking at our credentials. "I believe arrangements were that no Americans are to be allowed in Tokyo until the formal occupation. Not all the Japanese have been disarmed yet. However . . ."

We thanked him, zigzagged through the barrier, and rode on through the endless devastation. There was just enough left of Tokyo to be able to recognize our whereabouts and to guide us to the business center where most of the big buildings of the industrial corporations, banks, and shipping companies were still standing in stony splendor across from the Imperial Palace. We turned into the circu-

10

lar driveway of the Imperial Hotel and the clerk at the desk recognized me at once. He didn't offer to shake hands.

I signed the register as "the first newspaperman to return to Tokyo," and asked for my old room, No. 312. Harry Brundidge, my fellow correspondent, pulled out the key to 384 which he had taken as a souvenir back in 1940 and held it up for the clerk to inspect. "Don't bother to send bellboys up with us. We have no luggage. We'll just have baths and come down and eat lunch."

The regular lunch hour was over, but they opened the doors and we went into the uninspiring room which even before the war could never have ranked with the gay places of the world. Now it looked definitely run-down. The tablecloths and napkins were dirty; the head waiter was wearing a patched and mended civilian suit that was really filthy. Gone were the bright-colored kimonos of the waitresses, replaced by dull-colored, baggy mompei—the one-piece overalls that women were forced to wear in wartime. The Japs treated us attentively but without extra fuss, as if it were a common thing for Americans to be eating in the Imperial. We found a few old friends among the customers at the ten or twelve occupied tables, consuming with appreciation an atrocious meal of watery soup and fish garnished with a horrible, thick soy-bean sauce—this in the best and at that time only restaurant in Tokyo, a place where only war profiteers and black-market operators could afford to go.

What the Japanese considered black-market luxuries in food and clothing would be regarded by Americans as a starvation diet and rags. Tokyo's industrialists and others who made money from the war could buy more rice for their families and occasionally lobster or a piece of meat, or perhaps a piece of cloth for a kimono to be worn in the house. They could also get small quantities of gasoline or charcoal for their automobiles. Those were their luxuries. It was not until GI goods began to circulate—soap, cigarettes, tinned stuffs, everything that had disappeared from wartime Japan—that a real black market sprang up and flourished.

After lunch we went down a half-flight of stairs to the barber shop of the Imperial. A Japanese gentleman, or so he looked and acted, was just climbing into the chair but he signaled Brundidge to go ahead and I got into the other free chair. Jim McGlincy stared from the doorway. "You mean to say you are going to let those Butchers of Bataan put a razor to your throats?"

"Why, sure. Shave, please!"

11

"Not me," said Jim, disappearing in a hurry.

The hot towels were hot, if not exactly snow-white, the razors sharp, and the after-shave lotion as sweetly stinking as it was before the war. A telephone call from the office informed us, "Manager-san very anxious to see you."

Up in the lobby, the suave and middle-aged Inamaru-san came out from behind the counter, bowing and hissing in obvious pleasure. "Ah, Mr. Brundidge, Mr. Ree, so happy that you have come back to stay with us. It's been a wrong, wrong time. And how are your wives?" Something old had been subtracted from Inamaru. He had formerly been one of the most impeccably dressed men in the Far East, always in perfectly tailored morning clothes in his office and in fine tweeds when he strolled outside or played golf. Now he wore the "national uniform," a semi-military, two-piece khaki suit of flimsy material, a garb that originated in Manchukuo and became compulsory in Japan after Pearl Harbor.

"Ha, ha, ha," Inamaru threw back his head and laughed. That was our introduction to Japan's national salute to the conquerors. In liberated countries the welcome had been "Victory," in conquered areas a sullen silence or a self-pitying whine. In Japan, the greeting was a re-echoing chorus of "ha, ha, ha's." We found it a bit disconcerting to be met with hilarious laughter instead of the Kamikazes or hand grenades we had more than half expected. And doubly so as we learned that the mirth usually preceded a tale of bomb damage from those so-funny B–29s.

"Ha, ha," Inamaru went on. "My wardrobe destroyed when B–29 dropped bombs on hoteru." A plane, crashing in flames after being hit by ack-ack, had jettisoned its bomb load in this central area of Tokyo near the Imperial Palace. One wing of the hotel caught fire and was partially destroyed, but the damage was not apparent from the outside or from the lobby.

Every Jap had a bomb story, and each one was just screamingly humorous. They even had pet names for the Superforts that destroyed their homes and businesses and killed or maimed members of their families. "B–ko" (Miss B), they called the big bombers, using an affectionate contraction. After a big attack, Tokyo Rose would jest about a "raidy night." The kids in the streets could identify a Mustang fighter that flew up from Okinawa on an escort mission, and distinguish it from a carrier-based Grumman Hellcat.

In all Japan I met only two people who were resentful about our

12

bombing. One was the English-speaking manager of the Japan tourist bureau, who didn't mind so much when his two Tokyo residences were burned but who complained bitterly at the destruction of his house in Yokohama. The other was a doctor in Hiroshima, of whom more later. The rest of the Japanese simply were not angry about it. They accepted it as the fortunes of war and held no grudges, made no post-war speeches about the barbarity of attacking civilians.

Contrary to my own expectations and those of many others who had lived in Japan, the bombing did not cause any panic. I investigated this as carefully as possible and the only reports I heard were of some people "who ran out of their houses in panic and contrary to government orders just stood on the street corner instead of throwing sand on the fires." They called that panic in Japan! They should have seen Manila under the bombs, at first, or France or Poland or Germany, or the hysteria along Broadway when the cops chase a robber around Times Square.

After the fires consumed their homes, the Japs went back into the rubble, gathered what possessions remained, and either started to build a shanty on the ruins or packed up the family and went down to the station to wait in line, sometimes for days, for a train back to the country where everybody had a father, a cousin, or a brother. Some four to five million people evacuated the capital in the four months covering the period of the heavy fire raids and they were still leaving when we reached Tokyo, standing in columns ten wide and a half-mile long around the railway stations.

One of the people we met at lunch the first day in the Imperial was young Bobby Vargas. His father was the Filipino politician, Jorge Vargas, whose fate it had been to remain in Manila as mayor when the Japs came and who later made the mistake of joining the puppet government and going to Tokyo as ambassador of the Jap-proclaimed "Republic of the Philippines." Bobby said he would guide us out to the embassy, and on the way we detoured to make a sentimental journey.

I had once planned to get married in Tokyo (developments in the Sino-Japanese war transferred the marriage to Hong Kong) and, because my wife's ancestor King Kalakaua of Hawaii had once paid a state visit to the Emperor Meiji (whom he roused out of bed in the palace after a night of roistering), the Japanese press had taken a great interest in her arrival. The papers reported, "After their marriage Mr. and Mrs. Lee intend to build a love nest in Tokyo and live

13

happily for many years. That is their plan." Actually it had been our plan to rent the home of Captain Maxwell Taylor of the U. S. Army, later major general and commander of the 101st Airborne Division. We looked now for the house but "love nest no stop, all burning down." So had almost everything else in the residential districts of Tokyo, which for me has always been the most depressing city in the world. If the city is eventually rebuilt with more parks, more light and air for its millions, without the drab wooden slums, then the bombing will have done some good. There were a few pre-blitz modern apartments and I had volunteered to post a sign on the Nonomiya building reserving it for USASTAF. From aerial photos it looked intact, but we found it gutted.

The Philippines "Embassy" nearby, facing the Yasukuni Shrine where the spirits of Japan's war heroes were honored, was still in one piece but its occupants were the most unhappy men I have ever met. Jorge Vargas and his colleagues who had bet on the wrong horse felt themselves thrice traitors—to their own country, to the United States, and to MacArthur who, whether the reader likes him or not, is regarded by the Filipinos as pretty close to God. In other circumstances, Vargas might now be holding a high position in the government of the new Republic of the Philippines.

Talking to us in Tokyo, Vargas said, "President Quezon requested me to remain behind in Manila after he left for Corregidor with General MacArthur and to try to make the occupation easier for our people." Seeing the forces of Bataan go down, feeling his country deserted by the United States, Vargas and a handful of other Filipino politicians had then taken the next step of outright collaboration in the puppet regime established by Japan. "If I could only see General MacArthur now," he said pleadingly, almost in tears, "I feel I could make him understand." Then wistfully, "Do you think he would receive me face to face?"

I don't think Vargas got his interview. His son Bobby took up residence in the Imperial after making friends with an American signal-corps sergeant who roomed there until the hotel was requisitioned for "colonels and above" and for visiting V.I.P.s. One morning some C.I.C. men knocked on the door and asked, "Are you Bobby Vargas?" "Yes, I am." "Come with me," a lieutenant ordered. "Why don't you take my brother Eddie who is in the next room?" Bobby suggested. "He's much better'n me." By "better," Bobby meant that his brother had worked more openly for the Jap cause. "I'll take you both," said

14

the lieutenant, ordering his men to "pull 'em out of here." Later the entire Vargas family was jailed.

We found the reporters in Domei's big newsroom busy that first day sending out news to the world or laboriously translating, and character-writing with pencils, items about the occupation. They took time off to greet us as professional colleagues and then turned back to their work. Their attitude was that the occupation was something that had to be put up with, but they made it apparent that they expected the Americans to keep hands off, thank you, and not disturb working men performing essential duties. On the first day, they had already dispatched reporters to apply to MacArthur for "credentials" to cover the occupation and surrender, side-by-side with American correspondents. The credentials were granted, in line with MacArthur's ideas of free speech and an informed Japanese press. Domei however was soon put out of business and replaced by a new agency.

In anticipation of the arrival of American troops in Tokyo, the Japanese government had been busy trying to organize matters so that the womenfolk would be spared from rape, which, so the populace had been informed throughout the war, was a specialty of GIs. In one part of the capital the police located a cluster of fifteen or twenty houses which were still intact—no mean feat in the burned-out city. The occupants were rooted out to join the other homeless, and the houses reconditioned as brothels. Police advertised in the papers for "600 experienced or inexperienced prostitutes" and went into business. They also ordered the one undestroyed brewery to start producing beer, and a distillery to manufacture a fiery liquor which was poured into beer bottles and indiscriminately labeled "gin" or "whiskey." These moves were the forerunner of the beer and dance halls that later sprang into existence amid the ruins of the Ginza, once Tokyo's Fifth Avenue, under the sponsorship of private enterprise.

We went out one night to inspect the original police-operated prostitution quarters and, although Tokyo was then out of bounds to troops, the entryway was jammed with jeeps. GIs and MPs were running around excitedly, waving guns, and we thought for a moment that at last the long-expected anti-American uprisings had started. But an MP explained:

"Some lieutenant and sergeant just stuck up the cashier of the joint with a tommy gun and got away with about six thousand yen."

It developed that the two Americans had purchased at the central cashier's office a ticket for seventy yen which allowed them to go into any of the houses. Dissatisfied, they later demanded their eleven dollars back and then, apparently on a whim, took all of the money at gun point.

The officially sponsored houses of prostitution did not altogether do away with rape. I heard of three cases, involving some twenty Americans, in the first three weeks in Japan when a few of our troops took out their long-nourished anger and let loose their appetites with helpless women as victims.

But in the first hours in Tokyo, as more and more Japs saw our small group riding or walking through the streets and discovered that we did not intend to rape the women or kill the children, the tension gradually wore off. Although they did not show it in their faces, the Japanese were badly in need of reassurance about our conduct, and the first contact, their first glimpse of the strange uniforms and white skins, always gave them a shock. We walked past the Takarazuka Theatre. About a thousand people, drab in their mompei, were standing in line waiting to buy tickets for the next performance. Seeing the photographers with us, busy snapping pictures of the ruins, about half the crowd abandoned the show and tagged along gingerly behind us. After walking for an hour we had picked up nearly a thousand curious people, who chatted among themselves about our every move but kept a cautious distance behind us, except for some irrepressible small boys who had to touch our clothing and carbines.

On a smaller scale similar scenes were enacted all over Japan in the areas successively occupied by our troops. At first there were fear and caution on both sides, tentative contacts, and then a swift coming together that developed into the most amazing operation of its kind in history—an occupation in which there was not a single instance of sabotage, not a wire cut or a gas tank set afire, not—except when Americans took the offensive—a single shot fired or a clash of any kind between these bitter enemies. The whole thing was crazy, upside down, completely contrary to everything that experience led us to expect. The war was erased, forgotten, it had never happened. Japan and America had always been good friends. These ruins? Oh, so sorry city not beautiful, have very bad earthquake and everything burned down.

The people walking in the streets of Tokyo, turning to stare at us,

16

were the sons, daughters, brothers, and sisters of the men who tortured and killed our captured fliers, who staged the Bataan death march, who starved 25,000 Australian and Dutch prisoners to death, who bayoneted little Filipino babies. Their relatives had died under our bombs. A few hours before we landed at Atsugi we had hated them bitterly and been thirsty for revenge; we had expected them to hate us. Yet at the end of our first day in Tokyo our arms were weary from returning the salutes of soldiers and from waving at babies.

We had anticipated malice, treachery, whining, such as we heard in Germany and Italy, and there was none. In one of the early days we went up to the Foreign Office press section, now occupying a portion of the new Navy Office in lieu of its blitzed quarters. The spokesman, Mr. T. Kase, who had taken the job only a few hours before, greeted us cordially in his Harvard accent and said, "Japan is anxious to do everything possible to start on the long road to—shall I say—friendship. As Stevenson said, It takes two to kiss and it takes two to be friends. Japan is ready on her part. We expect to be treated firmly because we know we are the vanquished, but we hope now you won't be harsh with us."

The Japanese did have some trouble getting the idea that we were complete bosses. They tried to hedge, to stall, to tell MacArthur how to word his directives in the light of Japanese psychology. The newspapers got away with as many articles in this tone as they could, but as soon as they saw MacArthur meant business and was cracking down, they changed their tune and played the *Star-Spangled Banner* and *Democracy March* as loudly as possible, turning their hatred against the militarists and the big businessmen who "led us into the war." In explaining their defeat, they could always say that they were ready to fight to the last—as indeed they were—and quit only because the Emperor so ordered. To protect their own feelings, they wanted us to exhibit all respect for the Emperor.

"There is one bad thing going on," the naval interpreter Mizota said to me, "and that is those planes flying over the Imperial Palace. Why don't they tell those aviators not to buzz the palace? They can circle the city all they want but they shouldn't go over the palace. The people don't like it."

The people soon got used to it, however, after MacArthur summoned the Son-of-Heaven to the American Embassy and the Emperor obeyed the command of the barbarous infidel. Afterward, when Hirohito "democratized" himself and moved about to visit factories

17

and public gatherings, and then declared himself that the idea of his divinity was a myth, the stage had passed in which the Japanese needed an excuse for their capitulation. But that came later.

Mizota had one other complaint. "The American Army people we dealt with in arranging for the occupation have been splendid, firm but courteous. On the other hand, the American admiral whose ship we boarded at Yokosuka the other day kept us sitting for five hours in his cabin without offering a glass of water or a cigarette, or suggesting that we might like to visit the head." The Japs expected all the amenities. They knew they had to pay the price, but they wanted to talk terms over tea and cigarettes.

After the first two days, I was able to return to Tokyo only intermittently until we finally moved in from Atsugi, but Brundidge held court in his room and on my visits I met many callers, from newspapermen to nobles. One Japanese ex-Army major passed out gold-plated lapel pins entitling the wearer to life membership in night clubs he intended to open—the U. S. Army permitting. He also had a good supply of sake and freshly killed beef. A baron who was manager of the beautiful Kawana Hotel and Golf Club offered to turn the place over to us, explaining that only one of the two courses was in shape, the other having been used by the Army to grow vegetables. "I'll fix up a game for you with Prince-Prime Minister Higashi-Kuni," he volunteered.

"What's his handicap and has he had any practice? I haven't played much during the war."

"He shoots to a sixteen on the long course at Kawana. Sure, he practiced during the war. We kept on playing the whole time, even though balls were a little difficult to obtain. We had all the rubber in Malaya and Java," the baron laughed, "but very few golf balls."

The big worry of the civilian officials and businessmen who came to see us at the Imperial was over the "slowness" of our occupation. "Why don't you hurry up and get more troops into Tokyo?" they asked. "The hotheads will start something if they think they can get away with it." These men wanted to see an overwhelming display of American strength. They cheered inwardly when hundreds upon hundreds of our planes flew overhead, not only because they represented protection from the diehards but because here was one more reason to justify, to themselves, the surrender. If you are going to be beaten, you like to think the other guy is the toughest opponent in the world.

18

Despite their fears, we became quickly convinced that nothing dangerous was going to happen. At the request of Inamaru-san, we checked our carbines and revolvers in the Imperial, and didn't bother to take them out as we walked unarmed around the city. Looking back, I do not believe that there was at any time any real danger of a serious outbreak. The men who might have led it, the last-ditch fanatics who could not bear to live in their shattered world, preferred hara-kiri by knife, or suicide by pistol or poison, to organizing a Kamikaze corps to kill MacArthur. We were kept busy in Tokyo reporting the suicides of generals and statesmen, but when the self-immolation was ended the total number of those who took the easy way out was surprisingly small.

None of our visitors could do too much for us. They bore us no enmity, no ill will for the late unpleasantness that had ruined their country and their lives. The war was seldom mentioned, and then only jokingly. Everybody agreed that it was high time those rascally militarists got their come-uppance.

One of our frequent callers was Massaguchi Moriyama, a wiry, intense man of thirty who had gone to school at Columbia and represented the Domei news agency in New York before the war. "Massa," as he introduced himself, was a reporter for the Yoimiuri newspapers and he came to report that two wild buffaloes which William Randolph Hearst had presented to the Yoimiuri some years before no longer existed. One had been killed in the bombing and the other slaughtered and its meat distributed among the homeless. Through his friends in the police department and elsewhere, Massa was able to arrange transportation for us about ruined Tokyo, to produce some liquid nourishment from time to time, and occasionally to arrange a dinner party at a geisha house where, instead of serving the delectable national dishes of Japan—raw fish, fried shrimps, sukiyaki—the hosts went to all kinds of trouble to obtain beef (or horse meat) and potatoes, which the mama-san cooked hours ahead of time and put on the table stone-cold. After a few days of acquaintance, Massa also told me the story of his younger brother, who had been a Kamikaze pilot.

The boy was seventeen, a student of aeronautics in a technical school in Tokyo. "About the time of the invasion of Okinawa," Massa said, "a Navy officer visited the school and announced he was looking for volunteers for Special Attack Corps. He pointed to my brother and about twenty other boys and said, 'You are volunteers. You have

19

one week of freedom before reporting to headquarters at Atsugi for flight training for your glorious mission on behalf of our Divine Emperor.'

"My brother came home and announced to mother, my wife, and myself, 'I am a Kamikaze.' Then he went into our living room and shut the sliding doors. For five days he squatted there on the mat with his knees crossed, never speaking, facing the family shrine. Occasionally he sipped the tea that mother set beside him. Then on Friday he came out. He embraced us all, and to me he said with tears in his eyes, 'I do not want to die. I am too young to die. I want to live.'

"Next morning he went off and we have never heard from him since, no word from the Navy Department, nothing. We believe he was killed diving his plane into an American ship."

Now, it is possible that Massaguchi made up the whole story, knowing our interest in Kamikazes and their psychology and wanting to identify himself with such a newsworthy enterprise. It is equally possible that it was true.

On an airfield at Osaka I talked with one Kamikaze whose number did not come up. "It was a great life while it lasted," said this husky, bright young member of the Special Attack Corps. "Being in the Army and an experienced fighter pilot, I was going to be one of the last to go, as my orders were to train as many men as possible for flying. The Army was saving its planes to beat off the invasion of the Japanese islands, while the Navy sent a good many of its planes to attack your ships at Okinawa."

On their induction into the Kamikazes, the Japanese went through a funeral ceremony and from then on considered themselves living dead men. In the event they crashed behind our lines and faced capture, they carried a short sword with which they were supposed to take their own lives. There was a regular procedure for suicide: first, a token slit in the stomach and then, because cutting open the abdomen often fails to bring prompt death, a slash at the veins in the side of the neck.

Some of the suicide pilots were given sufficient training only to enable them to get a plane into the air and reach its target. Others were veteran pilots. When the fledglings went out, they followed a "mother plane" equipped with navigating instruments, and in their tanks was enough gasoline for only a one-way trip. "No use bringing them back," the Japanese lieutenant said. "They couldn't land any-

20

way without killing themselves." On the other hand, the experienced aviators had plenty of gas for a round-trip in case they were unable to locate targets due to bad weather. No disgrace attached itself to returning alive in such circumstances.

"Once you took the Kamikaze oath," my informant said, "you were given increased pay and better food, including such rare delicacies as an occasional bit of sugar or candy. You could send those things home to your family. We were envied by the other troops and now the war is over they are saying, 'How lucky you were! All those nice things and you don't have to die.'"

The lieutenant tried to explain the "mystical exaltation" that one felt on becoming a Kamikaze. We found it hard to follow. But we could understand the interpreter when he said, "The Japanese are perfectly willing to die for their country but they are human like anybody else and much prefer to be alive. The Kamikazes are glad that they did not have to die crashing their planes into your invasion ships."

So were we.

But we kept our fingers crossed as we went out to the U.S.S. "Missouri" on Sunday morning, September 2nd, for the surrender, still worried that the Kamikazes might turn up as uninvited guests.

Chapter Two

Japan Surrenders

MacArthur THOUGHT THE CEREMONY WAS ALL over when he walked out through the bulkhead door, put his hand on the railing, and looked down on the lower deck of the "Missouri" where the Japanese surrender documents had been signed a few minutes before. But there had been a mix-up—the Canadian delegate had signed on the wrong line—and the Japs and General Sutherland were still straightening it out.

MacArthur watched them for a brief moment. He took a cigarette from the pocket of his open-necked shirt, lit it, and inhaled deeply. All eyes on the deck below were turned up to watch him. He blew out a long streamer of smoke.

And out of that cloud of smoke came a thousand American airplanes! Giant B—29s and other big bombers; then formation after formation of Navy fighters and torpedo planes. They roared over the great, somber ships lying in Tokyo Bay and on toward cloud-shrouded Fuji. Watching them, I recalled a wish of three years before to be in Tokyo while American airplanes flew overhead in clouds so thick that they hid the Rising Sun. The sun was thoroughly hidden now on this morning of September 2, 1945.

Well, all right! MacArthur didn't actually produce those planes by magic. But there are plenty of people who claim that he could have if he'd wanted to. And there are plenty more who would argue that he staged the whole show in advance, even to the mix-up in the surrender signing, to the timing of his puff of smoke, in order to have all eyes centered on him just when the airplanes came over.

People feel that way about MacArthur; either they admire him with extravagance approaching adoration, or they think he is a highly polished poseur whose every move is rehearsed. As our most controversial figure of the war, nobody is neutral about him. Never were those differences of opinion more noticeable than on that historic morning.

When his launch approached the dreadnaught, before the ceremony, I heard one reporter say:

"What's the matter with Dugout Doug today? He's riding in a boat. I thought he always walked across the water."

Another turned on him angrily. "Call him General MacArthur! And don't be irreverent."

"Irreverent about whom? MacArthur, I suppose. You pro-MacArthur guys put him ahead of Jesus Christ."

That row had scarcely died down when there was another hubbub. A Soviet cameraman had taken the seat on the gun turret reserved for a representative of the capitalist press, in this case the publisher of the *New York Times,* and he refused resolutely to surrender it. The Russian still had the seat when the ceremonies started, but a lesser light had yielded his place to the *Times* delegate.

It was at this point that the forlorn GI to whom this book is dedicated appeared and then disappeared from our view, and shortly afterward the band stopped playing its triumphal tunes, the Japanese delegates scrambled from their small boat up the long ladder and assembled on the deck, and MacArthur came out to meet them.

Regardless of their previously conceived opinions of MacArthur, everybody on the "Missouri" that morning agreed that the ceremony was impressive almost beyond description and that MacArthur was great. There were generals with their bright stars and gleaming brass hats. But nothing seemed to happen until MacArthur came on the scene. He looked a foot taller than the other Americans, the Russians, the Chinese, the French, and the English; and the Japanese were small children beside him. His intensity, his sincerity, the absolute perfection of every move he made and every word he spoke gave a sense of high, historic drama to every one of the eighteen minutes which were required for the official recording of our great victory and for the brief words of the conquerors.

It was not until it was all over that his critics could voice their cynical opinions: "A very fine bit of acting!"

They were certainly correct about the quality of performance, but I think they were definitely wrong in their analysis of MacArthur. An actor goes on the stage for three hours a night, steps into a char-

23

acter, and, if he is good enough, lives his part; but for the other
hours of the day he has another life outside of the theatre—a life
in which he eats, sleeps, makes love, reads, and writes. MacArthur
does not turn his characterizations on and off. He lives his role every
minute of his life, so that it is his life, and not an act in the sense of
part-time make-believe. Perhaps one key to MacArthur's character
lies in his prose. A great many Americans describe it as "purple"
and, applying the critical terms of jive, think that his communiqués
are corny. MacArthur does not think it purple. It does frequently
sound anachronistic, as if such words as "valor," "treachery," and
"our flag," should be spelled with capitals. You cannot imagine him
answering a surrender demand with a succinct "Nuts!" In the sense
that he does not think like a bobby-soxer or the average ward-heeler,
MacArthur is an anachronism. He is not only literate, but literal.
When he writes of "grim, gaunt, ghostly men," he sees those specters
of Bataan. When he thanks God for victory, he is doing just that:
thanking a God who is a very personal and important part of his
daily life. His words are a completely sincere expression of his
thoughts.

And so it was that morning on the "Missouri." MacArthur saw not
only the immediate scene in front of him—the ships spread under the
murky sky, the militarists of a dozen countries lined up on the
battleship's deck, the reporters perched on the sixteen-inch gun
turrets, and the sailors high on the ship's platforms. Clearly in his
mind was the whole pageant of the war: the ships exploding and
sinking in Pearl Harbor; the black defeat of Bataan; the deathless
loyalty of the Filipino guerrillas; the struggle up through the islands;
the gathering of American power for victory. When the Japanese, at
his orders, stood motionless on the deck and then stepped forward to
sign the surrender documents, he saw not only the seven men in
rather shabby uniforms and the four tight-lipped civilians in morning clothes. He looked back through the centuries of history at a
Japan that had grown strong by its fanaticism, that had never before
surrendered, and was now yielding its ancient way of life.

When MacArthur spoke, it was not merely as a general. His was
not only the voice of the commander-in-chief of the American forces,
but of all of the forces of freedom triumphing over the hordes of
darkness and savagery. I believe that he thought of himself then as
an elder statesman, risen above the strife and passions of battle. He
was on Mount Olympus, seeing clearly the whole world spread be-

neath him. He was forgiving toward his enemies. He was brilliantly aware of the vistas of the future when he spoke clearly of the prejudices of race and color: "In the Philippines, America has evolved a model for this new free world of Asia. In the Philippines, America has demonstrated that the peoples of the east and the peoples of the west may walk side by side in mutual respect and with mutual benefit."

But MacArthur, high on Olympus, was mortal too. His hands were shaking as they held his manuscript. That morning his words sent a cold thrill through your backbone, and the most hard-boiled sailor glimpsed for a minute the vast sweep of the historic drama in which he had played a little part.

"And so, my fellow countrymen," MacArthur concluded, "today I report to you that your sons and daughters have served you well and faithfully with the calm, deliberate, determined fighting spirit of the American soldier and sailor. Based upon a tradition of historical trait, as against the fanaticism of an enemy supported only by mythological fiction, their spiritual strength and power has brought us through to victory. They are homeward bound—take care of them."

Millions of Americans saw MacArthur in the newsreels taken that morning. Not so the Russians. In the Muscovite edition of the pictures, MacArthur and all of the other officers except the Russians were blotted out, as were all indications that the "Missouri" was an American battleship. Soviet citizens saw the Japanese delegation surrendering to two bulky Russians whose chesty uniforms were covered with medals.

To many of us on the "Missouri" who hadn't believed that the Japanese would surrender short of total defeat, and who had been sure that we would have serious trouble with individuals or even with large military formations refusing—in the Emperor's name—to obey the Emperor, the scene was incredible. Even when the Japanese stood there, we feared that they had concealed some secret, ultra-destructive weapon which would blow us all higher than Fuji. When Mamoru Shigemitsu, the foreign minister, stumped forward on his artificial leg and affixed his signature to the documents, and General Hoshijiri Umezo, the Army chief of staff, followed to sign his name, we expected them to pull out knives and slit their bellies, or at least to jump overboard.

But to MacArthur, the surrender was no surprise. In his Christmas

25

Eve prediction to me back in Tacloban he had said, "They wouldn't believe me. For years, I told them in Washington. I told them these Philippine Islands are the key to the western Pacific. In broad strategical concept, the Jap has a defense line along the Asia coast from their own islands down to Formosa through the Philippines to the Dutch East Indies, and then over to Singapore, where it turns the corner up into Burma. They had an outpost line, which we have now overrun. We have hit them in the center by coming back to Leyte and the Philippines. The battle of the Pacific will be decided here. Holding the Philippines, we can turn either north or south at our convenience.

"I believe Japan will then ask for peace," he went on. "Japan is the most feudal nation in the world. For centuries the Samurai have been the feudal overlords and the people followed them. But now there has arisen a new class of industrial feudalists. There are five or six groups that funnel the wealth of the country into their own channels. They hope in the next years to supplant the military feudalists.

"The Jap won't collapse in the field. Not the individual soldiers. If there is a collapse, it will come in Tokyo. And it may be so complete that they will accept peace terms involving occupation of the country by American soldiers, knowing that they will be kind to them, as they were to the Germans, and can be soft-soaped.

"Mind you, they won't quit unless Germany is beaten or about to be beaten."

MacArthur's vision was prophetic. Less than a month after the Germans collapsed, and two months after we had secured the Philippines (having landed meanwhile on Okinawa), the Japanese made their first overtures for peace. Accordingly, MacArthur was prepared when he was given the job of governing Japan. Likewise, it was typical of MacArthur to emphasize the recapture of the Philippines, where he himself was fighting, as the decisive factor in the decision of the Japanese to surrender. He may also have been considering the B-29 raids, then still in their infancy, and the Iwo Jima and Okinawa campaigns still to be fought but he did not mention them in his summary of the Pacific situation.

From the first day of war in 1941, I was at intervals in the immediate vicinity of MacArthur. I saw him in Manila in the first desperate days; in Bataan and Corregidor when his forces were fighting without food and without hope; in Australia during the time that he felt hopeless and frustrated and persecuted by his "enemies" back home

26

who supposedly denied him supplies; later, when he triumphantly returned to the Philippines and his beloved Manila—and finally in those first great days in Japan. In those four years, he talked to me at length possibly six or seven times. I do not say we conversed, or that I interviewed him, because you don't do that with MacArthur. He does the talking and you the listening, and the only time you can get in a word is when he is lighting his pipe or a cigarette. That is not as unsatisfactory as it sounds, because you only have to speak a few words before MacArthur knows exactly what is on your mind, whether a complaint or a question, and he picks up the talk from there. I remember most of those talks, but the one that is perhaps most representative was that Christmas Eve at Tacloban. It was at a time when MacArthur was well on the way to victory but when the defeats were not too far in the background—a period emotionally halfway from the bitterness of Bataan to the calm of Olympus.

In reproducing it, I am not violating a confidence, because the general said much the same things to several other people who are no longer under the censor's injunction that MacArthur, like the President of the United States, must not be quoted directly. There was in MacArthur then more than a trace of the bitterness he had frequently expressed at certain admirals, at the New Dealers who feared him as a presidential candidate, and at other individuals. He had not yet scaled the mount of the Immortals.

I had finally returned to the Philippines after eighteen months in Europe and after some time in hospitals in France and on Saipan. The atmosphere around headquarters at Tacloban was even more one of megalomania than I had remembered. When you got to MacArthur himself, that all disappeared and things were clear, reasonable, and logical. But between the general and the outside world stood a ring of guards who conceived it as their duty to protect him from emotional or physical disturbance. A few of his staff, like Generals Sutherland and Marshall, dared to speak up to him and give him a true picture of events and he respected them for it. Many of the others were toadies and bootlickers, who took it upon themselves to interpret his moods and desires. Thus, a gesture of his cigarette, at times, resolved itself into an order which in the case of his public relations staff was reflected in the stories that millions of Americans read in their morning newspapers. The Palace Guard determined which letters should reach MacArthur, which critical stories he should be permitted to read. They wanted to "protect him."

27

On Christmas Eve, the general's aide led me through MacArthur's bedroom, with the mosquito net over a white bedspread, and out onto the porch at the Tacloban residence that was MacArthur's headquarters. MacArthur was pacing up and down, smoking his corncob pipe and gazing at the mud-filled streets and the army barracks beyond them. He had just been promoted to General of the Army, but he had not obtained his new insignia and was wearing only four stars on his khaki collar instead of the five to which he was entitled. He seemed a little less intense than when I had seen him last in Australia, but no less determined. Apparently because he knew that many people were momentarily flustered on meeting him, MacArthur had a habit of bending his head for a moment and clasping your hand in both of his before looking into your eyes. He did so now. Then he said, "I'm glad you're back, Clark."

"I'm glad to be back, General." After that I listened for an hour and a half. He motioned me to a chair, and sat down himself in a rocker. His pipe went out, but he kept it in his hand and used it to emphasize his gestures.

"The last time I saw you was in Melbourne. We've come a long way since then. I was afraid you were lost in the first B–29 raid over Tokyo. Jean [Mrs. MacArthur] sent a clipping from a Melbourne paper telling me of that, and it took eighteen days for me to receive another dispatch saying your plane had finally returned to Saipan. You and Frank Hewlett are the last survivors of the original reporters who were with me on Corregidor and are here with me now." MacArthur has one noticeable peculiarity of speech. His "rais" become "r's." Thus "afraid" is "afred." Not that he uses that particular word very frequently.

Then MacArthur discussed censorship, speaking with all his usual sincerity but making statements which, as will be shown in another chapter, had very little connection with reality. "I want you to know that we have the same basic policy of censorship here as when we were back in the tunnel on Corregidor. Our policy is to let the press tell everything. Censorship has been used for political purposes in other theatres. It won't be here. There are some silly rules that we by-pass. You can write what you like, no matter how critical. If there is something wrong I like to know about it myself. The only thing we can't do is tell the Jap what he doesn't know about us— things that would hurt us.

"Now, about the next show." He leaned forward, holding his pipe

28

in his right hand, acting out his words. "The press doesn't know about it yet [actually, reporters had been briefed] but I'll tell you in confidence. I am going to hit the Jap right where he hit me back in December of 1941. In Lingayen Gulf. I'm going to land with four divisions. I am counting on the Navy for air cover and I am fairly confident they'll give it to me.

"My intelligence tells me the Japs have one hundred and fifty thousand to two hundred thousand men on Luzon. I personally think they have only four divisions, and only one of them is a good division [MacArthur was right]. If they retreat into Bataan and Corregidor, I will wipe them out within five days, with air and artillery. I'll show them what they could have done to me in 1942, if they had had the imagination."

That sounded to me like sheer braggadocio, and I thought Mac-Arthur was talking through his hat. But when the time came, he sealed off Bataan in a single day by an end-run amphibious operation at Mariveles, something that General Homma had never quite dared attempt although he went halfway to his decisive objective. And in one day, by parachute and seaborne landings, MacArthur sealed the fate of Corregidor and put most of the island in our control, although it took some time to mop up all the Japs in the caves and tunnels.

The general went back to the forthcoming Lingayen landing. "If I'm wrong about the number of Jap troops on Luzon, I'll be the first to call the turn on myself. The reason I am hitting there is to cut off Jap reinforcement from the north. I'm shutting his back door. Of course, with his forces on Formosa, he's at my back door too, and whether he can bring down enough to neutralize me depends on the developments of the campaign.

"It is a long chance, longer than I would ever take again—but I'm absolutely confident it will work. This is my best Christmas in years. I am happy now to be at death grips with the Jap."

Then he sized up what he considered the weakness of his plan, which called for a 700-mile amphibious jump from Leyte across the Surigao Sea to the western edge of the Philippines and then up north to Luzon. Japanese Kamikaze attacks had been especially vicious and effective in the preceding weeks, and there were still considerable numbers of Jap airplanes in the northern Philippines despite Admiral Halsey's carrier-plane sweeps of the airfields.

"I have to depend on the Navy to cover my back door," MacArthur

29

said, "and for much of the air cover in the early days, although I think I can bring up the fifth and thirteenth Air Forces to the fields we now hold on Leyte and on Mindoro, and thus have land-based air cover for the landing and future operations. The trouble is that not all the admirals are like Bull Halsey. I love the Bull. He is always ready to close with the enemy. His signal is to attack. He is not afraid of losing ships."

The general's voice got hard. "I am not sure what the Navy will do. They were very badly shaken by their losses in the Mindoro operation, when the Kamikazes sank a good many ships. But I had to go across to Mindoro to get airfields nearer Manila, so that in going on up to Lingayen I would be dependent on Navy air for only a short time. You may not believe this, but I had to threaten to court-martial one admiral to get him to send convoys to Mindoro. Now, I am afraid that if things get too hot up at Lingayen, they may want to pull out."

MacArthur was partly right about that too. Exactly fourteen days later, on January 6, 1945, our advance bombardment force of some sixty-six American ships, plus a few Australian vessels, steamed into Lingayen Gulf to shell shore positions in preparation for the landings. That first day, one hundred suicide planes attacked the advance force, and nineteen of the Emperor's pilots dove their explosive-laden aircraft into sixteen of our ships. That night, the admiral in command sent back a message to the flagship on which I was a passenger. It said in effect, "The intensity and severity of the Japanese attacks has been such as to suggest the advisability of postponing the whole operation." Without consulting MacArthur who was on another ship, Admiral Kinkaid wirelessed back, "Stay in there and fight." Next day there were only about twenty Kamikazes, and from then on the suicide assaults declined rapidly to zero as the carrier planes and the aircraft from Mindoro paralyzed the Japanese fields in the Philippines and on Formosa.

The general continued his rocking, pipe in hand. "Yes, we've come a long way since Melbourne, despite the Navy cabal that hates me and the New Deal cabal. Since the last day I saw you our total casualties to date have been exactly twenty-eight thousand killed and wounded. On Leyte alone, we've killed one hundred thousand Japs. We've done it by using our brains and artillery, not flesh. I have larger forces now than when I saw you last, but it's not as much as you'd think. I have left behind, by-passed, and isolated more Japs than the fourteen divisions I now have at my command. I had to by-pass them, because if I had tried to wipe them out they'd have wiped me out instead.

"I couldn't have come here without the air. I got rid of those incompetent, bungling, nincompoop airmen who were with me in the early days of the war. General George Kenny is the finest airman in the world and Whitehead [Lt. General Ennis Whitehead, 5th Air Force commander] is another assassin. Don't be misled by their appearance. Their airmen are a rough, hard-talking, hard-drinking bunch. They are casual about their dress. They talk tough and they are tough. And when the chips are down, they never fail me. They always hit a home run when the bases are full. They make their errors when they don't count."

MacArthur rocked in his chair for a few minutes, made one futile attempt to light his pipe, and then leaned forward. "Yes," he said, "I am happy to be back here. I only hope that I am spared to reach Manila. But we are not going to find our old companions, the men who were with me on Bataan. We will, perhaps, get two thousand white men back [the Filipinos who survived the death march had been paroled by the Japs] but time and disease and brutality have done for the rest.

"But I am going to avenge them, as far as possible! I am going to wipe out the Jap in the Philippine Islands. In other places, I have by-passed them. Here they are going to die. We are going to take our losses and kill them."

Now, MacArthur let his heart overrule his head. What he wanted more than anything in the world at that time was for the Japs to give up Manila without a fight so that he could recapture his beloved city intact and with his beloved Filipinos unharmed. So he said, "I believe they will declare Manila an open city when I land behind them at Lingayen, cut them in two in Luzon, and advance on down to the capital. You understand, though, that this is just speculation. I think the Jap will declare Manila an open city because he wants to do something to erase part of his record of bestiality and brutality. If I told them back in Washington what I believe they would think me crazy—some of them do now. But I believe the Japs will ask for peace after they lose the Philippines."

He correctly predicted that the collapse would come in Tokyo, and not in the ranks of the Japanese army. Then he said, "I would rather fight the Boche than the Jap. There is something in the Jap's

31

spirituality that makes him fight bravely to the death. Something that is not in our Christian spirituality. He gets frightened, too. I've seen them with their teeth chattering with fright and yet they wouldn't quit. They kept on until they were killed. If they weren't so yellow—and by that I mean so brutal and bestial—I would be compelled to admire them as soldiers. The fact that we kill six to one, or sometimes thirty to one, does not mean that the American soldier is six times as good or thirty times as good as an individual Jap. It means we use our brains as well as our flesh in fighting them.

"The history of the Jap's contacts with the white man proves that he suffers from an inferiority complex. That is behind many of his actions. If he gets the upper hand of you physically, he cannot treat you mercifully. Something in him makes him act with brutal violence. He can't resist kicking you when you are down. But at heart he is yellow. He is afraid of the white man."

He paused to rock, and this time the match flared up and he lit his pipe. "I left Jean and Arthur in Brisbane. I didn't think public opinion would stand for them undergoing the dangers here. But as soon as I get to Manila I will send for them. They can help take care of the civilian refugees in the camps there. The civilians liked Jean and Arthur. Jean," he smiled, and then flattered me by showing that he recalled a phrase I had written about her three years before, "is still my finest soldier."

This was just at the time of the German breakthrough in the Ardennes, and MacArthur turned his thoughts to the European front. Even at this late date, the subject is still a little touchy, but I will quote what he said.

"They are fighting a different war there—a war of brute strength. Knowing Eisenhower and his stubborn egotism, I have expected this German counterattack for a long time. Eisenhower was asking for trouble, as always. He was my Chief of Staff for many years and I know him well, as you know."

I did know that, and of the disagreement that sent Eisenhower away from the Philippines some months before the Japanese attack in 1941. And I was not surprised at MacArthur's words, because the only time I had seen Eisenhower angry was when he discussed the Pacific commander. That was at the time of the Salerno landings in September, 1943, when I was covering Eisenhower's headquarters at Sidi-Bou-Said in Tunisia. The general received me every morning at 7:30, and his customary greeting was, "What's the news?" One morning I answered, "The radio says that General MacArthur has made the biggest parachute landing in history at Lae and Salamaua, down in New Guinea, and that MacArthur himself watched from a B–17 while his troops jumped."

General Ike hit the desk a crashing blow with his fist and glared at me. "Do you believe that?" he demanded. I was on the spot. Eisenhower's parachutists had just made landings in Sicily and more recently at Salerno, and I didn't know if Ike wanted my opinion as to whether MacArthur's operation involved more men, or whether MacArthur actually had flown over the scene. I tried to dodge the question by saying, "I just heard it on the radio, General. I don't know whether to believe it or not. It's just a radio report." "Well," said Ike, "I don't!" Then he changed the subject and in a few minutes he was smiling and cordial as ever.

As far as I know, MacArthur and Eisenhower, those two former friends, both men of great ability and integrity, never exchanged messages of congratulation during the war. Eisenhower, as he told me, believed that MacArthur blamed him personally for America's failure to attempt to reinforce the Philippines in strength in early 1942 when Bataan was nearing its end. "The truth is," said Ike, who was then Chief of Plans in the War Department, "that from the first day of the war I battled to get help to the Philippines. I took it to the President himself, and was overruled in my plan for a major effort to aid Bataan. I was however given some money and a few ships and I tried desperately to get them through the blockade. I worked night and day and sweated blood over this." The silence between the two men was finally broken when MacArthur sent Ike a friendly message on his appointment as Chief of Staff, and later they met face to face in Tokyo and no doubt straightened out their misunderstandings. . . .

MacArthur went on with his analysis of the European war. "I told Churchill that the plan for Europe was all wrong. I told him we would have some initial successes in Normandy and probably liberate France. But then we would hit the real hard core of German resistance. We are doing things all wrong there. I know that country where they are fighting now. It is terrible terrain. I was in there after the last armistice. I told Pershing we never could have broken the German line without losing four million men. He would not believe it. But it is a country of narrow passes that you can get through only by using up men and men and more men, killing a

33

battalion and then replacing it with another and going forward that way foot by foot. [MacArthur might well, without knowing it, have been describing the Battles of Huertegen Forest, then in progress.]

"In war, you have to fight with brains as well as muscles. In war you lead from strength, just as you do in bridge, in football or baseball. Where is our strength in Europe? On the sea and in the air. Where is the enemy's strength? On the ground. Then what should we have done in Europe?

"I could have landed with twenty divisions on the north coast of Germany and had Berlin in two weeks. You can't tell me that it is impossible to navigate in those waters off the coast. The German navy has navigated there. With our fifteen thousand planes, we could have established air control long enough to get our troops ashore. Then it would have been a question of protecting the convoys coming in. I don't say we could have driven the German air force completely out of the air, but we could have held control long enough to get our men and supplies ashore. The distances aren't great, only several hundred miles. Out here we came many hundreds. And the Jap has air, too, and uses it—you've seen those Kamikazes.

"I had a wire from Churchill in the past few days," MacArthur continued. "It is only three words: 'You were right.'"

Unless memory misleads me, and the notes made at the time, I asked MacArthur at this point, "But where did you meet Churchill, sir? I didn't know you'd seen him." MacArthur's reply was "Brisbane." But, of course, Churchill has never been to Brisbane, so my memory must be faulty—or the general was romancing a little.

"I told Churchill, too," MacArthur went on, "that the Russian could not be beaten on his own soil but would be a different man off it. History shows that Russia has never lost a war on Russian territory and never won one off it. Now the Russian aims are changed. They are politico-military. They want the northern Balkans and so they are fighting there right at this time, instead of attacking in East Prussia to relieve the pressure on Eisenhower.

"Eisenhower, by the way, is not a field soldier, although of course he has gotten a lot of experience in the past two years. As for our generalship in Europe, it seems to me that in France the Third Army very cleverly exploited the breakthrough after St. Lo, moving with speed and imagination. Also Montgomery—or probably it was Alex-

34

ander—did a good job of logistics in the drive across the desert after El Alamein."

I asked him about the Italian campaign. "It was timid and unimaginative. It was a good idea to go in there perhaps, because we needed victories at that time. But it has not helped to defeat Germany. Anzio was a classic military mistake. It was probably not Eisenhower; but whoever it was handling the soldiers made the mistake of trying a short envelopment. They should have gone way up toward the Riviera for a landing. Even if Anzio had been successful, it wouldn't have meant anything. It would have been far easier to go all the way north, and I won't believe that there weren't sufficient carriers available to cover that operation from the air."

What we were doing in Europe, MacArthur concluded, was engaging in a slugging match and—"That's no good! If we fight that way we may lose three to four million men. That means we'll lose the war a hundred years from now.

"The bad part is that in war, Death changes his selectivity. Ordinarily he picks the weak, the old, the infirm, the diseased. In war he takes the cream—the brave and fine men: the future poets, painters, scientists, engineers. Not the professional soldier, because the professional soldier"—he smiled—"has a habit of keeping on living."

In reporting any interview with MacArthur it is impossible to reproduce his presence and his hypnotic personality. But it is not his personality that wins him followers—it is the clear, forceful words and the logic that carry his listeners along almost irresistibly, no matter how prejudiced they were before he started to speak. MacArthur made several history-changing talks during the war, but the most important was probably in a house on Waikiki Beach in Honolulu where he met President Roosevelt back in June, 1944. America's best military brains were gathered in a room cooled by the trade winds, and one by one the admirals got up to advocate their plans for defeating Japan. The President listened and then began a summation, citing casualties in the war to date. Suddenly MacArthur rose, shook his long finger dramatically and said solemnly, "Mr. President, whoever gave you those figures—lied!" He went on to outline his own plan; the drive into the central Philippines, the final assault on the Emperor's homeland. For three hours he spoke, and no one moved very much except to light a cigarette.

The general's reaction to Roosevelt's acceptance of his plan was typical. Until then he had been convinced that Roosevelt was one of his "enemies," one of the "New Deal cabal" depriving him of supplies for political motives. Afterward, he spoke of the President with affection. "You know that the President is a man of great vision—once things are explained to him." However, a good many of MacArthur's staff officers didn't get the word about their chief's new state of mind and they continued to keep F.D.R. in No. 1 position on their personal hate lists. Like the major general who said in Tokyo, six months after Roosevelt's death, "Yes, I'm going home now. I'm *almost* ready to forgive the American people for the third term." Not the fourth term, which had been a fact for many months, but "the third term."

MacArthur described the Honolulu meeting to me. "I talked for three hours and afterward the President said, 'You know, Doug, you told me more about the Pacific in that time than I ever learned in my whole life.'"

MacArthur said, "Thank you, Mr. President."

"Doug," the President went on, "when you were in Washington as Chief of Staff you fought with me more than any other person in America. But I always liked to have your opinions, because you represented the conscience of the Army to me. And now you are the conscience of America for me."

The quotations reproduced here contain enough of MacArthur's sentiments to make it clear why the general has had enemies. But nothing MacArthur said or did could justify the wave of vilification that swept the United States from early in the war until long afterward, even when most people were convinced the general was doing a first-rate job of governing Japan. Ridiculous, petty, and frequently shocking charges were made against the general and glibly repeated wherever our citizens gathered or our troops were fighting. Part of this was the self-conscious reaction of the United States on recovering from the shock of the early war days. In those days the country had desperately needed a boost for its shaken ego and had found its stimulus in the Bataan campaign and in the person of MacArthur, who was elevated by the press and public to the stature of a godlike hero. When MacArthur was no longer needed, many people vented on him their shame at their own overemotional reactions.

The gossip and scandal circulated about MacArthur threatened for a time to obscure the great military feats of his comeback from Australia, the campaigns in New Guinea and up through the islands to the Philippines and Manila. For decades to come, military histo-

36

rians will be discussing those battles and MacArthur will be given the credit he deserves for using "brains and artillery instead of flesh," as well as for the nearly incalculable inspirational qualities of his determined leadership and his matchless personal courage.

In the days right after the surrender on the "Missouri," MacArthur was criticized for not moving faster, for failing to arrest the war criminals. It is my belief, as will be shown later, that some of the criticisms of our policy in Japan are justified—that we are making some important mistakes. But no fault should have been found with MacArthur's seemingly slow moving in those first days. There was good reason for it, as MacArthur himself explained, "I have taken chances before, but never anything like this. Just think! We are a few thousand men surrounded by seventy million people who have been our fanatical enemies and who may turn on us overnight. We have got to secure our position."

It is unfortunate, in my opinion, that one of the "security" steps ordered by Washington and followed by MacArthur was the retention of the Imperial system and of Emperor Hirohito.

Chapter Three

Democratic America and Imperial Japan

ADOLF HITLER'S PLAN OF WORLD CONQUEST WAS spawned in a cellar beer parlor in Munich.

Japan's scheme of armed expansion was built around a palace: the sprawling, now bomb-damaged, wood, paper, and glass edifices that are the earthly abode of the one-time Son-of-Heaven, Hirohito.

And when Japan's scheme started to fail and defeat loomed, the running of the war was moved directly into the palace and Hirohito himself publicly seized the leadership of the fight. "Publicly" in Japan, that is, because the American public was never allowed to know Hirohito's true war role. Our State Department was plotting to use him as our puppet and their plot has succeeded—for the time being—over the vigorous objections of our war allies.

The ex-divine Emperor, descendant until recently of "a line unbroken from ages eternal" of the Sun Goddess Ameterasu, was far luckier than Hitler. He not only survived the war but despite all propaganda to the contrary continues to be the god and leader of a majority of his 70,000,000 Japanese subjects.

Since our occupation of Japan, Hirohito has declared in his own words that he is not a divinity. Shintoism, the mystic religion that placed him as the No. 1 god of a race destined to rule the world, has officially been divorced from the state. A constitution has been drawn up which strips the Emperor of most of his temporal powers. He is pictured in the papers visiting factories, getting his feet wet in the Pacific at Hayama Beach, or reading the comics in the *Stars*

38

and Stripes to his son and heir, Prince Akahito. He looks like a funny little man with a mustache. (Remember Hitler?)

This propaganda, of course, is an effort to prove to the world and to his subjects how "democratic" he has become. Part of the world believes it. Most of his subjects do not, except for the Communists whose objections to the Emperor system were tied in with their hatred for the Zaibatsu, the big family trusts in which the Imperial household was the largest stockholder. For the others, Hirohito has stepped back in to fill Japan's "spiritual vacuum." He is doing business at the same old stand.

Nearly every nation that fought Japan—China, Russia, Australia, New Zealand—declared that Hirohito was just as much a war criminal as Hitler and demanded that the Imperial system be smashed once and for all and the Emperor placed on trial for his war guilt. The United States, backed by the Churchill Tories both in and out of Whitehall, insisted that Hirohito be kept on his throne.

This American insistence was the fulfillment of a promise that our State Department kept making to Hirohito throughout the war. It was Washington's policy to protect the Emperor from all criticism, picturing him as a doll-like zombie secluded in the palace at Tokyo, and as a prisoner of the naughty militarists. The State Department, which secretly controlled operations of the OWI and censored radio intercepts from Japan, forbade any American official to refer to the Emperor and if his name was mentioned at all he was not to be associated with the brutalities and atrocities of the soldiers who fought and died—and committed those brutalities and atrocities—in his name.

It was the State Department's policy, as carried out by the OWI, to concentrate on the Gumbatsu—the War Lords—with Tojo as the vicious dictator and villain of the piece. Through our secret broadcasts to Japan, the ruling class was given to understand that we thought the Emperor a very fine man, as were his business associates, the Zaibatsu. We let them know that if they surrendered, we would not make things too difficult for them.

All this merely emphasized our acceptance of the clever propaganda that the Japanese had been thrusting down our throats for years, building up Hirohito abroad as a harmless, innocent little man, while inside the country he was the Son-of-Heaven and the real leader of his people.

Now, during the war, there was a sudden and startling change in

39

the Japanese propaganda beamed overseas. The Japanese radio and press came out openly and said that Hirohito was in fact and in person leading the war, it was *his* war, he personally urged his soldiers to die for him and win for him. The mask was torn off; Hirohito was revealed in his true role.

So what did the State Department and the OWI do? They deliberately kept this all-important revelation from the American people. They continued to picture Hirohito as a harmless, innocent little man. In their radio broadcasts to Tokyo, they followed the same line.

Tokyo, annoyed to the extreme, screamed back, "You're nuts! Hirohito *is* our leader. He *is* running the war!" Washington turned a deaf ear and, ignoring all the facts, continued to insist that Hirohito was a very nice guy. So it was that we paved the way for prolongation of the Emperor system in Japan.

What is the truth about Hirohito's war role?

To go back briefly: Hirohito in his third year as Emperor appointed General Baron Giichi Tanaka as premier. Tanaka produced his famous memorial to the Emperor, this same Hirohito, outlining the successive steps that Japan must take to conquer the world, beginning with the seizure of Manchuria, then China, war with Britain and America and Russia. Perhaps Hirohito never saw or heard of this document. Perhaps!

Hirohito approved the seizure of Manchuria and the war on China. In preparation for the war on America and Britain, he approved the Axis alliance with Germany and Italy.

Three months before Pearl Harbor, a new General Defense Headquarters was set up in Tokyo. Hirohito took personal command of this organization. His action was interpreted in the American press as intervention by the throne to "curb the military." Events promptly proved this interpretation fatuous. They proved that Hirohito took direct command to unite the military in preparation for war.

Then came the Imperial Rescript declaring war on the United States and Great Britain—complete sanction for the plans of the war lords.

After the rescript, Hirohito temporarily retired into the background. He emerged again in the role of leader when things got tough for Japan. From mid-1943 Tokyo's propaganda began to feature the Emperor and, beginning in 1944, Japan proclaimed to all the world, *"This is the Emperor's war."* It was obvious to Japan's leaders that the Army and Navy had failed, and in this crisis Hiro-

40

hito stepped personally into the breach. While American propaganda was still playing him up as the friendly little victim of the vicious military, he took over control of the war machine.

Beginning in early 1944, all councils of war were held in the Imperial Palace. The chiefs of the Army and Navy attended, war maps were unfurled, decisions were made in the presence of Hirohito. In fact, the top admirals and generals moved into rooms in the spacious palace grounds to be nearer to the Emperor who had actually taken over command of the military and who himself decided how to meet the growing American pressure.

This is not a matter of conjecture on the part of the author. It was all proclaimed by Radio Tokyo or in the Japanese press in declarations that were known to the State Department and the OWI but which were hidden from the American public by those agencies in their determination to keep Hirohito on his throne after the war was won. Churchill—in his defense of Italy's monarchy—was not more adamant!

War cabinet meetings were held regularly in the palace and on the eighth of each month the nation observed "with trepidation" the Imperial Rescript issued at the time of the Pearl Harbor attack. Hirohito expressed keen interest in the feats of the Special Attack Corps, the Kamikazes, who dedicated themselves, in the terms of a nationally popular song:

> *"For His Imperial Majesty*
> *Today we are a shield.*
> *To defend the Empire's glory*
> *We depart forevermore."*

The Kamikaze legend implicit in this song was Hirohito's favorite story. On May 25th of 1944, he was given advance notice of a Kamikaze attack on our massed ships off Okinawa. Radio Tokyo reported this in the following words: "When plans for this operation were conveyed to the throne, His Imperial Majesty granted special Imperial approval. His brief message moved the pilots deeply." So deeply that they killed hundreds of Americans.

Hirohito was obviously firmly in the saddle, yet the American people were not allowed to know it. In defense of the Emperor, Ambassador Joseph Grew told the Illinois Educational Association at Chicago that there would be peace with Japan "when once Japan

41

is under the aegis of a peace-seeking ruler not controlled by the military."

To this, Radio Tokyo cracked back, "When Grew says that the Emperor of Japan is peace-loving, he is completely right, but when he tries to make a distinction between what he calls the military clique and the rest of the nation, he is utterly wrong since there is a complete, insoluble unity of the entire Japanese nation under the binding leadership of His Imperial Majesty."

Mr. Elmer Davis, the director of OWI, did not share the view of Radio Tokyo; instead, he declared, "The Emperor has no more to say about Japan than I have."

One is therefore entitled to ask why Mr. Davis did not save us two and a half years of agony and bloodshed by telling the Japanese to surrender in early 1942. They did surrender when Hirohito told them to, though Hirohito "had no more to say about Japan" than did Elmer—if you can believe what Elmer said.

The men who, like ex-Ambassador Joseph Clark Grew, interpreted Japan for us were not, of course, pro-Jap as opposed to pro-American. But they understood Japan's problems. They were pro-Jap as opposed to pro-Chinese or pro-Filipino or pro-Indonesian. The businessmen who invested millions in Japan—and sold millions in war-making machinery, oils, scrap iron, and machine tools to Japan— saw a neat, orderly, organized country that appealed to them far more than did a sprawling, disorderly, disorganized China or the vague countries of southeastern Asia. Too many times to be counted I have heard discussions of the subject: "The Japanese are honest and straight forward. . . . You can't trust a Chinese. . . . Those Chinks are filthy people. . . . I'd much rather deal with a Japanese than a Chinaman."

The British Ambassador to Tokyo, Sir Robert Craigie, even said it officially and publicly in 1940 when Japan's armies were over- running China. "Already," Sir Robert told a group in Tokyo, "There is growing up [in Japan and Britain] an appreciation of the extent to which the actions of the other have been vilified and misrepre- sented. . . . I have a definite feeling of confidence in the future of Anglo-Japanese relations." He went on to refer to the "deep-seated similarities" between the two countries, both of which he asserted were striving for a lasting peace and "the preservation of our institu- tions from extraneous and subversive influences."

Sir Robert's speech was followed shortly by Britain's closing of the

Burma Road—China's last lifeline—and through such actions and through the words of Grew and men of like mind we got a picture of Japan and of Hirohito which made us completely incapable of judging the real significance of such steps as Hirohito's assumption of command of the new General Defense Headquarters on September 11, 1941, which action was taken, as Tokyo announced, for the defense of Japan's "national territories in view of the growing tension in East Asia." The *New York Times* saw this action as "consolidating and unifying the supreme leadership of the nation in the hands of the Emperor himself." Which, indeed, it did, but for war, not for peace.

It is my personal belief, based on what numerous Japanese told me, that Hirohito signed the Imperial Rescript ordering the war not later than the fourth week in November, notwithstanding the Japanese government's claim that the Imperial seal was not affixed until three hours after the Pearl Harbor attack. After the surrender, Baron Kantaro Suzuki, who was prime minister just before the capitulation, told reporters that Hirohito was fully cognizant of war plans and gave his full approval. I believe Hirohito helped Tojo and the Army faction overrule the somewhat reluctant admirals. I believe the Emperor knew of and approved of the law under which American airmen were beheaded or executed by firing squads.

No one with any knowledge of Japan could possibly believe that the admirals and generals would take such a momentous step as to go to war against America and Great Britain without informing the Emperor of their intentions and getting his approval. In the face of all this evidence, the State Department would still have us believe that Hirohito was "forced" into acquiescing in the Pearl Harbor attack when it was already a *fait accompli*, that he objected to the war all along and was a peace-loving, innocuous little individual.

Actually, at forty-four years of age, Hirohito is a competent and capable man, well able to make decisions and carry them out. He showed his strength of will when in defiance of court circles he chose his own wife, Princess Nagako, and forced the courtiers to give their approval.

Physically, the Emperor is no weakling. He is good at fencing, riding, skiing, gymnastics, swimming, plays golf and tennis. His body is lithe and well-toned.

As a boy of ten, he had his first airplane ride with James C. (Bud) Mars who barnstormed Japan in 1911. He underwent vigorous mili-

43

tary training, and climbed to the top of Mt. Fuji. In 1921 he visited Europe where he became chums with Edward, Prince of Wales, and toured France, Holland, Belgium, and Italy. Returning to Japan with new self-confidence, he became Prince Regent to rule in the name of his father, Emperor Taisho, a sick man and a weakling by comparison with Hirohito's grandfather, the great Meiji who Westernized Japan and made it able to survive in a modern world.

The Emperor is the richest man in the world through his ownership of lands and stocks in the companies and corporations of his friends, the Zaibatsu. He had billions in war industries and despite the eventual defeat of his legions, the war was his most successful financial adventure.

He has been "democratized" now, but he was and still remains the keystone of the Japanese religious, political, and economic structure. For the present he is not in a position to exercise the power by which he ordered 70,000,000 people to go to war for him and whose sole word was enough to make still-undefeated armies surrender on a 10,000-mile front.

For the future, we should remember a five-letter word spelled *hoben.* It means, anyway you translate it, "The end justifies the means." The Japs have a kindred saying, "Hang out a sheep's head and sell the flesh of a dog." *Hoben* adds up to double-talk and deceit—to a long-term view that can admit defeat today in order to prepare for victory tomorrow. Cordell Hull got caught on the chin by a *hoben* haymaker when he listened to Kurusu and Nomura talk peace while the Jap task forces were steaming toward Pearl Harbor.

Under the concepts of *hoben,* Hirohito or his successor can at some future date turn to his people and say, "We, the Divine Ruler of the Divine Race, outwitted the stupid barbarians who temporarily occupied our sacred land, knowing that our subjects would not be deceived by our stratagem of seeming to obey the invader's wishes. We were never defeated. Now let us get on with our mission of conquering the world."

Some annoying subjects, especially the Japanese Communists, might raise the seemingly embarrassing point that Hirohito himself proclaimed the surrender in August, 1945. To answer this, Hirohito would have only to quote from the Imperial Surrender Rescript, which the Australians called a "defiant, diabolically clever" document, but which the Americans accepted at somewhat more than face value.

In the Rescript, Hirohito in no sense admitted defeat. Instead, he slapped our faces by saying, "Indeed, we declared war on America and Britain out of our sincere desire to insure Japan's self-preservation and the stabilization of East Asia, it being far from our thought either to infringe upon the sovereignty of other nations or to embark upon territorial aggrandizement." He spoke of the atom bomb, and then went on to express "The deepest sense of regret to our allied nations of East Asia [puppet China, puppet Philippines, Thailand] who have consistently cooperated with the empire toward the *emancipation* of East Asia." (Italics mine.)

And, "having been able to save and maintain the structure of the Imperial State," he said, "let the entire nation continue as one family from generation to generation, ever firm in its faith in the imperishableness of its divine land, and mindful of its heavy burden of responsibilities and the long road before it. . . . Keep pace with the progress of the world."

Hirohito expressed no shame, merely regret at the failure of Japan's Holy Mission to emancipate the people of the Orient, to unite them against the white man. Plus an admonition to keep an eye on the long road ahead.

After a few months overseas, GI Joe cries to go home. The Japs are accustomed to thinking in terms of centuries. The imperial myth is so deeply rooted in them that it cannot, by our present policies, be dug out by a short-term occupation. We missed our chance on V–J Day. It will take many years of training in democratic processes, many years of anti-Shinto education to change them from the 70,000,000 people who, as one man, obeyed unquestioningly the commands of a single individual—an individual who could in the future once again order them to fight as easily as he did in the past.

As long as we coddle Hirohito and protect the Emperor system, instead of destroying it, the danger will exist of a new, rebuilt, remilitarized Japan—this time with all the modern weapons it needs—going on the warpath again in the holy name of the Emperor.

If the chance to reinstitute Japan as a world power does not come to Hirohito within a reasonable time, if he decides that *hoben* can best be served by withdrawing from the picture, it is not unlikely that he will yield his throne to his son and heir Akihito Tsugu-no-miya, who was twelve years old in 1946. In this case Hirohito would be following the respected but little-known Japanese custom of Inkyo, which means "living in the shadows." When the male head

45

of a family grows old, he may retire from active participation in its affairs and turn them over to his son, but meantime continue to advise and mold from the shadows. If Hirohito does follow this custom he would be entitled to his own court and household, and could direct his heir according to his wishes.

Who is Akihito? He is a youngster who recently has been introduced through the *Stars and Stripes* to Blondie and Moon Mullins. Perhaps this influence, plus his American tutor, and attendance at semi-public high schools will erase the training he has had since birth as the son of the Son-of-Heaven. During the impressionable years of the war, this training was directed toward military ends. For instance, he "visited a certain air base and listened to explanations about general conditions concerning naval aviation." During the visit "he was reminded of the fierce air operations on the battle-fronts by the splendid training of the young eagles over the airfield."

The purpose of such visits was to impress the youthful heir-apparent with the seriousness of his duties, as well as to inspire the pilots with awe at the sight of the royal personage. Akihito responded enthusiastically, expressed his deep concern "with the war situation and was deeply moved by the loyal ferocity and courage of the imperial forces." Like any other boy, he became interested in constructing model airplanes and battleships. He went to aircraft plants, inspected labor service forces. Like his father, he concentrated on physical training as well.

This semi-military background of the prince was, like his father's war record, carefully concealed from the American public in the pre-peace buildup of the royal family. Between the capitulation and our actual occupation of Japan, the Tokyo press got busy picturing Akihito in a childlike way and the OWI passed this concept on to the American people. The Tokyo propaganda was a precaution in case Hirohito could not survive the storm of defeat and occupation and Akihito had to step into his shoes.

But Hirohito, supported by the Americans, rode through it with no trouble at all. In fact, it is no exaggeration to say that his position became stronger than ever, for he received the wholehearted backing of General of the Army Douglas MacArthur. The two great men got along well together from the moment of their first meeting in Tokyo, when MacArthur summoned Hirohito to the American Embassy and the Emperor obeyed the command.

It was a meeting chocked with drama as the Son-of-Heaven stood face to face with the man who was giving orders to the Son-of-Heaven. Hirohito and Douglas MacArthur both realized the great historical import of the moment. Hirohito wept. MacArthur wept.

From then on there was no need for Hirohito to think of immediate abdication. He had lost the battles but he had won the war. He had convinced MacArthur that our State Department propaganda—persisting in the face of all the facts—was correct and that Hirohito was in truth a peace-loving individual who had taken no active part in the battle but had been a helpless prisoner of the militarists.

MacArthur thereafter took the initiative in defending the Emperor's position, insisting that to destroy the Tenno system would be a gross violation of our "pledge at Potsdam" and would only result in firing the Japanese with an unquenchable desire for revenge. MacArthur declared that the love and reverence which the Japanese felt for the Emperor as a symbol, not a man, was something beyond the poor powers of Americans to understand. This last was, if you read it correctly, an admission that we could not and did not defeat the Japanese, could not by killing hundreds of thousands and destroying their cities wipe out their fanatical faith in the Son-of-Heaven. We had to confess our failure by allowing them to retain the Emperor system which was the core of their national spirit and their beliefs in their divine mission.

The Russians, Australians, Chinese, all contended that what we were doing in Japan would be identical to retaining Hitler (if alive) as the ruler of Germany while destroying the Nazi Party and the Wehrmacht. They thought we were being stupid.

MacArthur thought otherwise. He thought that by substitution of "good" advisers for the militarists who formerly "controlled" the throne, the Emperor could be made a powerful force for the democratization of Japan. He argued that the "divorce" of Shinto from the state would put an end to the idea that the Japanese were superior to other peoples, so the divorce was put through. However, as of this writing, the Emperor still dons his ceremonial robes and attends the major religious festivals in the Shinkaden Temple in his palace grounds. So perhaps the decree is not yet final and there may still be a reconciliation at some future date.

MacArthur, acting through directives from above as well as on his own initiative, has in the months since the surrender worked efficiently and with brilliance to reform Japan. He has:

47

Disarmed the military forces.

Broken up the military and "thought" police.

Supervised an election, at which women exercised their new right to vote.

Initiated agrarian reforms to give the small tenant farmer a better chance for a living.

Instituted educational reforms.

Begun the punishment of war criminals.

Guaranteed free speech and the right of assembly (although he cracked down hard on a "riotous" demonstration by a handful of Communists).

Taken steps to break up the big corporations and trusts and put the Zaibatsu—the giant monopolies—out of business. But, inasmuch as we have decided not to kill off all the Japanese but to let them live and work and feed themselves, I predict that the Zaibatsu will regain at least a share of their powers because they are the only group in Japan with the experience to put the country on its feet again.

Further, MacArthur has directed the promulgation of a new constitution, modeled on our own, by which Japan renounces war as an instrument of national policy and promises that it will never again maintain an army or navy. It has been deprived of civil aviation.

For the present, Japan lacks the means to build a war machine, having lost its sources of iron and oil and coal. Its war industries have been destroyed. Its people are too preoccupied by the necessity of just living to do much thinking about revenge.

But the men who built Japan into a mighty power still exist and the ideas that supported the plans and dreams of world conquest will never be wiped out in a brief occupation—three to five years as MacArthur now suggests.

And the very core of Japanese militarism still exists in the Emperor system and in Hirohito, who is still the richest man in the world, who, through the blind devotion of all but a handful of his 70,000,000 subjects, is still the most powerful man in the world and who—despite the State Department and now MacArthur—has never proved that he was a "peace-loving" man.

I know that the argument for keeping the Emperor is that it avoided the armed conquest of Japan and thus saved many, many American lives. This is the same argument that was used to justify the deals with the Fascist rascals, Peyrouton and Darlan in North

Africa, with Badoglio and his Fascists in Italy—where we likewise insisted on retention of the monarchy until the Italian people themselves threw it out. The State Department naturally never goes on to the next step in this argument which is that if we saved so many thousand lives by making a deal with Fascism in North Africa, we could have saved hundreds of thousands by coming to terms with Hitler. Deals like that simply make a mockery of the deaths of the thousands who fell before the deal was made.

I did not want to see one American die unnecessarily in defeating Japan. But I think the State Department, which has long shown a tendency to favor monarchical and reactionary regimes, was anxious to preserve the Emperor setup in Japan and thus failed to drive as hard a bargain as was possible. I think Japan was much nearer complete collapse than we imagined, and that a few more atomic bombs on Tokyo would have made them accept any terms—including the abdication of the Emperor and termination of the Emperor system. It was that system we were fighting, and all it stood for. As long as Hirohito rules, there will be no rest for the men in the graves on Bataan and Iwo Jima and Guadalcanal.

Chapter Four

Millionaires with Patched Pants

Picture, if you can, the imaginary scene as Mr. Thomas Lamont, head of the House of Morgan, greets the coming of a September morn in the city of New York, year 1945.

The banker is living for the nonce in the home of the late Mr. Charles Schwab at Riverside Drive and 73rd Street, and in answer to the soft-voiced summons of his valet he opens his eyes and looks out through the paneless windows at a smoky and misty morning.

He arises from the floor of the master bedroom, throwing back a none-too-clean blanket, and climbs into a patched pair of striped morning pants and a sleeveless white shirt, over which he dons a shiny black coat. He goes down to the lawn, not by the stairway because there is no stairway, but by means of a ladder leaning against the window. Laying aside his coat, he performs his ablutions with grimy water scooped up from a tin basin.

From the yard he can see through occasional breaks in the fog and smoke, all the way to Central Manhattan, and even to the lower districts of the island. The buildings which formerly blocked the view are no longer standing, and on their sites is a jumble of tin shacks and wooden lean-to's thrown together from the wreckage of apartments and once-imposing office edifices.

After souping up a few spoonfuls of watery oatmeal, without sugar or milk, and drinking some plain tea, Mr. Lamont walks up to Broadway where, after a long wait, he climbs aboard a trolley car and rides for two hours through a wilderness of wreckage down to Wall Street. Here most of the buildings are still standing.

The door guard at the House of Morgan tips a shabby hat and

50

greets Mr. Lamont, "Ah, good morning, sir. Bit of a raidy night, what!" Mr. Lamont, who has counted some thirty fires burning while on his way downtown, is not amused.

Up in his second-floor office, Mr. Lamont pushes a buzzer and a male secretary appears, handing over the four-page *New York Herald Tribune* and a tabloid-sized *Wall Street Journal.* The headlines say, ENEMY IN BERMUDA. CUBA FALLS TO ENEMY. CASUALTIES HEAVY IN NEW ORLEANS INCENDIARY RAID. PITTSBURGH DESTROYED BY NEW ENEMY WEAPON CALLED ATOMIC BOMB.

"The news," says the secretary superfluously, "is not too good this morning, Mr. Lamont."

"Well, Sanderson, let's skip it. I have some orders for you. Tell the automobile plants in Detroit . . ."

"Sorry, sir, but the plants were burned down."

"Ahem, Sanderson. Direct our ships to proceed to Newfoundland to pick up . . ."

"So sorry sir, but we have no more ships."

"You mean they are all gone?"

"That's right, Mr. Lamont, and not only that but a flash just came on the ticker saying the enemy landed in Canada this morning. As you know, all our harbors have been mined by enemy airplanes."

"How are we going to eat without food from Newfoundland?"

"That's what my wife was asking me, sir. She said that after all I work for J. P. Morgan and Company and I should be able . . ."

"All right, Sanderson, you may go now. But first bring me my pencil sharpener."

From a desk drawer, Mr. Lamont pulls out a bundle of pencils which he proceeds to sharpen. The job done, he takes a tray from a closet in the oak-paneled room and arranges the pencils neatly. He puts on a pair of dark glasses and goes out onto the street to pick up a dime or so peddling his wares. . . .

Transfer that scene to Tokyo in September, 1945, and you have a reasonably accurate outward picture of the position of Japan's industrial and financial rulers at the time of the surrender. We met the great Japanese tycoons in the Imperial Hotel for an unprecedented press conference at which they told us why, from their point of view, Japan had been defeated and what they hoped to do in the future to put the country back on its feet.

Inamaru-san, the dapper manager of the Imperial, arranged the meeting. (He was dapper once more after bringing some of his prewar wardrobe out from a hiding place.) It might be better to say that he "staged" it, for it was a superior production considering the difficulties he must have encountered in rounding up the props. And in rounding up the participants, for the Japanese who met us had once been so rich and powerful that no foreign newspaperman could get within a hundred yards of their oak-paneled offices.

Inamaru set the time for six o'clock "sharp." He must have told the Japanese to be there early because they were already present in the second-floor conference-and-banquet room when we arrived. At the door we were handed typewritten sheets headed, "American Side"— listing the names of the reporters—and "Japanese Side," with the identity of the Japanese participants. Chairs had been arranged in a semicircle, with places in the middle for the Japanese and the Americans on each flank. Mr. Inamaru had, during the war, taken some liberties with the originally austere decor given to the Imperial by Mr. Frank Lloyd Wright, and some indirect lighting gave just enough illumination to produce a cozy, homey atmosphere. Most of the Japanese were dressed in business suits, with one or two in kimonos.

I looked down the list of the "Japanese side."

Royzo Asano, president of the Asano Cement Co. and of the Nippon Kokan Kabushiki Kaisha, which means Japan Steel Tube Co., Ltd.

Aiichiro Fujiyama, president of the Japan Chamber of Commerce.

Kiyoshi Miyazaki, President of Mitsui Company, Ltd.

Ichiro Hattori, Managing Director, Mitsubishi Trading Co.

Hisanobu Terai, President of the Nippon Yusen Kaisha (N.Y.K. steamship lines).

And so on. With the exception of Mr. Asano, most of the conferees were *banto*, or managers of the affairs and fortunes of the great wealthy families—the Zaibatsu—that monopolized Japan's economy. There were representatives of Yasuda and Sumitomo, in addition to Mitsui and Mitsubishi, those four firms comprising the largest of the Zaibatsu. In the extent of their control, they had no counterparts in any other country. Mitsubishi, for instance, was in shipbuilding, munitions, coal mining, machinery, aircraft, shipping, and trading. Sumitomo controlled metals and machinery. Mitsui did one-tenth of all Japan's internal business, plus forty per cent of the country's foreign commerce. And the firms were further interlocked by marriage, by investment, and by directorates into an all-controlling monopoly.

Mr. Miyazaki was, all rolled into one, Thomas Lamont and Tom Girdler, Henry Kaiser and Henry Ford, plus a Rockefeller or so.

I felt more at ease when I saw that Mr. Miyazaki was wearing shoes which were definitely not mates.

The mismated shoes, it must be said, and the poorly fitting clothes that some of the other *banto* were wearing were so much baloney. So was the hissing and bowing that the Zaibatsu put on for the benefit of the representatives of the barbarian press. A wealthy Japanese girl, whom I had known before the war, told me that immediately after the Saipan invasion, word had passed around among the financial and social leaders in Tokyo that it was time to get out of the capital. "We knew you had a big bombing plane that could reach us from Saipan," said Yuriko-san. "In fact, we even knew that it was named the B–29." A dozen other Japanese acquaintances confirmed this information.

As a result of the tip, the rich got their best personal possessions out of Tokyo and stored them in their beach homes at Kamakura, their mountain places at Myanoshita or Kurizawa, or in Kyoto—which escaped bombing. So when their Tokyo homes were destroyed, they were down to their last half-dozen houses. As for money, they had only some $30,000,000,000 among them when the war ended. Enough of this was liquid and hidden away so that the freezing of bank assets did not cause them to starve to death. On the other hand, it did not take a master mind to look over the ruined cities of Japan and see that a great share of their plants and shipyards, mills and factories was desperately in need of repair.

Their good manners toward the press represented something new. Before the war they were overweening and arrogant toward those not their financial or social equals. American stenographers and clerks who worked in the New York branches of Zaibatsu firms have told me their bosses were decidedly unpleasant toward their underlings, although very suave and polished in the presence of Wall Street friends whom they entertained at expansive and expensive banquets at the Waldorf, with a hundred-dollar tip for the waitress and another hundred dollars for the hat-check girls.

At our meeting in the Imperial, the members of the Japanese side decided to create a friendly atmosphere by relating their favorite bomb stories with masochistic pleasure.

"Ha, ha," laughed the trim Mr. Asano. "My house was burned down by the B–29s. I have been living in a tin shack." His voice was cultured New England.

"Ha, ha, ha," giggled Mr. Miyazaki. "My home likewise burning to ground."

"Ha, ha, ha, ha," chuckled Mr. Hattori. "My cousin was killed by the B–29s. He was standing on the roof of his house, composing a poem describing the wild beauty of the air raid, when an incendiary bomb came near. He tried to catch it in his hands. He didn't. Ha, ha, ha, ha."

Their efforts at clowning were not too convincing. We already had proof that these men were shrewd, skilled, with plenty of business and industrial know-how and unlimited drive and ambition. They and their predecessors, starting from scratch in a backward and isolated agricultural country, had built Japan into a formidable industrial power, not quite top-notch, but near enough to enable Nippon to hand the Western powers their greatest defeat in history.

With their cheap (by Western comparisons) standards of living they had competed with great success against our own industry, to such an extent that we had to pass laws limiting the import of electric-light globes manufactured in Osaka, shipped across the Pacific, and sold in Schenectady at prices far cheaper than similar articles manufactured in that city. They had excelled in the production of bicycles, flashlights, patriotic emblems, textiles, silk garments. Their cheap cotton clothes had been suitably priced for the vast markets of Asia. They had made seventy-five per cent of all the crockery used in the United States.

The Zaibatsu had been equal to the test of preparing for war. Since 1937 the industrialists had been the partners of the military, at first reluctantly under the compulsion of successively stronger national economic mobilization measures, and then willingly as the Army conquered new territories and new sources of raw materials. They and their trained engineers, with the help of the United States, Britain, and Germany, had built the guns, ships, tanks, and planes that enabled them to overrun the Orient in a few months after Pearl Harbor. No, they certainly weren't clowns when it came to business.

Mr. Fujiyama of the Chamber of Commerce, who had done this sort of thing before with American businessmen as participants, called the session to order and proceeded to the business of the evening which, since this was an American air-force party, was principally planned to develop evidence of how the B–29s defeated Japan. Mr. Asano translated, in his educated tones, for those of his colleagues whose English was scanty. First of all, Mr. Asano and his associates wanted to make it very clear that the war was not of their doing, that they had attempted to discourage the militarists because they did not think Japan could win.

"I knew your industrial production. Japan could not hope to match it."

"I traveled throughout America after studying at Cornell and M.I.T. I knew we could not win and told the Army so."

"On the face of it, our job was impossible."

"Here was Japan's problem. We lacked coal, iron, and oil, the very guts of modern industry. When the war started we got the sources of those things, but we could not bring them to Japan. To have brought in all the needed raw materials from the captured lands of the south we needed thirteen million tons of shipping. But we started the war with only seven and a half million tons and that was rapidly cut down. We had to devote forty per cent of our labor to raising food, and even that was not enough and we had to import more rice."

"Our battle was against time. If you had given us time to consolidate our conquests, we would have made Asia the strongest area in the world. But our outpost lines would not hold. You did not give us enough time."

Knowing that their position was potentially hopeless from the start, they had nevertheless kept on producing right up to the end, using makeshift methods when the fire raids destroyed their factories and the submarine and aerial blockade cut off the last of their raw materials. They gave us a dismal picture, which I believe was accurate, of Japan's economy at the end of the war.

Mr. Miyazaki said that Mitsui industries, representing a 10,500,-000,000-yen investment, had been fifty per cent destroyed. That included thirty to forty per cent destruction of chemical industries.

Mitsubishi put their total losses at well over fifty per cent. Nevertheless, both these great firms had set aside dividends for the American firms with investments in Japan. For instance, Westinghouse owned twenty to thirty per cent of Mitsui Electrical Engineering Co. Associated Oil of California was an equal partner in Mitsubishi Oil Refining Co., at Yokohama. "We have the funds set aside and saved for our American investors," said these farsighted Japanese businessmen. "They can have their dividends [profits from the war] when-

55

ever they care to come for them." Indeed, this was not at all surprising. It was not the first time in recent history that international business tycoons had placed their obligations to each other above those owed to their respective countries.

Steel production, they told us, continuing the song of woe, was down to fifteen per cent of the 1941 capacity of 5,000,000 tons annually.

There was very little aviation gasoline left—about enough for the last big Kamikaze sortie that the air forces had planned. The Japanese tried to make gasoline from sweet-potato alcohol, but the quantities had been small.

Railroads, and telephone and wire communications, were shot to pieces. There were no materials for repair of trains, street cars, or automobiles. Coal was lacking.

There had never been enough clothing after the textile industries were converted to war production. China had supplied only a trickle of cotton compared to the vast amounts Japan formerly purchased in the United States and Brazil.

Rice was short. There was no salt.

Plane production had reached a maximum of 1,800 monthly and then fallen back to a thousand, where by heroic efforts it was maintained nearly to the end of the war, despite the fact that our bombing had been aimed at the aircraft industry. (If the Japanese had gone underground with their industry, as the Germans were starting to do, we would have had the devil of a time blasting it out. As it was, the Japanese made only one brief effort at the end of 1944 to dig in their plants, but by then it was too late.)

The captured overseas empire no longer meant anything because there was no merchant shipping left of the great fleet of 7,500,000 tons. In all, only about 130 merchant ships survived the war. Shipping losses had started in early 1942 as our submarines prowled the enemy sea lanes. In 1942, Japan had been able to build 425,000 tons of new ships, but had lost nearly five times that amount.

N.Y.K., once one of the greatest merchant fleets in the world, had exactly *one* of its well-known passenger ships left, the Hikawa Maru having been spared because it was used as a hospital vessel. Mr. Terai of N.Y.K. told us this, with the customary laughter at his own expense. He also confirmed what we had believed back in 1940 and had reported to our Naval Intelligence at that time, that the new N.Y.K. ships were built for quick conversion to aircraft carriers.

My wife, daughter Kay, and I were on the luxurious "Nitta Maru" on its maiden trip from Kobe to Shanghai in the summer of 1940. It was a beautiful vessel to see, airconditioned throughout, furnished tastefully. But it was also top-heavy, rolling like a barrel in the slightest sea, and when you touched a doorknob, it came off in your hand; the showers didn't work, the rails were of wood and very frail, and it was obvious that the whole superstructure was designed to be knocked away in a hurry and replaced by a flight deck.

"Yes," said Mr. Terai, "that was what happened. 'Nitta Maru' was made into carrier and was sunk by your airplanes. Likewise the 'Asama,' 'Tatsuta,' 'Kamakura'—all the big trans-Pacific liners."

Mr. Asano-san summed it all up. "There was no doubt that Japan's industry was very badly beaten. We told the government leaders that we could not continue."

"Which government leaders?" Ah, well, said Mr. Asano, he and the other industrialists hadn't actually dared to bring the subject up with the generals; they feared arrest or death if they took a defeatist attitude, but they had tried from April of 1945 "to let the people know that victory was impossible" and were very happy when the atomic bomb "gave us an excuse to quit."

His summary was interrupted by the sudden appearance in the conference room of Major General Victor E. Bertrandias, who was given a rousing welcome by the Japanese and was obviously somewhat embarrassed at being greeted as an old friend. The Japanese sitting nearest to me was studying the two stars on the general's collar.

"What do they mean?" he asked.

"Bertrandias is a major general in the American Army Air Corps."

"Ah, so," he hissed interestedly, "he was only a major in the reserve when he used to sell us Douglas airplanes. He made many trips to Tokyo before the war. My company, the Nakajima aircraft, was the licensed manufacturing agent of Douglas in Japan. I am glad to see Mr. Bertrandias back again. We big businessmen understand each other."

Victor E. Bertrandias, major in the U. S. Army Air Corps reserve and vice-president of Douglas Aircraft in charge of exports, had been a familiar figure in Japan for ten years before the war, as had been many another American salesman of airplanes, oil, and machine tools which the Japs were buying in great quantities to build up their war machine. I used to see Bertrandias and company in the lobby of the Imperial in Tokyo, chatting with their Japanese friends, or climbing into the big limousines sent to call for them by their acquaintances in the Zaibatsu.

It was Douglas, followed by Lockheed, who furnished Japan the most assistance in building up her pre-war airlines. In New York, Department of Justice investigators told me how they had traced the relations of Douglas and the Zaibatsu through the files of Japanese companies in New York.

One of the most important Japanese purchases from Douglas was the original of the DC–4 (C–54), the four-engined transport which succeeded the DC–3 as the workhorse of the air on *our* side in the war. Originally, the Japanese Army Air Corps tried to purchase the plane, but when it was learned that Secretary Hull planned to embargo the export of military aircraft, the name of the purchaser was changed to Japan Air Transport and the deal went through on schedule.

The DC–4 was shipped to Japan as deck cargo on a Japanese freighter, shepherded by Douglas employees who assembled the giant aircraft in Japan. It was the Japanese intention, of course, to convert the DC–4 into long-range bombers with which to attack the United States. A Japanese air-force general told me that this plan was abandoned for a peculiar reason. "You see," he said, "we did not have any runways built solidly enough to handle the four-engine planes. So we stopped attempting to make them." No explanation as to why the runways were not strengthened.

However, the Japs appreciated getting the DC–4 so much that they wrote Bertrandias a letter in which they thanked him for his efforts. The Japs had obtained many other airplanes from us in the days before it was illegal to export them, our State Department being blind, and when American big business took the attitude that money was money and an order an order, and what the hell if the Japs were bombing the Chinese—that was none of our party. Douglas granted licenses to Nakajima to manufacture planes from Douglas patents, and I made many pre-war trips in Jap-built DC–2s and DC–3s.

Shortly after we saw him in Tokyo, Major General Bertrandias returned to the U. S., was discharged from the Army, and returned to his export job in Douglas where, of necessity, he began to look for

58

other customers than the Japs. At least for the time being, the Japs were not buying any airplanes, although aircraft manufacturers would no doubt be ready to supply them once more when the hour was ripe. The night of our conference in the Imperial Hotel, Bertrandias retired from the room in some confusion and in rather a hurry, thereby missing an excellent dinner.

Our stories had been describing the hunger in Japan, and just before we sat down at the long table our hosts had been telling us that "seven million people will die of starvation this winter" unless rice were brought in from Korea and French Indo-China, and soy beans from Manchuria. So we rather expected austerity rations.

Instead there was a full-course dinner: soup, fish, steak, salad, a fancy dessert, white and red French wine and brandy afterward. The talk was friendly and charming, the war forgotten as our hosts looked to the future.

"What next?" I asked my dinner partner, Mr. Fujiyama.

"First of all, our hope is to recover a little industrially, to learn the reparation terms so that we may know what we can and cannot do. The Potsdam declaration is our golden rule now, and at Potsdam it was promised that Japan would be allowed to live. We must pick up the pieces."

Mr. Miyazaki came in from the other side, "We rather expect that it will take five to ten years to restore our foreign trade to some extent. We hope to export silk, and buy food and cotton. Mitsui formerly held many cartel licenses, and had agreements with other countries on shipping rates. We will start building ships, if permitted, and try to resume our trade."

And Mr. Asano put in from the head of the table, "Unless our people are given food and work, there is grave danger of socialism. We do not believe the United States wants that in Japan. Besides, who will fill the vacuum in Asia's economy caused by the destruction of our industry? America cannot sell to the Asiatic market at prices the people are able to pay. Nor do you want the rice that we formerly took from the Philippines, China, and Indo-China in exchange for our manufactured products. You have found substitutes for rubber, so your trade with Malaya will decline.

"Those countries," he went on, "cannot buy from you unless you buy from them. But Japan needs their products and we in turn can sell them things they need. So, I rather think, Japan must be the middleman between America and the rest of the Orient because you

59

can buy from us and we can buy from you, process your goods, and sell them in the Asiatic market."

And so, Mr. Asano!

China, the Japanese pointed out, was in need of technological assistance and Japan could furnish it. Indeed, after eight years of war the old enemies, China and Japan, were in fact getting together in this respect. Japanese engineers remained on the job in China long after the surrender—until the United States protested vigorously and even after that.

It was when the party was finally breaking up that Mr. Asano made the classic remark of the night. In a series of shocked stories written in Manila in February, telling of the atrocities suffered by our prisoners at the hands of the Japanese, I had predicted the approaching collapse of Japan and said:

"What we must expect from Tokyo shortly is for a group of suave, Harvard-educated businessmen and diplomats who have many old friends in America, to come forward with their hats in their hands, bowing with that unexcelled Japanese politeness and hissing, 'So sorry, please. It was all a very bad mistake.'"

Now, bidding us farewell, Mr. Asano said, "The whole thing was a very sad mistake. And by the way," he added, "are any of you from Harvard?"

No, we said, Rutgers, Columbia, Missouri, Penn, Yale, Jersey City High, West Point.

"Ah, so sorry," said Mr. Asano with a slight hiss. "I was hoping to get news of my friend and Harvard classmate, Mr. Robert Benchley."

The meeting broke up amicably amid a fresh burst of ha-ha's.

What these gentlemen did not know was that the United States had the last ha-ha on them, at least in the late hostilities. They had outsmarted us for a long time before the war, through their industrial and economic spy ring in the United States, but finally that same spy ring had provided us with the information that made it possible for us to pinpoint their great centers of production and blast them from the air. How we put this information to work for us is a story that has been told only briefly.

For four years prior to Pearl Harbor, the Japs spent a half-billion dollars in the United States for the purchase of the latest American machinery and highly specialized tools needed to establish assembly-line production of airplanes, tanks, submarines, and guns. At the same time, they purchased manufacturing rights to the machinery

60

and hired American experts to go to Japan to help in the organization of assembly lines. Many leading American companies actually entered what amounted to partnership with Japanese companies. By an astute, careful survey of our machine-tool situation, the Japanese discovered that it would take the United States at least two years to get into full production for war.

They frequently made their inquiries with disarming frankness. They would write to a large American machine-tool producer, informing him that a $2,000,000 order was to be placed in the United States, and inquiring how long it would take to turn out the necessary products and, incidentally, asking what foreign and domestic orders were already on hand that would delay fulfillment of the Japanese order. Or they would ask a manufacturer how long it would take to enlarge his plant to fill an order from Tokyo. In this way they obtained (and passed on to Germany) an accurate picture of our production and potentials.

Machine tools and specialized machinery were selected and purchased in the United States under the direction of Japanese Army and Navy technical missions which used the offices of Mitsui and Mitsubishi as their American headquarters. Our big companies showed no compunction whatever about filling Japanese orders, and even after President Roosevelt finally cracked down, ways were found for getting around the executive order. When the Japs were banned from exporting technical blueprints, they could still go to the offices of airplane companies and obtain access to the blueprints. Our firms continued to ship oil and cotton to Japan by such devious means as delivering cargo to a phony go-between company in Haiphong, French Indo-China, where the goods were transferred to Japanese ships.

What was to trip up the Japanese in the long run was the fact that they kept complete records in their New York offices of purchases of United States industrial machinery and tools and other vital equipment, for oil refineries, steel mills, airplane engine plants. These records showed the destinations in Japan of these materials. On the day of Pearl Harbor, the Japs suddenly slipped into their downtown offices in New York and tried to burn the most revealing of their records, but the F.B.I. had been trailing the Mitsui and Mitsubishi big-shots and stepped in in time to preserve most of the invaluable documents.

These files became America's leading sources of military information about Japan. Careful sifting of the material enabled our experts to pin-point nearly every war factory in Japan, and to determine what and how much it was making. This enabled our Strategic Air Forces officers to select targets in order of priority, first smashing the key factories and then turning the bombers loose against remote and hidden industrial centers which had been located through a prolonged and intensive search through thousands and thousands of purchase orders, shipping invoices, and similar documents.

The Zaibatsu were amazed at the success with which these targets were tracked down, not knowing that it was due to their own passion for detail.

In later talks with the big men of Japanese business, I came to understand what they thought of their nation's past and probable future. They thanked Theodore Roosevelt for helping them get their start as a modern nation. Under pressure from England, ever fearful of Czarist Russian expansion in the Far East, Teddy had stepped in to halt Russo-Japanese hostilities in 1904–05 at a time when Japan was near industrial exhaustion in her war against Russia. Thanks to Teddy's Portsmouth Conference, the Japanese had come out of that war the victors, with Korea in their grasp, and well on their way to expansion and modernization.

Then England, fearing China as well as Russia and fearing that Wall Street capitalists would get a foothold in Manchuria and a grip on that country's railway system, had signed the Anglo-Japanese Alliance. It has been England's policy to keep Japan strong and China weak. The British estimated that they could risk having one Asiatic nation well armed and industrialized and employ it as a partner in the subjugation of China, Malaya, and India. Of course, this goes for the Dutch and French, too.

It likewise applied with equal force to our own industrialists and men of money, and to many of our diplomats—past and present. We did not go to war with Japan over China. Of course not. We were making too much money from our trade with Japan and for three years after 1937 (when the Japanese invaded China) we kept on dealing with Japan, selling the goods needed to overrun the Chinese, the airplanes with which they bombed, the scrap iron in those bombs.

A prominent silk man told me over beer and sukiyaki in a Tokyo restaurant in the fall of 1945, "History will, we rather think, repeat itself. The United States had heavy investments in Japan, which we have protected as far as possible, and the only hope for the United

States to get a share of the Orient's trade in the future in competition with China as it becomes industrialized, and with England—will be through the industry of Japan. We rather expect that the United States will make private loans to help us back on our feet, so that you may profit from our industry."

And, having obviously discussed the question among themselves and agreed on a definite line, all of the Japanese big-shots brought up the question of American fears of Communism—the old Hitler-Tokyo line. "Japan stands as a buffer between Soviet Communist expansion and the United States," they said. "You can use our country and our manpower to fight Russia, which you must inevitably do. In the meantime, it will be to your advantage to see that we are fed and to restore our productive power, so that we will be ready to take our places in the front lines of the next war."

This bill of goods was sold very easily to certain of MacArthur's generals, who were all for fighting Russia but *now*, at once, before the guns cooled off, and while we had an atomic jump on the Reds. Also, it was inevitable that certain of MacArthur's staff should find such men as Mr. Asano-san very charming gentlemen.

Despite this comradeship of ideas, MacArthur's drastic order redistributing the holdings of the four largest of the Zaibatsu—Mitsui, Mitsubishi, Sumitomo, and Yasuda—was a stunning blow to the big families. MacArthur declared the companies abolished and directed that their assets, amounting to the amazing total of $30,000,000,000, be held for the public. The purpose of the dissolution was to create an "equal economic opportunity" for everybody to make money. The Zaibatsu were included, and with a jump of fifty years on prospective competitors it was a cinch that they would not be long in getting back in the swim, after shaking off the effects of the dissolution and subsequent orders imposing heavy retroactive income taxes, and a capital levy on property.

The key to the future, as the silk man and others of the Zaibatsu said, was some distance beyond those immediate, crippling orders. It was bound up with policy toward Russia, on the one hand, and on the other with the likelihood that Wall Street and the City could find means to restore Japan's industry and her place in the cartel system. American firms, they pointed out, had a direct interest in seeing Japan get back on its feet.

And, they pointed out, Germany recovered after the last war. Japan could do it too, although, of course, without those nasty militarists. The Zaibatsu had the knowledge, the organization to get things running again. I predict that they will, even though their first steps were small indeed in comparison to their pre-war power. N.Y.K. organized a fishing fleet. Mitsui asked permission to establish a shipping line to New York. Mitsubishi started cornering silk, as well as tuna and crab, in anticipation of the day when they could start trading again. Employees were rounded up, ready to be put to work.

One of the Zaibatsu, in fact one of the Mitsui family, went to work as an office boy in the INS bureau in Tokyo at a salary equivalent to about ten dollars a month. Obviously he didn't do this through necessity, despite MacArthur's regulations limiting bank withdrawals. In the evening after work, he entertained foreign newsmen at parties which cost him ten times his monthly pay. He was a Cornell graduate, an aviation engineer, and he admitted with no false modesty that he had designed the last and best Nakajima fighter-plane engine. He had been working on jet-propelled planes when the war ended.

It did not take long to learn Mitsui's real reason for establishing himself in the news-agency office. He was put there to watch the war criminal lists and to get pre-publication notice of MacArthur's economic decrees.

Nor did it take long to learn the Mitsui attitude toward democracy. Sitting in the office one day, he pointed out the window at the street crowds three stories beneath us. "To hell with freedom of speech, the ballot, and all the rest of that stuff," he said. "Just look at those dirty guys in the street. Even if they were permitted free speech, they wouldn't know what to say. Keep their bellies full, keep them warm this winter, and you won't have to worry about giving them a democratic government. What they need is the Emperor."

Well, they still have him.

Chapter Five

Why Japan Quit

THE ZAIBATSU HAD TOLD US THAT AMERICA'S SU-
perior industrial production defeated Japan.

From other Japanese—generals, admirals, politicians—we got a
variety of answers to our question as to what brought about Japan's
surrender. In many cases, these answers had to be taken with a considerable dosage of salt, because the questions put by the American
Navy and our Army Air Forces were decidedly leading. Right after
Japan's surrender, both the admirals and the army airmen set out to
prove to the American people that one branch or the other of our
services had single-handedly brought Japan to her knees. The Navy
and Air Forces were bitter opponents in a battle revolving around
the proposed merger of our armed forces and each sought to round
up evidence that would enable it to claim exclusive credit (except for
an occasional side-of-the-mouth acknowledgment) for winning the
war.

The top Japanese were quick to grasp this situation and they
played off, very suavely, one side against the other in this all-Ameri-
can fight. Under interrogation by our strategic bombing experts, the
generals, admirals, and businessmen would reply, "Your strategic
bombing beat Japan." Asked the same questions by our Navy investigators, the same Japs would answer, "Your Navy carrier planes sank
our warships. Your Navy submarines destroyed our merchant shipping, and, of course, we could not fight without warships and without shipping."

The Japs were more than willing to be obliging. They told our
people what they wanted to hear. Thus one night I heard Rear Admiral Taoshita Takata tell General Barney Giles, deputy commander of Strategic Air Forces, "The B–29 was the biggest single

factor in defeating Japan. Your strategic bombing destroyed our industry and made it impossible for us to fight longer. When your planes mined our harbors and established the aerial blockade of Japan, we were finished." General Giles beamed.

Then, not wishing to offend Major General Wurtsmith, commander of the 13th Air Force and a participant in the Bismarck Sea Battle, Admiral Takata added, "Of course, the greatest surprise and shock to us in the entire war was the engagement in the Bismarck Sea where your planes came in en masse at mast-level against our ships. We lost our entire convoy of between thirty and forty ships which were enroute to New Guinea." General Wurtsmith beamed.

Having gone into Japan with the Strategic Air Forces, quite naturally I heard more pro-Air than pro-Navy statements by the Japanese. In presenting a few of these for what they are worth, I wish to point out that the tragic result of the Air-Navy struggle is that the American public has never been given a true and thorough picture of the lessons of the war against Japan. No organization in Washington, no commission without an axe to grind, no impartial body ever evaluated without bias the efficiency and weaknesses of our various weapons and branches of service. No such organization can exist in our present system of waste, duplication, conflict, and rivalry. The full facts never were and never will be laid frankly and clearly before the people by either the admirals or the generals, because each group has a selfish interest in seeing that this is not done.

In any case, here are some of the one-sided bits of testimony collected by the Strategic Air Forces:

Prince Fumimaro Konoye, thrice premier and a member of the imperial family, said before his suicide by poisoning, "Fundamentally, the thing that brought about the determination to make peace was the prolonged bombing by the B–29s."

The former president of one of Japan's largest concerns, Mr. Moto of Mitsubishi Heavy Industries, declared, "The first bombings of Mitsubishi occurred on December thirteenth, 1944, when the airplane engine factory at Nagoya was bombed and then again on December nineteenth, 1944, when the air frame factory was bombed. By April, 1946, one-third of the production of Mitsubishi had been destroyed and from then on there was a general feeling of helplessness and hopelessness. . . . Our company did not think that Japan could win the war because, despite increased production of fighter planes, the B–29s kept coming in greater and greater strength."

And here is a statement by an American-educated Japanese propagandist, Dr. Kawai, chief editorial writer of the Nippon *Times,* who holds B.A., M.A., and Ph.D. degrees from Stanford University:

"When the B–29 raids began the people really knew the war was lost. Before that they knew some islands had been lost, but islands mean nothing to the ordinary man. When the big raids came, the feeling of defeat began."

Looked at impartially, there is no question that airplanes and submarines were our most effective weapons against Japan. Nearly one half of Japan's principal industrial cities—in all some sixty-eight targets with a population of over 21,000,000—was wiped out by fire-bomb raids (and it is incidental, to me, that American *Army* pilots were flying the planes). Japanese figures placed the total dead at 260,000, with 412,000 injured and 9,200,000 made homeless. Airplanes (they happened to be U. S. Navy planes) smashed the bulk of Japan's sea power. Submarines sank 148 combatant ships and 1,041 noncombatant ships, on the basis of official reports which are probably reasonably accurate. Our aircraft sank 1,000,000 tons of enemy shipping in 1944 alone.

Add to this the fact that on island after island our troops overwhelmed the supposedly invincible Japanese, and that we were coming ever closer and closer to the home islands, and it is not difficult to understand how matters reached a point where highly placed Japanese statesmen decided in the spring of 1945 (several months before the atom bomb) that the time had come to find a way out of the war, and began the complicated negotiations that led finally to surrender.

A highly important factor, too, was one of "spirit." The Japanese were great believers in the invincibility of spiritual strength. They thought it more powerful than any other weapon, that it could surmount any material disadvantages. I think what stopped them short of annihilation was our own greater determination, even more than our material power. That is what a Japanese air general said in so many words, "We lost because of your greater spiritual strength."

An admiral told me, "We were surprised to learn your fighting spirit."

Even Tojo said, "We had to admire your spirit as fighters. You were worthy opponents for us."

I believe this is what convinced the Japanese most, even though it is obvious that all the determination in the world could not have won without modern weapons. To the Japanese, war is as much a matter of spirit as of firing a rifle. The outstanding characteristic of the Jap soldier was not his marksmanship, intelligence, or initiative, but his Banzai fanaticism. He thought this spirit could conquer the world. Then, as time passed, he saw that America's will to win was stronger than his own.

The Japs had been taught to think of us as an immoral, materialistic race, lacking courage, soaked in alcohol, neurotic, devoted to sissy sports and languorous pastimes. Gradually, they learned that our "unconquerable spirit" was more unconquerable than their own. Looking back, it is difficult to translate this into terms of scared guys crawling onto beaches (not "storming them," which is a newspaper term) under machine-gun and mortar fire, of men lying wounded and crying and bloody on the deck of a ship just hit by a Kamikaze, of kids whose nerves cracked up in the hell of jungle foxholes, of the conscientious objectors raising turkeys back home, of black markets and night clubs. But it was there all the time; in Sergeant Schmidt behind his machine gun on Guadalcanal, and the Sullivan brothers, and MacArthur and "Rosy" O'Donnell, and Nimitz and Halsey, and the Americans who kept fighting, regardless of what uniform they wore.

Americans have the spirit it takes to win wars. Unfortunately, they don't seem to know what to do about it afterward.

On the "non-spiritual" side, I liked best the comment of my old friend, Rear Admiral M. Kanazawa.

"I think so," said Kanazawa in his best English. "Whole war very big mistake, ha, ha."

I found Kanazawa when we visited Hiroshima, locating him by chance in a house on a pine-covered hillside overlooking naval headquarters at Kure, where he was commander of all naval forces in the southern half of the main island of Honshu and on the island of Shikoku which forms the seaward flank of the winding Inland Sea.

In the fog-shrouded harbor of Kure was about three-fourths of what remained of Japan's once-mighty fleet which, on the afternoon of Pearl Harbor, had been the second largest in the world, potentially outgunned only by the British fleet 12,000 miles away and with no intention of deserting European waters to travel to the far Pacific. In all, some fifty Japanese war vessels survived the Pacific battles. We saw some of them in the harbor at Kure, as we drove from the airfield through the fire-blitzed town and on down the shore road to

Hiroshima. There was the beached hulk of the ancient battle-cruiser "Idzumo," Scotland-built, which in the battle of Tsushima Straits in 1905 had been Admiral Togo's flagship in his victorious fight against the Czar's fleet. The "Idzumo" was resting on the bottom with a port list of about fifteen degrees, and on its funnels were painted the silhouettes of nine American planes, fighters, and bombers, which its gunners claimed to have shot down.

Across the rainswept bay was the big bulk of the battleship "Haruna," which Colin Kelly bombed in the early days of the war off Luzon, and which our naval carrier pilots had finally holed and sunk in shallow water in one of the last raids on Kure. Farther out were anchored a number of submarines, a few cruisers and destroyers, and through the mist we could see men working to dismantle their guns.

After a telephone call had identified me, Admiral Kanazawa invited Bob Brumby and me up to his house. I didn't recognize him at first when he came to the open door in the gray-green summer uniform with a single star on his collar. He was a compactly built man of about fifty, energetic, with a shock of thick black hair and a face deeply seamed from a lifetime of laughing. He laughed now, "Ha, Ha. You don't know me. Kanazawa! Maybe the war made me look older."

He told us to keep on our shoes as we followed him into a large living room with the inevitable round table, sofa, and deep armchairs which are part of every European-style Japanese house, office, or conference room.

He called for tea, then for Shanghai Scotch-type whiskey, and finally as we talked on he invited us to share his dinner. It turned out to be a bowl of rich bean soup and some small, peeled boiled potatoes, very tender but half cold, served with butter and salt. That was what a Japanese admiral was eating at the time of the surrender, and Kanazawa apologized repeatedly for the meager fare, recalling with a chuckle the feasts he formerly presided over in Shanghai.

Kanazawa admitted in so many words, "We were defeated," and went on to discuss the war from the practical naval point of view rather than one of Kamikaze mysticism, although he had some of that in him, too. I know that he was telling the truth about Japan's war plans, because he had outlined them to me in Shanghai four years before.

He said the plans had been carried out exactly as laid down for

69

years. They had not included any idea of attacking the mainland of the United States. The plan was to take and to hold a line running from Attu and Kiska down through Wake and the Gilberts to the New Hebrides and New Guinea. This was the outpost line of defense, and behind it were the Marshalls, Carolines, Solomons, Bonins, Okinawa, and Iwo Jima; and behind them the territory for which Japan went to war—the Philippines, Dutch East Indies, Siam, Malaya, and Burma.

It was the belief of Japan's war leaders that they could hold us at most points along the outpost line and, failing that, could check us at the second line with such great losses that the war would become a stalemate and we would agree to a compromise peace that would permit the Japs to hold on to a large share of their conquered territory.

The attempt to go into northern Australia, which was frustrated by the Coral Sea Battle, and the belated effort to take Midway and the Hawaiian Islands were inspired by Japan's early successes and by the realization that the farther east and south the outpost line was pushed, the safer they would be. They saw us coming back in Hawaii, building up forces in New Caledonia and Australia, and they recognized that they had not gone quite far enough. Guadalcanal brought the realization home to them.

"Guadalcanal." Admiral Kanazawa held up one index finger and with his other hand bent the finger slowly halfway over. "Guadalcanal was the turning point of the war." Once Japan lost there, it became a question of fighting defensively, of holding scores of widely scattered outposts, and "defensive war, I think so, is rather difficult." It was for this reason the Japanese fought so desperately to hold Guadalcanal, losing scores of ships and thousands of men. They realized that all their island bastions were interlocking and interdependent, and they tried at all costs to keep the line from being pierced at any point.

Kanazawa said that from the naval point of view Coral Sea and Midway were major setbacks for Japan. They robbed the Imperial Navy of the initiative, caused its first serious losses, and further than that taught the Japanese for the first time that Pearl Harbor and Bataan had not crushed America's will to fight. Kanazawa said it this way, "We learned the fighting spirit of the Americans in combat. We had underestimated your will to fight."

"The plans went wrong at Coral Sea and Midway," we pointed

70

out, "and then your whole plan failed. What was the primary reason?"

"Japan made very many tactical and strategic mistakes," Kanazawa answered with a laugh. "I think whole thing very big mistake." Then he went on, "I think so, too many airplanes defeated Japan. If we had more airplanes, we might have won."

If Japan had the war to fight over again, she would have done these things, he said:

1. Attacked and seized the Hawaiian Islands in the first days. The Japanese had thought this impossible, but had learned from later statements of American commanders that these highly strategic islands were wide open and would have fallen after a brief fight. This would have driven the American Navy—or the small remnants of it—back to the United States mainland.

2. Massed thousands and thousands of airplanes in underground hangars in Hawaii. When the Americans made their first attempt to recapture the Islands—and it probably would have taken two years because shipbuilding facilities would have been transferred to the east coast in a panicked flight from the Pacific coast—the airplanes would be turned loose in Kamikaze attacks in such strength as to force us to turn back.

3. The Americans could not have made land-based airplane attacks on Hawaii for a number of years, perhaps six. Neither the B–17 nor the B–29 had enough range for round-trip flights from the mainland. Meanwhile, Jap submarines based on Hawaii could have patrolled our west coast, and suicide planes flying from carriers might have succeeded in blocking the Panama Canal.

4. Simultaneously with the seizure of Hawaii, the Japs would have taken such satellite islands as Johnston, Palmyra, and Midway, plus Penryhn and Tahiti, and behind them New Caledonia and New Zealand, and in the north, the Aleutians. This would have moved their outpost line thousands of miles east of the one they did occupy, would have deprived us of the principal bases from which we later mounted our attacks, and made it necessary for us to come 2,500 miles across open water from California to get at them.

5. Occupied Singapore, as they did, and then gone on to take Ceylon as a stepping stone to Calcutta which, when seized, would have isolated China. The oil they needed immediately could have been picked up at Balikpapan in Borneo. The Philippines and the Dutch East Indies could have been cleaned up at leisure. We could not have reinforced them.

"Yes," said Kanazawa wistfully, "I think so, if we fought that way we would have won—at least until you got atomic bomb."

The Japs had no reason to apologize for the war they did fight. It is the custom as soon as wars are won to forget how difficult was the achievement of victory. In the Kamikaze plane, the Japs had a very effective weapon, both in its damage to ships and to morale. With more Kamikazes, they might have turned the tide as they came close to doing three times—at Mindoro, in Lingayen Gulf, and off Okinawa. If they had opposed our landing on the Japanese mainland—scheduled for October, 1945—we might have lost as many as 2,000,000 killed and wounded before the islands were brought under control.

Kanazawa said the Japanese had realized very early that the war would be decided by airpower. Their Navy had swiftly converted the battleships under construction into makeshift aircraft carriers, with a flight deck aft, and (unlike the United States) had not built a single battleship during the war. But desperate efforts to turn all construction facilities to the production of aircraft had fallen short and at the end of the war Japan had only 5,000 naval planes. The Army had another 5,000.

Kanazawa confirmed that there had been a serious Army-Navy schism at the time of the Okinawa battle. The Navy had wanted to fight the last battle of the war there, using every available plane and ship, and the Army had insisted on hoarding its remaining planes until the invasion of Japan proper. The result had been a compromise, with the Navy losing its last battleship, the "Yamato," to our Navy planes when the "Yamato" and its escort vessels made a bold but futile attempt to sally out to Okinawa.

"Some of the Navy Kamikaze planes, I think many hundreds [the American figure is close to 4,000] were thrown into the battle of Okinawa," said Kanazawa. "But after it was seen that the island was lost we discontinued the attacks. All the planes in Japan, both Army and Navy, were being saved to attack your landing ships when you invaded. My job was to defend with my marines and sailors, and with suicide boats, the beaches of Shikoku and of this part of Honshu. We were getting ready for the battle, digging in, setting up defenses, when the Emperor ordered the war to stop."

We had seen some of those preparations on the road to Hiroshima. At the entrance to one tunnel, our car skidded on the wet concrete and careened sideways into a pile of packing boxes. Two of them were torn open and we saw that they contained brand-new airplane engines, of which there were perhaps five hundred in the tunnel. The other tunnels along the highway were stocked with bombs, shells, ammunition, guns, mines—all hidden away to escape our bombing and waiting to be pulled out and used on the D–Day of our invasion.

Except for small, fast, explosive-laden boats concealed under camouflage and up rivers and creeks, the Japanese had not expected to have much naval strength left to fight off the landings. "We had only some fifty ships left," Kanazawa said, "including the badly battered battleship 'Nagato,' three damaged carriers, three cruisers, ten submarines, and twenty destroyers. Only about half the surface ships were in condition to fight. We rather expected that all our ships would be sunk by your planes before the invasion."

He said Japan lost one-third of her naval strength at Coral Sea, Midway, Saipan, and in the battle for the Solomons, so that the equivalent of two-thirds remained at the time MacArthur sliced back to the Philippines in October, 1944.

"That was the most clever move, strategically, of the war," Kanazawa declared. "The Philippines were the key. When we lost them we had no hope of winning because we were isolated from our sources of raw materials. As you know, Japan is a rather narrow country (geographically) and could not exist without raw materials. Loss of the Philippines cut the Empire in two." Kanazawa and General MacArthur should get along very well together.

Accordingly, when the Japs learned that our forces were moving toward Leyte, they assembled every available ship in a desperate attempt to hold the islands. The result was a three-pronged battle in which (1) Halsey defeated the Jap carrier forces north of Luzon, (2) at Surigao strait Admiral Kinkaid trapped and destroyed powerful Jap forces, and (3) in Leyte Gulf our third force of baby carriers was in turn surprised, caught in the gunfire of the Japanese heavy ships, and then fought back so hard while fleeing to the south that the Japanese were finally slowed down and never attained their original objective of getting into the transport area of Tacloban and sinking our troop and supply ships.

"Most of the ships that we have left are out there in the harbor," the admiral went on. "You can have them all. I surrender them to you and am glad to get them off my hands." We declined the offer with thanks, Brumby pointing out that we were rowboat men, and

73

suggested that Kanazawa wait until the American naval forces came along in a month or so to make everything shipshape and legal. There was no chance in the meantime, the admiral assured us, of the Japanese scuttling their ships as the Germans had done at Scapa Flow. "My ships are all disarmed, my men, too. I have even told the school girls in my command to be polite to the Americans. The troops will be orderly because the Emperor ordered us to surrender. As you know, we obey only the Emperor. If he had decided that the war should go on, we would have died fighting. My wife, too, would have died at my side."

We thought the last part of the program a little extreme, and wondered why Kanazawa had not sent his wife to the country for safety. "No," he insisted, "her place is here. She stayed through the B–29 attacks on Kure. If I was to be killed, she must die with me. My daughter also." So there was some fanaticism in Kanazawa, as he proved again when we discussed the future of Japanese prisoners of war taken before the end of the conflict. We told him about half of them wanted to come home and live in obscure villages. "Oh, no," said the admiral. "It is better that they remain on those islands, if you will allow them."

"But," we protested, "all they did was surrender, many of them after being badly wounded. Now all Japan has done the same thing."

"It is not the same thing. They were not ordered to surrender by the Emperor, but were commanded to die for him. They did not do their duty. The Japanese code makes it a disgrace to surrender. They will be ostracized at home. They cannot atone for what they have done."

We changed the subject, and the admiral was nearly speechless with laughter at his own expense as he described his discomfiture at Rabaul. Bob Brumby had been in one of our bombers on the Christmas Day raid there in 1942. "Oh, yes," Kanazawa recalled. "I think I lost rather many ships that day. Ha, ha, ha."

He had ordered his troops at Rabaul to plant vegetables and tobacco and after the garrison was isolated by our air attacks and he himself left by submarine, "I did not worry too much about them, knowing they had plenty to eat and smoke."

Frequently during our talk, the admiral had referred to my games of golf with him in Shanghai. Now he said, "In future, it must be like after golf game at Sekinjao or Hungjao. Americans win or

British win or Japanese win, everybody sit down afterward, take drink together. We must be friends."

"The trouble with this game, admiral," I said, "is that your handicap wasn't big enough."

He went into another spasm of laughter, "Ha, ha. That's right. To fight war with small number of airplanes is like playing golf with only niblick and putter against man with drivers and irons."

As we got up to leave, Brumby admired a print of Fuji on the wall and made some courteous remark about its beauty.

Kanazawa thought it over for a minute and then, chuckling, shook his head, "Ah, yes, very pretty mountain. But I think so, in this war, Fuji not too good for Japan. Your airplanes could find way by locating mountain.

"In fact"—you could see he thought it was a good line—"Fuji in this war was America's co-pilot."

Chapter Six

Hiroshima Doesn't Hate Us

THE SUPERFORTRESS "ENOLA GAY," A TINY SPOT OF silver against the morning sky, had not used Fuji-san as a co-pilot on that fateful August 6, 1945, when it came in over Hiroshima to drop the first atomic bomb and to change the course of history and the ways of the world.

Japan was already beaten. Negotiations for surrender had been opened through Moscow¹ two months previously. In a matter of weeks at the most, Tokyo would have found a way out.

Even before it was subsequently disclosed that Japan would have surrendered without the atom bomb being dropped, many people were shocked and horrified at the action of the United States in making all-out war on civilians. Preachers, priests, and pacifists shouted against this foul deed and against the bombing of Nagasaki a week later, even though most of them had kept silent when the B–29s killed hundreds of thousands of civilians in their "orthodox" fire raids on Japanese cities.

Their protests rose even louder than did those of the Japanese government against the employment of this "inhumane weapon." The Men of God said we should not have used this terrible killer.

Their attitude was a pain in the neck to GI Joe. Not knowing Japan was nearing the breaking point, what the humanitarians were demanding—of course, without really realizing it—was for millions of Americans to die or be crippled in invading Japan. These unwittingly bloodthirsty people would have preferred to see countless Americans killed or torn to pieces in "orthodox" warfare rather than to give this new and terrifying weapon a chance to end the bloodshed. Such people failed to realize that there is no such thing as a

76

humane war and no longer are there noncombatants; every man, woman, and child on the other side is an enemy. There is only one rule in war—kill or be killed—and the more of "them" you kill, the fewer on your side get killed. It is futile and foolish to try to make "rules" for the organized murder that is war. There is no polite way to kill a man; a bayonet in the belly or the scorching, agonizing breath of a flamethrower is no less painful than being blown to bits by an atomic bomb. What we have to do is stop wars, not attempt to humanize them.

Actually, if the Japanese had carried out their threat to fight to the last and the war had gone on, there is no doubt that our casualties would have been so appalling that we would have used every weapon at our command—gas, chemicals, bacteriological killers —and to hell with humanitarianism, which is a luxury you don't enjoy in the front lines.

I disagree completely with those who would have had us refrain from using the atom bomb, whether for humanitarian or any other reasons. It is true that the Japanese would have surrendered shortly, atom bomb or no atom bomb. If the bomb had been hidden, concealed, kept secret, there might have been a postponement for a few years of the race by other nations to manufacture it. But only for a few years. By using the bomb, bringing it out into the open, we brought civilization face to face with its greatest decision—to live or to perish. Because there can no longer be any doubt that man has finally achieved the means of extinguishing himself from the face of the earth.

It was unfortunate for the human guinea pigs in Hiroshima that their city had to be used as a testing ground, a death laboratory. The city had been deliberately spared fire bombing for just this purpose; its geographical setting was suitable, it was flat, open, with the sea on one side and the nearest hills about six miles from the central section. Coldly, the scientists and the scientific killers of the United States Army Strategic Air Forces selected it and said, "This is the spot." In a way, Nagasaki was even more unfortunate than Hiroshima. Another city had been chosen as the target for the second and bigger bomb, but on the date selected there was bad weather over Japan, the crew of the B–29 could not find their number-one target through the clouds, so they bombed the secondary target of Nagasaki.

We were the first Americans to fly low over Nagasaki after the

77

bombing and the first to reach Hiroshima, many days before our scientific investigators got there. Before going to Hiroshima, we were awed by the Japanese stories of the terrible destruction. We expected that the survivors of Hiroshima would, at least, wail and weep and cry out at our inhumanity. We also feared we might expose ourselves to lethal doses of radiation.

We flew from Atsugi down to Kure, twenty-eight miles from Hiroshima on the Inland Sea, in the midst of heavy storms and had to make two separate attempts on different days before we could find a hole through the clouds and land our big B–17 on a tiny fighter strip at the Kure naval base. The Japanese gave us automobiles and a naval surgeon as guide, and we drove on down to Hiroshima over slippery roads lashed by winds and heavy, though intermittent, rain.

"I am glad that it is raining," said Dr. Taira, the naval surgeon. The rain, he explained, "soaks up the radioactivity, so it is less dangerous to enter the area today than if the weather were clear." The Japanese at that time were insisting (erroneously, on the basis of future evidence) that the bomb had left radioactivity which would make Hiroshima uninhabitable for at least six years. They claimed that people going into the bombed area were afterward, in many cases, affected by symptoms for which there was no cure and which resulted in death in days or weeks.

They described these symptoms, which had already killed many thousands: a sharp decrease in the white-corpuscle count in the blood, loss of appetite, intestinal bleeding, bleeding of the gums, hair falling out, severe headaches, high fever. In addition, they believed, although this was not yet known as a fact, that exposure to the gamma rays caused sterility.

Our own scientists declared that because the bomb had been exploded some 1,500 feet in the air, the ground had not been impregnated by deadly radiant energy, and said that the sufferers who exhibited such symptoms later had actually been burned in the first blinding flash at 8:16 A.M. on the sixth of August. In fact, our scientists seemed terrified by the destruction they had let loose, and we got the impression that, at first, they were attempting to minimize the terrible effects of the bomb.

Colonel Stafford Warren, the Army's crack radiologist, even went so far as to say that "if the Japanese had been eating sounder diets and had been given proper treatment, thousands of them would not have died." Of course, this is true, but it is even more true that they would not have died if the atom bomb had not been dropped.

Our scientists, under Brigadier General R. F. Farrell, were convinced that the Japanese were exaggerating in reporting post-bomb radioactivity. The American investigators went to Hiroshima and Nagasaki fully convinced beforehand that there would be no prolonged radioactive effects, and that the persons fatally burned or infected by the gamma rays were stricken at the very moment of the blast, and not afterward.

A group of reporters asked one of the scientists point-blank if he had been instructed to make findings in Hiroshima and Nagasaki that would support the American investigators' pre-announced conviction that there would be no fatal radio after-effects. Instead of becoming angry at this reflection on his scientific integrity, he answered quite calmly:

"We did not have such instructions from the Army and we would not have accepted them. We went there with open minds. We took the best instruments and our foremost experts on the subject. Their findings are that no person has died or become ill as a result of gamma-ray infection suffered after the actual moment of the explosion." Some Japanese doctors still disagreed, and now, after the Bikini tests, even Colonel Warren admits there is such a thing as lethal, lingering radioactivity.

These American-Japanese scientific differences seemed a bit pointless, like a legal argument over whether a killer had thrust his knife three inches into his victim or three-and-one-quarter inches. There was no denial by the Americans that if the bomb had been fused to explode on contact with the ground, it would certainly have left radioactivity for years to come. And no one could deny the nearly unbelievable casualties produced by that single missile.

As we drove into Hiroshima, the American scientists had not yet reported their findings and we had to take the Japs' word for it that there *was* radioactivity. We passed a number of large, undamaged factories on the outskirts of the city, and then as we went on along a narrow street we began to see blast effects. Some four miles from the point where the bomb had exploded over the exact center of the city, there were houses and stores whose shingles had been torn away by the concussion. A factory wall was caved in here, a steel fence twisted out of shape there. The blast had obviously been fickle at this distance; one house was collapsed and its neighbor intact.

With each block, the number of damaged buildings increased.

Then, turning a corner, we came suddenly into an area of complete devastation, plainly marked, well defined. It was nearly square in shape, approximately a mile and a half long on each side. Along each boundary of the area the houses and buildings stood nearly as formerly, except for occasional damage.

Within the square, as far as the eye could see, the ground looked as if it had been gone over with a gigantic rake that had left a brown residue of churned-up soil and ashes. From this wilderness rose the frames of a dozen concrete and steel buildings, some of them burnt and blackened and partially torn apart, and some apparently structurally undamaged. Of the wooden, paper, and glass homes and shops and small factories, there was nothing left except that brownish rubble, ground up fine. Trees still stood—or what had been trees. Now they were broken and gashed as if by shellfire, blackened, charred, and completely stripped of leaves. We saw, though, that grass was growing amid the scattered fragments of corrugated-tin roofing scattered on the ground.

The total effect was of a terrible hurricane and devastating fire, and indeed that was what happened to Hiroshima—that and the gamma ray. Our scientists estimated that the blast pressure at a distance of 2,500 feet from the center of the explosion was more than that of a 15,000-mile-an-hour wind. In a single, flashing millionth of a second, thousands of people fell dead, some charred to a crisp, others horribly burned by the greater-than-sun temperature generated by the bomb. In a few seconds more, other thousands died as the blast, moving slower than the flash, brought debris tumbling down on their heads.

Fires started by the searing sheet of heat sprang up in a hundred places, and other flames licked at the ruins as cooking fires and factory blazes were scattered by the winds.

Everybody within a square mile below the point of the blast was dead within a matter of seconds, either by heat, by radioactive burns, or by concussion and falling debris. Three weeks after August 6, 53,000 dead had been counted, 30,000 more were missing and probably dead, 14,000 were seriously injured and 43,500 less seriously hurt. A total of 137,500 casualties in a city of 333,000 people— all caused by a single bomb.

As we drove along concrete streets from which the rubble had been partially swept to clear a path for automobiles, we saw an old woman poking in the rubble, and a lone soldier trudging along through the rain, his back bent under the weight of a heavy bundle. Then, suddenly, we came up a small rise and there were some 500 people standing in line and waiting, believe it or not, for a street car. The car came along presently, already overloaded, and a few people squeezed off and raised their parasols and umbrellas, and a few others stepped on.

For most of these people, we were the first Americans they had seen in their lives, and for all of them this was the first contact with Americans since the bombing. Each of them had lost relatives and friends, home and possessions. Yet there was no hatred in their eyes when we walked over to talk to them. A few youngsters frolicked around us, holding our hands, feeling our clothes, making friends. One of them was bald, his hair lost in the blast, but he chatted with us self-importantly as he told of seeing the explosion, "I thought the moon had fallen down on Hiroshima," he said.

Dr. Taira, our guide who had been a naval surgeon in Manila and treated casualties from the second Battle of the Philippines Sea, was an exception to the friendly people. "Who invented the atomic bomb?" he wanted to know.

"Whoever did it," said Dr. Taira, "did wrong. I don't mind battle casualties but it was dreadful to see the women and children killed and wounded here. I don't think women and children should be involved in war."

So what do you answer: France, Poland, London, Nanking, Manila? We made no answer.

If the world were composed of sane people, we would have sat down after Hiroshima and said to each other: this has gone far enough, we must stop now. Instead, the world is engaged in an atom-bomb race and as long as it goes on it is inevitable that within a few years man will blow himself and his world to fragments. As long as atom bombs exist, and as they are placed in firing positions in widely scattered underground rocket chambers, aimed at New York and Moscow, Washington and Leningrad, Buenos Aires and London, it is certain that some day the buttons will be pushed. If we do not have atom bombs, if their manufacture is prevented by international control and supervision, then nobody can push the buttons because there will be no buttons. That is the choice: If we make bombs, they are going to be used. If we don't make them, we can't use them.

81

The scientists—it is said—now have it in their power to make bombs one thousand times as powerful as the baby bomb that hit Hiroshima. Atom bombs, as the scientists and military men have pointed out, can be loaded into stratospheric rockets which within a few years will be capable of reaching any part of the globe. Millions can be wiped out in a few minutes, all the cities of the earth destroyed in a matter of hours. There is no defense against such rockets.

Even if rockets could be stopped, another way would be found to deliver atom bombs to their targets. In a few years it will be possible to pack atomic explosives into an ordinary artillery shell. That means that submarines, surfacing some midnight off the coast from Portland, Maine, to Seattle, could loft atomic missiles from their deck guns onto our great cities. New York, Boston, Miami, New Orleans, San Diego, Los Angeles, and San Francisco would, in a few minutes, no longer exist.

The scientists have very calmly set down the facts about the atom bomb. It is all there to read in *One World or None*.

Why does man do things like Hiroshima to his fellow man? I have my own theory. Setting aside for the moment the immediate excuses for war—economic, geographic, patriotic—I think that the cause of war is rooted in man's fear of death. Paradoxically, by challenging death he can obtain a momentary illusion of immortality. Man can split the atom, move mountains, build cities, invent philosophies, make and smash nations, but he can never escape the presence of death. He can never discover what is beyond the black curtain guarding the door through which he must pass. He may not worry morbidly, consciously, and continuously about death, but the fear of the unknown is always there, the mystery unsolved and insoluble.

The condemned man who takes his own life twenty-four hours before his execution embraces death because he is afraid to wait for it. The waiting is intolerable. The Japanese soldier clutching a hand grenade to his guts prefers that known death to the torture he expects if captured. The Japanese glorification of death on the battlefield, and deification of the spirit, is an attempt to make death easy. Buddhism gives its followers the comforting belief of reincarnation, and hence the Oriental loses some of his fear of death. Christianity, although it is based on a similar myth of rebirth, makes death more difficult because it places so high a value on individual life. In battle, seeing death strike all around him and not take him, man says to

82

himself, "I've got the old boy licked. He's not coming for me after all. If I scrape through this, I'll live forever."

For some twenty-five years of his life, man does not need war: He does not need to thrust a steel bayonet into quivering flesh, to kill and shed blood. He has woman, and the domination of the supine figure, the victory, satisfies his needs for conquest. Then one day the game is over. The firm thighs are still there and the soft, warm flesh but the unlocking key is lost. Now death moves closer, the black curtain beckons. Half the journey is done.

What now? Well, there is horse-racing, Wall Street, that foreman's job, Catholicism or Fascism, power and wealth, crusading, reforming, atom splitting, philosophizing. And beyond them is war, and war is an old man's game. What greater, all-absorbing, death-thought-obliterating game can there be than to juggle the destiny of nations, to decide which millions shall die and which shall live, who shall starve and who shall eat, to play at being God? So roll down the map, General, the big map, the map of the world, and let us see where we are sending those millions. Strike up the band, unfurl the banners, let the chimneys belch white and black smoke and the assembly lines spew forth the death-dealing arms. Make 10,000 battleships, 100,000 tanks, a million airplanes. Blow this city off the map! Attack here, attack there! Move those blue pins, Admiral. Ah, what a fine, absorbing game!

The old men sucker the young men into it. They sucker them away from the warm women-bodies and the young men, who don't need war, follow the unfurled banners, chase after the marching bands. The general shoves the fat cigar into his fat face and tells the young men: Climb into those B–29s, boys, and go up to Tokyo and murder a million people and don't come back. The suckers do it. And in twenty-five years more the young men of this war are the old ones; the flesh calls and it is not answered. The black door begins to open. What now? You remember that war we fought, we weren't afraid of death then, we had it licked cold. And so it goes, the victrola needle sticking, every twenty-five years, every twenty-five years, every twenty-five years, every twenty-five years. . . .

Chapter Seven

Her Neck in a Noose

FOR TWENTY-FIVE YEARS OF HER LIFE, IVA IKUKO Toguri, a Los Angeles-born American girl of Japanese ancestry, kept her nose clean and stayed out of trouble. Then—for the sum of $6.66 monthly—she deliberately sold her services to a country with which the United States of America was at war and thus laid herself open to charges of treason.

Iva, who is also known as Tokyo Rose, was one of the first prizes of our occupation of Japan. There is a possibility that she may die for her crimes. But if the dimpled, soft-voiced Los Angeles girl ever does dangle from the gallows it will be a gross miscarriage of justice unless the next scaffold holds the frail, arthritic figure of an eighty-three-year-old American missionary known as "Mother" Topping.

Both Iva Ikuko Toguri and Mrs. Genevieve Faville Topping committed the same crime—if it is held to be a crime—of broadcasting radio programs aimed at weakening the fighting spirit of their fellow Americans in the war against Japan. Both worked for a Japanese victory; Iva for pay, Mother Topping for free. Tokyo Rose's programs were at least entertaining to our troops—and there the parallel ends. Iva was arrested for her sins and at this writing faces indictment by the Los Angeles grand jury, while Mrs. Topping is still presiding benevolently over her missionary nest in Tokyo and trying to convince American soldiers that the Japs were forced into an economic war that was no fault of their own.

What saved Mrs. Topping from arrest and trial may have been, in addition to her age, her close friendship for the Japanese "Christian leader" Kagawa. Kagawa, after the surrender, became a great favorite of certain of the American occupation authorities who chose

84

to ignore his violent anti-American broadcasts during the war. The "Christian," who with some reason had accused American soldiers of all kinds of atrocities, emerged as a "Liberal" leader and an active figure, while a *Stars and Stripes* writer who dared to expose his wartime activities got into severe difficulties with the American authorities. Kagawa continued to move around Japan, associating with his old missionary friends, while the man who attacked him, Corporal Bernard Rubin of *Stars and Stripes* was investigated by the Counter-Intelligence Corps on a "loyalty" check and exiled to Okinawa.

Tokyo Rose was the fall guy, rather than some other of Tokyo's broadcasters, because she was the best-known voice from Japan during the war. She had a tremendous following among GIs who listened to her program of recorded American music on Radio Tokyo's "Zero Hour," especially in the days before our own Army set up its broadcasting equipment on recaptured Pacific islands. Next to Tojo, hers was the most familiar enemy personality and there was great curiosity among our soldiers as to the identity of the Oriental Lady Haw-Haw. Various rumors had identified her as a girl from the Hawaiian Islands, a beautiful German, a St. Louis woman married to a Japanese and a Eurasian Mata Hari. The best guess made by Americans, as they heard her slangy inflection coming over the air to their foxholes, was that she was American.

Because of the widespread curiosity as to her identity, there was a race between American correspondents to try to locate her. We happened to find her first and sneaked her into the Imperial Hotel with her husband, a Portuguese-Japanese named Phillip d'Aquino who worked in Domei.

"Are you Tokyo Rose?" we asked.

"Yes," the girl said, "the one and only Tokyo Rose."

She was a little nervous at first, as she sat on the bed holding her husband's hand. She was a pleasant-looking girl, but by no stretch of the imagination a siren; her long braids made her look nearer twenty than the ten more years to which she readily confessed. She was wearing blue slacks tucked into American-made zippered rain shoes, to compromise with the ugly Japanese mompei-style garment, and a yellow blouse and a reddish vest. Her teeth were straight and white, and when she smiled you noticed a small mole on her upper lip.

"It looks like I'm on the spot," she said in a low, well-modulated voice. You could tell that she hadn't yet made up her mind just what

85

to do about it—whether to tell everything or keep silent. She went on, "I don't think I should talk to you. When the story is published I'll be arrested."

What she really wanted, we quickly found out, was a contract, promising her some money, signed before she told her story. When that preliminary was over, we sent for some tea, and while we were drinking it she debated with herself how much to tell. Finally, I believe, it was her vanity that decided her to give the full story. After all, she was thinking, I am an international figure known to millions of American GIs and sailors. I have become world famous during the war. This story will be in nearly every paper in America and in one of the biggest magazines, and my picture will be everywhere.

And so, talking on for hour after hour, she told us her story—that of a woman who was scholarly, intelligent in most matters, and fully capable of exercising judgment, who had sold out her country, with little regard for the consequences, for the sum of $6.66 monthly and for no other reason, motive, or reward.

In the case of Iva Ikuko Toguri, born in Los Angeles on July 4, 1916, there was no question of a smoldering resentment against her native land, no incident that had made her feel an alien. She had never been called "you dirty Jap." She liked life in the United States and hated the restrictions in wartime Japan, where she had been trapped by the war's outbreak while visiting relatives. Yet, night after night, she sat down to write and broadcast a script deliberately designed to make her compatriots lose their will to go on fighting. She attacked their morale by telling them their wives and sweethearts at home were out with 4Fs—something many of them guessed anyway but didn't like to hear on the radio. She created Allied disunity by telling the Australian soldiers, "Diggers, the Americans are taking all your women." And through it all Iva always felt herself still American, still looked forward to going home to Los Angeles and her family and old friends there, and steadfastly refused to sign a paper renouncing her American citizenship in favor of naturalization as a Japanese.

Sipping our tea in the Imperial but not smoking "on account of my voice, you know," Iva talked like a mixture of adolescent bobbysoxer and college professor. Her father, Jun, had come to the United States in 1899 and her mother a year later. Her father was a prosperous importer and exporter and her mother, unusually advanced

86

for a Japanese woman of her times, had wanted to become a doctor. There were three other children, Fred, a UCLA graduate and now a businessman, June, twenty-five, and Inez, nineteen. All of them were well educated.

"It was unheard of for a woman of my mother's generation to study medicine," Iva said, "and her ambition centered in me. I planned to become a doctor, like seven of my cousins in Japan, but finally decided on zoology." At school, she became a crackerjack in microscopic technique, joined scientific societies at UCLA, and on weekends camped out in the desert with student paleontologists looking for the Miocene horse which roamed in the Barstow region 3,000,000 years ago. The biggest day in her life each year was Independence Day, the birthday of the United States of America and of Iva Ikuko Toguri. Of all the birthdays the one she remembers most was July 4, 1941, the day before she sailed on the "Arabia Maru" of the OSK line, wearing a new suit made by her sister June and carrying presents of stockings, candies, sugar, and fruit, to visit her mother's ailing sister in Japan. Her aunt and uncle, cousins and friends met her at the pier in Yokohama. Everything Japanese seemed strange to her. She had never been in a Japanese home and couldn't speak the language, so she entered a missionary school to learn it. The food was strange, too. She couldn't eat rice and was beginning to lose weight when her uncle went to the police and by special permission had her ration changed to bread. Iva decided, after a few months, to go home.

She wrote her family and told them, "Japan is no place for an American-bred person to live. The sooner I can come home, the better." To her sister she wrote of the contrasts between the two countries, describing how the Jap school kids had to march and drill, how discourteous the Japanese were on public conveyances, and how annoying the police restrictions that required her, as a foreigner, to report for questioning every few days.

She was packing to go home in November when suddenly all shipping was halted. Pearl Harbor was a complete surprise to her. "My uncle came in and said, 'We are at war with America. I heard it on the radio.' The shock was so great that I can never explain it in words."

She watched the Doolittle raiders fly over Tokyo with mixed emotions. "I stood there and prayed that the anti-aircraft fire wouldn't hit them, but at the same time I didn't want them to hit me. If it

87

came to a choice between the two, I wanted the planes to be shot down." I know how she felt.

After a few months, Iva began worrying about money. She had $500 but was starting to eat into her savings. So she moved into a boarding house, continued school, and in July of 1942 got work in the English department at the Domei news agency. "I suppose," she said, "that working for Domei was just as much treason—if I am guilty of treason—as was my later broadcasting as Tokyo Rose. Domei paid me one hundred and thirty yen monthly." Her tuition was one hundred yen monthly, leaving only thirty yen for food and board, and in July of 1943 she gave up school.

It was while Iva was with Domei that the friend she had made through the missionary school, Mother Topping, went on the air with the first of her seven broadcasts to America. Perhaps that gave Iva the idea of becoming a radio star, too. In any case, she applied for a job with Radio Tokyo and was accepted in August, 1943, and given work as a typist and script arranger. One evening, two Allied prisoners at Radio Tokyo, Captain Ted Wallace, alias Ince, an American who had been one of the "Voices of Freedom" from Corregidor, and Major Cousens, an Australian, suggested to Iva that she take part in the Zero Hour program.

They outlined what they wanted, "A girl with a definite voice personality . . . a happy-go-lucky style, just talking to the fellows. Imagine they are the kids from next door in Los Angeles and sort of talk to them." Iva asked, "How much?" "One hundred yen [$6.66] monthly." "I'll take it," she said. "I can live on that plus my Domei salary and hang onto what's left of my five hundred dollars."

Iva caught on quickly. Soon she was writing her own scripts and inventing her own characters, the stars being a boy-friend named Abe (she said no religious angle was intended) and a good-looking sergeant of whom Abe was jealous. As the victrola ground out nostalgic tunes, she would pretend to dance with the sergeant and then tell Abe to run get them glasses of cold beer. She would imagine the GIs sitting in the jungles, sweating under the tropical sun and swatting flies. Then she would play cooling music. "Compared to what other hard-working girls were getting at the station," she said, "my job was easy. Just face the mike and go home. I was rather selfish, in a way."

Unlike some of the other Radio Tokyo programs, Zero Hour was never gruesome. The approach was pally and the propaganda was not too obvious. The theme was homesickness, and since this was so, it did not matter that the most recent musical recordings were late 1941. After the B–29 raids started, one of the plane crews parachuted some new records over Tokyo intended for Iva, but she never got them. So she stressed the nostalgic quality of the music she played.

Iva first learned she was famous about a month after she went on the air. Before that several Nisei girls had done the announcing but it was not until she took over that a dispatch came through from Switzerland telling how the American soldiers listened to Tokyo Rose. "Everybody in the station began to call me that, and notes were left on my desk addressed to Tokyo Rose. I never used the name on the air, though." She had to fight off others in Radio Tokyo who wanted to horn in on this popular program.

After a while she got control of the entire Zero Hour, and right up to the end she continued her programs, claiming great American defeats and Japanese victories, in accordance with instructions from the Tokyo War Office. Shrewdly, she burned her scripts ten days before the surrender, unaware that official American listening posts had made complete recordings of her programs in preparation for her trial some day.

Did she regret having turned traitor for $6.66 a month, I asked Tokyo Rose. "I haven't any particular feeling," she said dispassionately. "It was an education. If it weren't for the war I never would have faced the mike, learned radio technique, and had the thrill of listening to my own voice recorded." So the war did some good after all: Iva Toguri got a thrill out of it. "I have no feeling of being a traitor," she went on. "My husband often warned me to quit but you can't just do that. Even if I quit a year ago it would have been the same. If I'm guilty now I was guilty then. I often thought I was doing wrong but I felt I was providing as much fun as propaganda for the GIs."

The neat little girl smoothed out her pigtails, finished the last of a fresh batch of tea, and rose to go. She signed an autograph, laughingly, to "Harry Brundidge and Clark Lee, who may have put my head in a noose today." She was very chipper about it. You could tell she didn't believe such a thing could ever really happen to her. After all, you can't hang anybody for learning mike technique and having the thrill of hearing her recorded voice played back to her. Americans, Iva felt sure, would understand that.

89

Later, I asked six American GIs here and there in Japan what they thought should be done to Tokyo Rose. Three of the answers were unprintable. Two, slower workers, said, "I'd sure like a date with her." One thought she should be punished. "What the hell," the five GIs said, "she gave us a lot of good music and we laughed at her propaganda. Lots of us thought she was on our side all along. We got a big bang when she welcomed our unit to the different islands every time we'd move."

The story that Radio Tokyo invariably knew every move made by the American Army is one of the most persistent of the war. It began shortly after Pearl Harbor, and as far back as April, 1942, when a group of us escaped from Bataan and reached Australia, we were told that Radio Tokyo had reported our arrival and had said, "Glad you made it to Australia. We'll be down after you before long." When a fighter squadron or a bomber group moved to a new base, dozens of people reported that Tokyo Rose had said, "Hello there, you boys of the three hundred and nineteenth. Hope you'll enjoy the Philippines more than you did New Guinea." Every new transfer was supposed to be announced by Tokyo the day it was made. However, I never found any one who actually heard such broadcasts himself. It was always a guy in the next tent. For what it is worth, Tokyo Rose told me that the Japanese War Office had never furnished her such intelligence information, and it does seem reasonable that if the Japs did have such a reliable espionage setup, they would have kept that fact to themselves.

A few days after our interview with her, little Iva went to jail.

No such fate was in store for Mrs. Genevieve Fayville Topping who, in the tone of a minister's wife addressing the church women's club, had made seven overseas broadcasts to her sister Americans. "I tried to persuade the women of America," Mrs. Topping explained, "to move anyone and everyone to the realization that it was possible to negotiate peace if the Americans would only halt their atrocities." Jap atrocities? Mother Topping had never heard of them and was sure the Christian Japanese were incapable of committing them.

"Mother's" attitude is by no means unique among American missionaries. There were others who remained in Japan during the war who broadcast appeals to their fellow Christians to cease fighting against Japan's "just crusade." One American woman on the Tokyo Women's Hour turned on the tears in this fashion: "Yesterday I was

90

rummaging about the closets and I came across some dusty photographs taken in America . . . memories. of past joys, hopes and fears. . . . My daughter piped up and said, 'Do you think Edward's father, whose picture is there, will fly over here and throw bombs on us?' I looked at my children and couldn't answer."

Other missionaries like the Rev. Theodore F. Walzer, who returned to the United States by diplomatic exchange ship, were unshaken in their conviction that the Japs were really very nice people. Talking to fellow exchangees—American reporters who had undergone six months' imprisonment—Walzer warned, "If you send back stories about what the Japanese did to you, you will be playing them a dirty trick." At Laurenço Marques, where the Japanese exchange ship "Asama Maru" shifted its passengers to the "Gripsholm," and vice versa, a group of American missionaries massed on the afterdeck of the "Gripsholm" waved their handkerchiefs to the Japs on the "Asama," and shouted "Banzai! (Long live Japan!)." The Japs responded by singing a war song.

Talking to reporters after the surrender, Miss Elizabeth Kilburn, one of the followers of Mother Topping and of Kagawa, shrugged off the latter's vicious anti-American broadcasts. "Those were violent times," she said. "I was in an internment camp and I said violent things in my heart when American planes bombed Tokyo. You can't understand unless you were under the liquid fire of the American planes. If I could have reached a radio, I would have said violent things to the Americans, too."

Reminded that the Japs had done a bit of bombing here and there, Miss Kilburn gave her tardy advice that after Pearl Harbor America should have turned the other cheek. "Does one wrong," she inquired, "deserve another? Anyway, Japan didn't even start it." To which Mother Topping added sagely, "It was an economic war. The poor Japanese were taken from their homes and forced to fight."

Chapter Eight

We Meet General Tojo

Right after the Tokyo Rose story, the Army placed Tokyo out of bounds to correspondents. The C.I.C. had lost face when we found her first. The C.I.C. is the counter-intelligence corps and its job was to round up the war criminals, the traitors, and the suspected traitors. But most of the C.I.C. agents were newcomers to Japan and none too expert in their work. Consequently, they stuck pretty close to headquarters in Yokohama prior to the official occupation of Tokyo, and let newspapermen beat them to most of the badly wanted Japanese big-shots like Prince Konoye, General Homma, and a dozen others.

This had to be stopped, so the Army declared Tokyo off limits. They stationed sentries on the two highway bridges over the river from Yokohama to Tokyo, and turned back all vehicles except those carrying liaison officers en route to confer with Japanese government officials on plans for the formal occupation of the capital. However, they neglected to post MPs at the railroad station, so it was a simple matter to get on the express electric train at Yokohama and forty minutes later get off at the Shimbashi Station and walk around the corner to the Imperial Hotel. My room in the Imperial was still being reserved for me by the manager, Inamura-san, and down the hall was the room in which Harry Brundidge, apparently ignorant of the out-of-bounds order, had remained since the day of our landing at Atsugi.

In his room one day I found Masaguchi Moriyama, the American-educated reporter who by now had cards identifying him as the "special representative of the President of the Yoimiuri-Hochi newspapers to deal with the American press." The president was scared stiff that the pro-Axis, ultra-nationalistic, saber-rattling of his newspapers would result in his being branded a war agitator and war criminal, and he had assigned Massa to the fulltime job of assisting us, or at least hanging around, in the hope that he would thus obtain information from headquarters as to how the president stood.

Massa introduced me one night to a rough-looking, bald character with the build of a fast welterweight. "This is Mori-san, a member of the Yoimiuri police press club." I looked him over.

"Be your age, Massa," I said. "This gent's a copper. I remember when he used to lurk behind the pillars in the lobby downstairs, before the war, and listen to what the correspondents were discussing over their whiskey-tansan. He used to go into our rooms and go through our letters and papers, and if we found him there he produced a Yoimiuri card and pretended he came for an interview."

Massa tried to bluff it out. "No. You're mistaken. He's a member of the police press club." Which he probably was. There was also a "foreign office press club," which included the reporters assigned to the Gaimusho, plus special agents assigned to check on them and on foreigners. The police press club worked the same way.

"Nuts," I said. "He's a gendarme and we're going to call him 'captain.'" The captain was grinning.

I recalled a conversation with a C.I.C. officer who had insisted that General Hideki Tojo, Japan's first wartime premier, was in hiding somewhere in the remote hinterlands of Japan.

"Say, captain," I asked the Jap gendarme, "where's Tojo?"

"Ah, so," he hissed. "I think so, I don't know."

I took out a pack of American cigarettes and handed them to him. "Are you sure you don't know?"

He grinned delightedly, "Ah so, maybe living in Tokyo. I take you there." And take us he did a few days later. Perhaps the C.I.C. men were out of cigarettes or they could have found Tojo sooner. . . .

When he was Minister of War in the Imperial Japanese government, pre-Pearl Harbor, and before that as the head of the Army's military gendarmerie, General Tojo offered rewards of many millions of yen for the capture of Chinese patriots and other intransigent individuals who refused to recognize Japan as the savior of East Asia. After Tojo became Prime Minister, and as the guiding spirit of Japanese militarism led his country into war against the democracies, the United States and Allied nations would have gladly paid millions of dollars to any rifleman who could get within shooting distance of the head of the Tokyo government and the planning brains of the war. There was a big price on Tojo's head. Yet, ten days after the official surrender of Japan, we succeeded in being ushered into the presence of this feared and hated man at the cost of exactly five U. S. cents—the price of the American cigarettes I had given Captain Muto.

Muto gave directions as the jeep took us out to Tojo's house. John Henry, Brundidge, Massa, and I were crowded in with the gendarme captain and the GI driver who took us through the ruined streets of Tokyo, out past what formerly was the theatre district and to the Setagaya ward police station. One of the ward policemen jammed himself in with us, and we drove down a long, tree-shaded lane that might have been in Maplewood, N. J., or Maplewood, Mo., but looked like no part of Japan that we had seen before. We made a sharp turn between stone walls that retained two grassy banks, and stopped in front of a police box. A dozen policemen and soldiers materialized into the lane, some in shirtsleeves and others in uniform coats. If they were armed, their weapons were inconspicuous. They surrounded us curiously, but without evident animosity.

On the right, thirty feet from the road and partially concealed by trees, was the ex-dictator's home, a one-story house of half-Japanese and half-foreign style, built of wood and yellow stucco. A diminutive, blue Datsun sedan sat in the concrete driveway. While Massa and the ward gendarme walked up to the door, one of the police guards pointed out that two tall trees at the entrance were charred nearly to the top. "*America no hikoki*—American airplanes." Like almost everyone else in Japan, he thought it was funny to be bombed, and he laughed hilariously.

The house itself was more than modest by American standards, but typical of the homes into which Japanese commanders retired at the end of their terms of service as chiefs of the general staff. The idea had been that a general required no more of life than a modest salary—plus the opportunity to serve his Emperor. Austerity and abnegation had been the keynotes of the generals' lives. It was traditional that on completion of his service, a Japanese chief of staff repaired to a suburban or country retreat from which he offered his advice to his successors and from which he was always prepared to emerge to offer his life, if need be, at the Imperial command.

94

Yet when Tojo built the house in wartime there had been a major scandal. Whispers started that Tojo had received a very large monetary present from a group of industrialists, and the talk swelled to such a roar that Tojo had to go to the unprecedented length, while still premier, of denying that he had been bribed. This uproar had been only a symptom of the general's unpopularity, which reached a climax with his resignation in July, 1944, after the fall of Saipan.

Exactly why Tojo was the most hated man in Japan was hard to explain. As far as most Japanese knew they were still winning the war, and it was Tojo who had given them the victories. But it was likewise Tojo whose decrees had cracked down on both the little man and the war profiteer in Japan—taking a few more grains of rice out of the former's slim diet every month or so—and breaking up the gay whirl in Tokyo in the first two years of war when the Japanese were cashing in on their conquests and everybody had plenty of money and was spending it freely. However, the Japanese were accustomed to decrees and to belt tightening, and what seemed to make them loathe Tojo was the fact that more than any other man in the country's modern history he, as an individual, had been the government —the front man for the Emperor. In recent years, even with one or two outstanding men in a cabinet, the government had always been "they," and nobody knew exactly who ruled Japan. Now it had been not "they" but "he,"—one man, Tojo. When the war tide turned, the little man centered his hatred and his lost feeling on Tojo. He detested Tojo's mannerisms, his way of riding a horse, the fact that his wife was spending more money than seemed possible on a general's pay.

The trouble with Tojo was that he symbolized to the Japanese both their strength and their weakness. He was the best they could produce, the best field general and tactician, the most faithful servant of the Emperor, the most fanatical of the fanatics, the man who developed the modern air force, the man who stood against the Soviet threat to Japan, the general who had dared to challenge the United States and Great Britain. But he had failed, and, knowing they too were doomed to failure, his countrymen had hated him.

Tojo had been the most brilliant and successful Asiatic military commander since Genghis Khan. Nicknamed the Razor because of his sharp intelligence, he had helped to set up in Manchuria the military-controlled state that was a model for what the Japanese Army eventually hoped to extend over the entire world. He was a businessman, too, a brief-spoken but persuasive talker who had made a deal with Japan's leading industrialists so that they became co-partners in Manchuria and in the Army's larger plans for world conquest. To the outside world he was sinister, threatening, brutal, a Hitler with the added danger of Oriental mysticism. . . .

Now there was a slight bustle on the lawn and around the corner of the house walked a lithe figure in white shorts and shirt, gray socks that came up over his knees, and low black button shoes. His bronzed skin gleamed like a polished Buddha. Shifting a long stick from his right hand to the left, he motioned us to a table on the side lawn.

Riding out to the house, I had said to Brundidge, "Don't shake hands with him." Harry replied, "I wouldn't shake hands with the bastard for anything in the world."

But now the little Jap thrust out his hand to me, and as the others pushed up from behind I was so close that our hands were almost touching. I accepted his firm grip. What the devil, there was plenty of soap and water back at the hotel!

We sat down in iron garden chairs and admired the house and beyond it the green, extensive fields that Tojo told us made up his farm. He called for a round blue tin of Hope cigarettes (made in Japan) and passed them to us with the remark that "American cigarettes are very difficult to get now." It was apparent that he understood a good deal of English, although our conversation was through the interpreter. It was also apparent that he was nervous, not knowing what to expect next, although he was perfectly in control of himself.

"Is the general taking any part in politics or military affairs now?" we asked.

He answered genially, starting to relax, "No. None whatever. I am a farmer now and work in my fields." He looked hard as nails. But there was something wrong in his demeanor. If you had interviewed him ten years before, say, in Manchuria, or if it had been possible to interview him just before he dispatched the carriers to attack Pearl Harbor and started the invasion fleets for the Philippines and Southeastern Asia, his replies would have been gruff and condescending. He would have used the prescribed means of a Japanese general dealing with an American—a superior air, deceiving half-truths, denial of knowledge of any embarrassing matter. All his adult life he had studied that manner, and now it was gone and without it he

96

was only another little man. Outwardly hard as nails, but inwardly you sensed a softness—the hard something that had been his self-discipline, his beliefs, his power and authority, his life-and-death control over millions, wasn't there and the man was hollow inside.

"What are the general's plans?"

"I have no plans, just to go on farming. I cannot discuss politics or military affairs because it is not for a defeated general to talk."

He alternately smoked a cigarette in a glass holder and toyed with his stick as we talked. Except at the eyes, his skin was unwrinkled. His eyes were quick and bright. Brundidge asked his age.

"Sixty-two Japanese style. Sixty-one American." The Japanese begin to count from the day of conception.

I followed up the question: "Does General Tojo believe that Japan's cause was just?"

He answered emphatically. "Hai, Hai! I do believe that Japan's fight was based on righteousness. I realize that America will not agree with that. However, I believe that it will take time and an impartial third party to make the final decision as to whether America's fight was just, or Japan's was."

That struck me as a pretty fair statement, especially the last part. It is difficult to imagine a defeated American general saying to a representative of Hitler, "You may be right. Time will tell."

Now, Tojo leaned over toward the interpreter and went on: "I was responsible for the war. I accept full and complete responsibility. But I do not believe that makes me a war criminal. There is a difference between leading a nation in a war which it believes right and just, and being a war criminal. . . . But again, that is for the victorious nation to decide."

We asked Tojo then if the Japanese Army and Navy had co-operated fully during the war, and he turned the query aside with a suggestion that we submit it to our own Army and Navy. His humorous observation seemed to cheer him up and suddenly his mood changed. He smiled, sat forward in his chair, and picked up Brundidge's field cap. Like a delighted kid he tried it on, turning it this way and that. It fitted his bullet-shaped head like a washtub. He mugged, smiled a solid-gold smile out from under the American eagle, and murmured, "Oki, oki! (Too big.)" He might have been referring to American power, as much as to the size of the hat.

Tojo looked tired and we got up to leave. Again the war lord walked close to shake hands, but this time we had room to maneuver out of the way. He walked out to the gate and waved as we drove away. There he turned and walked back up the driveway to the house. It was the last time he did it. The next day he was carried out, feet first, on an American stretcher with a gaping hole in his chest and another in his back.

Chapter Nine

Who Couldn't Die

T HE NEXT DAY, AT ABOUT TWENTY-FIVE MINUTES to one, an officer came into the crowded, noisy dining room of the Dai Itchi Hotel and knocked on a beer bottle with a knife to attract the correspondents' attention. Then he read a brief announcement:

"The Supreme Commander has ordered the Counter-Intelligence Corps to arrest former Premier Hideki Tojo, who is first on the list of war criminals."

We grabbed a couple of apples off the table and ran outside, looking for transportation. There was one car, a brindle-painted diminutive Jap model which I recognized as the "liberated" property of George Burns, photographer for *Yank* magazine. I rushed back into the dining room and pushed past the screen behind which Brig. General Le Grand A. Diller, MacArthur's public relations officer, had segregated the enlisted men from the officer-gentlemen correspondents and public-relations staff. Burns was wrestling with a piece of camouflaged spam.

I called him aside. "What do you want to do, George, eat this spam or see Tojo kill himself?" Burns dropped his napkin, grabbed his cameras, and followed without a word. Six of us crowded into the little open car. Harry Brundidge and Ken McCaleb were in front with Burns; and our interpreter, Massa, a police reporter from the Yoimiuri, and myself in the back.

Burns kept goosing the car, trying to coax more than twenty miles an hour out of its straining engine as we directed him through the burned-out city.

Finally we swung around a last corner into the lane in front of Tojo's house. We jumped out, and Massa questioned a loitering gendarme.

"Where's the general?"

"In the house, of course. His wife is with him."

"The Americans get here yet?"

"There's one up there."

A correspondent was sitting in a chair in front of the driveway entrance. Some of the police were sitting on the grass, and others lolling by their tiny sentry box. They greeted us as old friends from the day before and we gave them cigarettes. Massa told them, in Japanese, "Tojo is going to be pinched by the Americans."

They weren't very surprised. One of them sucked in his breath wetly through his gold teeth, leaned back, and burst into laughter. "Ha. Ha! Bery funny." The others joined in the hilarity.

As time went by, and the C.I.C. still didn't show up, we decided to try to beat them to the punch and "invite" Tojo to accompany us to headquarters.

We walked between the stone pillars and into the small yard, pushing Massa ahead of us.

Massa had to be pushed. He still hadn't recovered from the shock of talking to Tojo face-to-face the day before, and he was very apprehensive about breaking in on him now. A manservant, in sloppy army pants and cloth slippers, motioned us around to the side entrance of the house, facing the garden where we had taken tea with Tojo eighteen hours previously. The doors here were sliding panels, and a woman came to one of them. She was rather tall for a Japanese, with a thick, sturdy body. Her hair was still coal-black, though she was no longer young, and she wore the unbecoming black pants and blouse which Tojo had decreed as the national costume as a wartime cloth-saving substitute for the kimono.

Massa told her: "Please advise the general that orders for his arrest have been issued. We talked to him yesterday and he already knows us. We will be glad to give him a ride in our car to General MacArthur's headquarters."

Tojo must have been just inside the room, listening, because he stepped into the doorway, half pushing the woman aside. From inside the house came the wet smell of burning incense. Somebody whispered, "Hara-kiri!" But behind Tojo we caught a glimpse of a man moving around, apparently arranging things to be packed in a suitcase that stood on the floor. It looked as if the ex-dictator was packing to go to jail, not preparing to join his ancestors by the process of honorable belly-slitting.

As on the day before, the little man was wearing shorts and a shirt, but this time they were greenish. He looked far less composed than when he had jokingly said "Gorru-bye" to us. He sighted Burns' camera and snapped in Japanese:

"No pictures! No pictures! I will not have any pictures." Burns smiled disarmingly and kept the camera at his side.

"General," Massa began, "we will take you to Field Marshal Mac-Arthur if . . ." The Japs never called MacArthur "general." It gave them more face to have their conqueror a field marshal.

"No," Tojo cut him off. "I will wait for the authorities!" He turned to go inside, and for a moment he was boss again. "No pictures!" he repeated. "No pictures!"

We went back out to the lane and found it was beginning to get a little crowded. There were two command cars, both with newspapermen, and one of the Australian correspondents had brought his shapely White Russian girl-friend along to see the sights. We chatted, smoked, took pictures of the gendarmes and the entrance to the house, and waited for the C.I.C. to show up. The minutes dragged into an hour and a half, and most of the correspondents wandered off to walk in the lanes, or drove back into Tokyo.

"Massa," I said finally, "it's hot as hell here. Go on up to the kitchen and ask for some beer. And try to work on Tojo again to see if he'll come with us."

The young Japanese hated to go, but he walked through the garden gate. In a few minutes he was back, without the beer but with some news. "Tojo says he'll consider going with you," he announced. We sat back to wait for the general to make up his mind.

The sun had gone behind a low layer of overcast, but it was still very hot and in the quiet lane the suspense seemed to grow and grow. Massa felt it more than anyone. His apprehension increased noticeably. He fidgeted, left his sentences unfinished, and even threw away a Lucky Strike after two puffs, which was convincing proof of his state of mind. American cigarettes were very valuable items in those first days in Tokyo. Perhaps Massa's native instinct told him what was going on inside the house. Brundidge had the same thought and put it into words. "I'll bet he commits hara-kiri. That incense . . ."

Idly, we questioned the gendarmes who were sitting with us in the long grass. They discussed the question without special interest. "Maybe he will kill himself. Maybe not. The incense makes it look as if he might. But it's pretty late for him to do it now. He should

101

have cut his belly either when his government fell or when the Imperial Rescript for the surrender was issued."

"On the day of the Rescript," one of them went on, "Tojo's son-in-law committed hara-kiri. He was twenty-nine years old and a major in the Imperial Guard. He slashed his belly at the guard headquarters. Tojo himself went down there and got the body and brought it back to the house. It stayed in the back room for two days, in front of the family shrine, and then the funeral was held. Tojo never made any comment, one way or the other, about what the major did. So it is hard to tell what his thoughts are."

Another gendarme started a serious discussion about the future of Japan and of the world. "We hope," he said intensely, "that we will never again have leaders like Tojo who get us into war."

The policemen explained that the sentry box had been set up, and they were assigned to the house, not to keep Tojo under surveillance but to protect him from Americans and from attacks by "foolish, hotheaded Japanese." Several attempts had been made on his life, they said, after his government resigned at the time American forces conquered Saipan.

We chatted on about Tojo as if he had been a long-dead character in history, instead of behind garden walls a few yards away. But all of us were wondering: What is he doing now—moving around? Praying? Preparing for hara-kiri, or just waiting silently for the sound of alien wheels that would mean the end of everything for him? He had once won a great empire in one of the swiftest military campaigns in history. Now a prison cell was ahead—trial by his conquerors—and then dangling death at the end of a rope.

We didn't know he was in his European-style room writing his last will and testament.

"Come on there, Massa," Brundidge suggested. "Go up again and see if he's got any sake. I'm dying of thirst."

Once more Massa dragged himself up to the house on reluctant feet. He stood at the kitchen door and argued with a servant and then came back to us empty-handed. In a few minutes the servant himself came out of the house with a message from Tojo.

"The general's final decision," he announced, "is that he will not accompany you." So Tojo had made up his mind to something at least.

A few minutes later, the woman in the black kimono came out of the back of the house. She walked down a path through the trees in

102

the side yard, with her face averted from us, and then shuffled stolidly away down the lane.

"There goes Madame Tojo," said one gendarme.

"No, Kato-san," another argued. "That is his sister-in-law, not his wife."

While they were still discussing the woman's identity, we saw a strange figure coming slowly toward us up the lane. It was an old woman, who bent far forward as she inched her way along with the aid of a stick. In front of us she stopped, caught her breath, and bid us polite good days in formal language. Her back, almost parallel to the ground, could not have been more than three feet above the grass, so that she resembled a T-square. Contrary to the orders of Tojo, she wore a cotton kimono and obi, and in her hand was a silk *furoshiki* of the kind the Japanese use to carry packages.

We lay on the grass as she gazed intently at each of us in turn, and Massa explained that we were Americans. Again she hissed politely, and formally expressed her pleasure at having us in Japan. Her face was seamed with years and cares, her gums toothless, but nevertheless there was a neatness and cleanliness about her, and her brain was clear.

"This is the day they issue our rations," she said, "and I am going now to get mine. It takes me all afternoon to get there and back, because I move very slowly. And it is a long way to go for so little rice. They keep giving us less and less."

We nodded our sympathy, and she chatted on. "I used to be very rich, but my three houses in Tokyo were burned down by the American bombers and now my daughter-in-law is very cruel to me." For five minutes she talked about the daughter-in-law and her son, "who used to be so good and dutiful until he married that woman, but now he is crazy about her and she twists him around her finger."

Then, with all good wishes for our health and the continued success and prosperity of America, she turned and moved slowly away. At the entrance to the driveway, she paused and bent even lower in a brief salute to the guards.

As she went out of sight over the hill, we looked again at our watches.

"That damn C.I.C. must have lost the way," somebody said. "It's been three hours now. You'd think they could find the house in that time."

"Yeah. This is a nice way to spend an afternoon, but it's not getting Tojo arrested and it's not getting us any stories."

'I left the group and, on directions from the gendarmes, walked down a hill behind the house and found a lumber mill. There was a telephone inside, and after a long delay I managed to get through to the Dai Itchi to dictate a story. The connection was terrible, and it was slow, tedious work. While I was trying to make myself understood, Brundidge walked into the factory. He was very keyed-up. "Cut it short," he insisted. "I have a hunch things are going to happen right away. Let's get back there." I felt the same way. All through the afternoon, tension had been building up inside of us, subconsciously. We had talked about many things, but always there was in our minds the picture of the little man in the yellow house, and in our nostrils the faint, lingering smell of incense. We ran back up the lane and around to the front of the house. Two jeeps were in the front driveway, and about twenty Americans were moving across the lawn toward the house. Leading the way were an American major and lieutenant, and a Nisei captain—the interpreter.

Suddenly, Tojo stuck his shaven pate out of the side window of the front room and said sharply in English, "This Tojo."

Through his interpreter, Major Kraus said, "Open the door so I can come in and present my credentials."

Tojo answered in Japanese, "Unless this is an official order, I will not discuss it." Kraus bristled. He directed the interpreter: "Tell him to quit this damn fooling around and let's get going. Tell him to open the front door so I can present my credentials. Tell him to prepare himself for a trip to General MacArthur's headquarters at Yokohama."

While this colloquy was under way, the photographers were busy. George Burns, who hadn't made a news picture all afternoon, exploded a shot and Tojo glared and slammed the window.

"What do we do now?" an American soldier asked.

"Pull the son of a bitch out by his heels," an officer answered angrily.

The Americans ran from the garden to the front of the house. As they reached the entrance a shot rang out. They crashed the door. Back at the rear of the crowd, some of the correspondents scattered hurriedly to look for cover, thinking that Tojo was shooting it out. Inside the hallway, Kraus smashed out the panels of the door into the living room and stepped in.

104

Tojo had shot himself in the chair and then partially risen, by a great effort. He was half on his feet, wavering, and in his hand was a .32-caliber Colt revolver. Kraus shouted, "Don't shoot." Tojo looked up at the American, let the gun slide through his fingers, and slumped back into his chair. It was 4:21 P.M.

I pushed into the room. Tojo lay back in a small armchair, his eyes closed and sweat standing out on his forehead. His open shirt outlined a V of hairless brown chest and flat belly. Blood oozed slowly from a wound just above his heart.

"The bastard has killed himself," an excited voice panted in my ear.

"No. The son of a bitch is still breathing. Look at his belly going up and down."

It was a small room, about fourteen feet long and ten wide, and Tojo's chair was just a foot or two inside the door. A small wooden table was beside him and a cluttered desk opposite. There was a sofa behind him, and above it a very large oil painting in somber colors, depicting this now bleeding soldier of Japan in one of his moments of triumph.

Into this room now crowded a dozen people, all but two or three of them Americans. One of the Japanese, who had been chauffeur and secretary to the war lord and had stuck to him after his fall from power, leaned over him now, sobbing and patting his shoulder. The American reporters pushed past Tojo, brushing his knees, talking loudly and excitedly. Photographers shoved their cameras in the wounded man's face. Some of the gendarmes came in for a look, and then walked out, laughing. The chauffeur followed them, his face contorted with grief. Then the show began, with Tojo—the man who wanted to die and couldn't—as an impersonal Exhibit A.

"The yellow bastard didn't have nerve enough to use a knife," a reporter said. "He knew he wouldn't kill himself with that small bullet."

"Don't be a jackass," another snapped. "You can't put a shot through yourself where he did and expect to live."

I took a good look. Tojo had changed his shorts for his army pants and polished brown boots and a clean white shirt. His uniform coat, with four rows of colored ribbons, twenty decorations, lay on the window sill beside a rack holding three swords in leather cases. There was a blue porcelain tiger on one window sill and a large Japanese dragon-scroll print on the wall. A cabinet held writing

105

brushes, although Tojo had told us the day before that he neither painted nor wrote poetry. Soon all the smaller objects began to disappear into the pockets of the reporters. I saw a hand come through the window from outside, feel along the sill for the leather case, and then disappear with one of the samurai swords. Outside, George Burns stuck the sword inside his pants leg and started to hobble toward his car. He almost made it when a hand fell on his shoulder and a C.I.C. officer said, "Nice work, kid. But take it back now."

Burns took the sword back and put it in the case, while the C.I.C. agents departed to seek reinforcements and medical assistance, leaving only a rearguard of two distracted GIs. A Japanese reporter or two came into the room to join the Americans. We stood around, smoking and talking, and making bets on how soon Tojo's small chest would stop heaving. The bleeding man's face was a mask on which showed neither pain nor emotion.

After a few minutes, I went out of the house and ran down to the telephone in the lumber yard. A Japanese helped me get the Dai Itchi, and Bill Dunn of CBS answered.

I shouted at him over the buzzing line:

"Please send a flash for me! Tojo just shot himself when the Americans came to arrest him."

"What's that?" Bill said. "I can't hear a word. Who's Jojo, the dog-faced boy?"

"Not Jojo," I shouted again. "Tojo. War. Japanese. General. Prime Minister. Shot himself."

"Hot," said Bill, his voice coming to me clearly. "I know it's hot. What the hell are you trying to tell me?"

After ten maddening minutes, he was just beginning to hear enough to get the gist of the story. Then, out of the window, I saw Massa run down the lane. He was soaked with sweat and his eyes were wild.

"What's the matter?" I called.

"Tojo is dead."

"What time did he die?"

"Four thirty-eight," Massa said slowly. "Brundidge is coming down to give you the details."

"Are you sure?"

"Yes. I saw him die. It's terrible. Everybody is taking souvenirs. They have no respect for a dead man."

106

I shouted into the phone again and Bill managed to hear enough of the information to write a flash: "TOJO SHOT HIMSELF WHEN AMERICANS CAME TO ARREST HIM AND DIED SHORTLY AFTERWARD."

When I ran back up to the house, Harry Brundidge was on the front lawn, getting a little air. "What time did he die?" I asked.

"Who die?" said Harry.

I thought he was being unnecessarily facetious. "Who? Why, Tojo, of course."

"He's not dead. He's still sitting in the chair."

I ran into the front room. Tojo was slumped in the same position. He was groaning a little, not loudly. The blood had spread a little more on the lower left-hand side of his shirt. He looked very weak and I hesitated, waiting to see if he would die and make it unnecessary for me to correct the flash. Then he began to speak, and a Japanese reporter took down his words. In a steady voice, repeating much of what was in his "farewell note," he said:

"The war in the greater East Asia region started right. It was a just war. That is my conviction. But with all our strength gone, we finally fell.

"It is proper that the Americans take over the person responsible for this war, but I do not want to stand before a jury or an Allied commission. As the former head of the nation, I do not want to be tried by the victors.

"While I believe Japan is right, I believe, too, that America thinks she is right. The righteousness or fairness of that will be decided by an impartial cool observer, a third person or party. I feel great regret both for the people of Japan and for the people belonging to East Asia. I now realize the war was bad for the people. I shoulder the whole responsibility and I hope the people will not go wrong in dealing with the situation.

"As for me I would have tried to commit suicide by hara-kiri but sometimes that is not fatal and I wanted to die. I tried to shoot myself in the heart, instead of aiming at my head because I wanted the Japanese people to recognize that it was Tojo and know that I had done this and that the Americans had not substituted somebody else's body for mine. I am very sorry I missed my aim.

"I hope the nation of Japan foresees the future and follows the right path with unshaken heart. First and last I pray for the prosperity of the Japanese empire. I am now happy to die. Here is my Banzai for the Emperor."

He stopped, his eyes closing, and a photographer shouted very loudly, "Hey, *Tojo!*"

Tojo's eyes opened slowly. "That's right," said the photographer. "Now, hold it!"

A reporter was arguing. "I told you there is a homosexual streak in these sadists. When I lived out here before the war, the statistics showed a greater percentage of homosexuality in the Japanese Army and Navy than in any other armed force in the world. And the women, too. They got damn little affection from their men, and they used to fall in love with the actresses who dressed in men's clothes on the stage. You'd see hundreds of girls crowding around the stage doors at the Takarazuka Theatre, opposite the Imperial Hotel.

"Now, this thing proves that Tojo was partly effeminate. Did you ever hear of a male suicide shooting himself in the heart? Hell, no. They always point the gun at the mouth, the ear, or the temple. But there isn't a single case on record of a woman suicide shooting herself in the face. They always dress up in their best and put the pistol to their breast. Don't want to die with their faces mussed up. Tojo didn't either."

And still Tojo couldn't die.

I ran back down to the lumber yard and twisted the phone handle savagely, trying to get Dunn at the Dai Itchi and correct the flash. The phone just squawked back at me. Massa got on and reached the operator by shouting loudly, but the hotel wouldn't answer. We were both soaked with sweat and I had tormented pictures of presses rolling all over America, even though it was early morning back home, of newsboys shouting extras and the radio quoting my dispatch, "Tojo dead." Finally, we gave up and walked back up to the house, too tired now to run.

On the lawn, I stopped Massa. "Why did you say he was dead?"

"The gendarmes told me so."

"But you told me you saw it yourself."

"Yes, I did, but I didn't know what I was saying." It was clear that, indeed, he didn't. Emotion had temporarily unbalanced him.

"What do the gendarmes think about it?"

"They say Tojo is a bungler, as stupid in this as he was in losing the war. They say he should have shot himself through the head, or taken a knife and cut his gut. They think he's pretty ridiculous."

The rest of Japan almost unanimously shared that opinion. From all over the country a sadistic chorus went up: "Tojo is to blame for

108

everything. He got us into the war. He is a miserable bungler. He should have killed himself months ago. He should have shot himself in the head. He should have used a knife." When he was taken to a prison camp later, his fellow prisoners ostracized him and refused to talk to him or eat with him. But right now, we didn't know he was going to live to reach prison.

We went back into the living room. Tojo was no longer in the chair. Brundidge had found a small iron bed in the back room and the reporters had carried it to the front part of the house. They picked Tojo up and laid him on the bare mattress, and pulled off his butterbean boots. A pink cover was thrown partially over him, but it could not hide the stain that spread over his shirt when they moved him.

"He bled like a stuck pig," Brundidge said.

The slight figure lay there quietly, while the room kept getting noisier and noisier and more filled with smoke. An American and an Australian reporter, seeing each other for the first time in months, embraced over Tojo's head and exchanged loud memories of Guadalcanal. Photographers climbed on the desk and shot down at the bed from every angle. A newly arrived lensman found a stepladder somewhere, squeezed it into the corner at the foot of the bed, climbed up, and focused. He pulled his trigger, and the bulb exploded with a vigorous pop. Reporters who were facing the other way didn't know what had happened.

Somebody shouted, "Booby trap!"

The knights of the typewriter made a line plunge for the door and then, discovering it was a false alarm, trooped shamefacedly back into the room, their heavy boots scuffing the polished floor.

I called Brundidge and McCaleb aside for a conference. "Look, I can't get through to the Dai Itchi. We've got to do something about my flash."

Brundidge misunderstood me. "Well," he said in a low voice, "there are too many people here for us to hit him over the head with a chair. But you should have seen him bleed when we turned him over. We could spin him once more."

I had to go back down to the factory to try to telephone at that point, but when I came back Tojo was faced the other way on the bed and the mattress was more bloodsoaked than before.

It must have been an hour after the shooting when the Japanese doctor, who had been summoned by the chauffeur, finally arrived.

He was a bespectacled little man in a white suit. He took one look at Tojo and sat down in a chair.

"Why don't you fix him?" somebody asked.

"Forgot his tools," the interpreter translated.

We questioned the doctor, and he told us his name, Tamemitzu Ebara, but little else. So we told him Tojo was shot through and Ebara looked and announced that the bullet had gone out Tojo's back. This we already knew. Brundidge, an old hand at police reporting, had surreptitiously explored the bloody chair back after we moved Tojo and the bullet which he found in a pillow behind Tojo's back was in his pocket. He showed it to me in the kitchen, for identification purposes. "Best souvenir of the day," he whispered. "There can't be two of these."

Back in the front room, the doctor made a brief inspection of Tojo and told us he had a very short time to live. Tojo protested in a strong voice when the doctor touched him.

"Leave me alone," he said. "I want to die."

The doctor left him alone and sat back again. Meanwhile, we had discovered a phone in the hall and gotten through to the Dai Itchi. Standing in the doorway, looking into the room, reporters called out a play-by-play to the man on the phone, only a few feet away.

Russ Brines of the Associated Press was trying to make up for lost time. He had gone away about two o'clock and come back about five, when he met Brundidge on the lawn. "What's all the excitement?" Brines demanded. "Tojo shot himself," Brundidge said. Brines got angry. "Don't give me that crap." But he ran into the house.

Now he was phoning: "Tojo is lying there with a pink spread on him. He just turned over. Now he's raising his knees. . . . No, knees, you bastard. . . . K for kangaroo. N for Nancy, double E . . . that's it." He gave me the phone.

From the doorway, Brundidge shouted in a singsong voice the dope he was getting from Massa at the bedside. "His pulse is weaker. The doc says it can't be long now."

Then again, "He's turning himself over. Pretty spry. He just groaned. Yeah, it was five thirty-eight when he groaned."

And inside the room: "Look at the muscles around the bastard's jaw tightening up. He can't last long now." Latecomers combed the desk and walls for more souvenirs, as outside it grew darker and the

110

light switches were snapped on. Brundidge called, "His pulse is stronger. Shall we turn him again?" I shook my head.

It was ten minutes to six when the doctor's tools finally arrived, brought by a nurse who wore the usual black pants with a striped blouse and who told us her name was Miki. A C.I.C. man who had come back from Yokohama took her into the kitchen to sterilize the instruments. The officer was just in time to prevent Brundidge from "liberating" two bottles of Johnny Walker Red Label. He took the bottles and at our insistence, since we didn't trust the C.I.C. in such matters, sealed them, and wrote in a neat hand: "Seized by the C.I.C. in the home of General Tojo. September 11, 1945."

The doctor approached Tojo. In a surprisingly firm voice, Tojo spoke. "Keep your hands off me. I do not want treatment. I want to die." Massa was right at his head, translating as he spoke, and from the doorway his words were relayed to the man on the phone.

"I only want to clean you up," the doctor said soothingly. I caught the word *kirei*, which in Japanese means both clean and pretty.

"Pretty me up after I'm dead," Tojo ordered. "My body belongs to me while I am alive."

But the doctor wiped off the wound on his chest, exposing the round hole an inch below the left nipple, and put a small bandage on it. Then two newspapermen grabbed Tojo's arms and two GIs took his feet. He fought away Brundidge's grip at first and then relaxed. Easily, the four Americans turned the small body over. As they did, a stream of blood spurted out of his chest, tearing away one edge of the bandage and spreading over the bed. The news was quickly passed on by telephone.

"Jesus," somebody said. "That'll finish the son of a bitch!"

"Yeah, that did it. Lookit him bleed."

On the phone a reporter laboriously spelled out hemorrhage.

The Jap doctor slipped off Tojo's shirt, which was messy with blood in the back, and put another bandage on the wound there. Tojo turned half on his side again, his knees partially drawn up. The doctor took his pulse.

"I give him three hours," he announced through Massa.

"But, Jesus, doc," somebody protested in a hurt tone, "you said one hour before and that was nearly an hour ago." The doctor looked embarrassed.

We demanded of the doctor, "Is there anything that can be done to keep him alive?"

111

"No, absolutely nothing. He is certain to die." So the doctor did nothing. The nurse knelt by the bedside and kept her hand on Tojo's pulse.

"Not a bad-looking babe," said a reporter. "Ask her how old she is, Massa?"

Miki-san dimpled as she replied, "*Ni-ju-ichi*. (Twenty-one.)"

It was after six now and completely dark outside. Tojo was quieter, and only occasionally did he groan slightly or move his feet just a little. His hands were clutching the sides of the mattress. Once in a while, a light grimace showed the pain he must have been suffering. Under the lights his body was smooth and hard and hairless. It might have been that of a young boy.

The Japanese doctor began to fidget a little. Then he called to Massa. "I am not absolutely sure that perhaps he couldn't be saved. He still seems very strong. Perhaps I should call in another doctor for consultation. . . ."

There was no opportunity for that. Within a few minutes there was a bustle outside and suddenly the house was flooded by a new surge of men; big, business-like American soldiers who had to duck to keep their helmets, which were marked "MP" or "First Cavalry," from hitting the low doorways. A doctor and two medical corpsmen hurried in the room. The doctor, who was Captain James B. Johnson, went to the far side of the bed and bent over. He was young and strong-looking, with a thick shock of brownish hair.

Tojo looked up at the doctor and spoke briefly, as Massa translated, "Don't make any trouble for me. I am going to die anyway." Then he seemed to shudder a little, and lay still. Johnson got busy.

With skilled fingers, he started to sew the chest wound. Massa stood beside him, talking in a caressing voice to Tojo, telling him in Japanese what the doctor was doing. It was doubtful that Tojo heard. He opened one eye slightly and winced when the sewing needle went into his chest, but apparently he was only semiconscious.

On the phone, the dictating went on. "Doc Johnson's sewing him up now. His first name? . . . Just a minute." Inside the room, a newspaperman leaned over the inert body, "What's your first name and home town, Captain?" Johnson answered without looking up.

In the same way he gave his diagnosis. "Sucking chest wound. Common in battle. We usually save most of them. He's in shock, now." And his prognosis: "He has a pretty good chance of recovery.

Of course, it would have been better if they hadn't let him lie here so long without doing anything."

The corpsmen turned Tojo over as if he had been a small child and Johnson fixed the wound in his back. While he was working, a wooden hat rack was brought in from the hallway; a bottle of plasma was hung to one of the pegs and American blood started to drip into Tojo's left arm. A morphine needle went into his other arm. The corpsmen fetched a checkered quilt they found in the back room and then a heavy gray blanket.

Then the show was over. The stretcher came in. Two men slipped Tojo onto it and put more brown blankets over him. With only his taut face showing, and his scarred bald head, he was carried outside. At the door of the ambulance there was a short delay. Everybody "held it," while the photographers took one last shot of the man who hadn't wanted to be photographed.

Back in the house, the C.I.C. agents were pasting labels on those articles that hadn't already been carried away. They sealed the back room, where the family shrine stood as it had during the days that the body of Tojo's son-in-law rested there. There were oranges on it, and chrysanthemums, which had been the dead major's favorite fruit and flower. Two agents were engaged in a scientific search for the bullet. They probed the chair back, shoving their fists into the bloodstained hole, measured the angle of entry and then ran their fingers over the oil painting, thinking the bullet might have gone in there. We left them kneeling on the floor.

Outside, Doctor Johnson was just climbing into the ambulance. He paused for a minute and addressed the reporters.

"I noticed a lot of blood in there. Looked like somebody turned him over on the bed and he had a big hemorrhage." He paused. "Who turned Tojo?"

"Well, doc," Brundidge spoke up, "Lee and I may have had something to do with it. There was a little matter of a flash. . . ."

"That was nice going," said the doctor. "If that blood hadn't been drained out, it would have gone into his lungs and drowned him. Best thing in the world you could have done for him. That saved him for the hangman. . . ."

113

Chapter Ten

Our Side Did It, Too

DRIVING BACK TO THE DAI ITCHI FROM TOJO'S HOUSE after the shooting, we nearly got ourselves killed. George Burns' Japanese car had no headlights and in the darkness he took a wrong turning off the roadway and onto some trolley tracks. By some miracle, the light automobile jumped a three-foot culvert into which it should, by all the laws of gravity, have plunged. We were shaken, but unhurt, and with the assistance of some Japanese who ran out with paper lanterns we pushed the car out of the way before it was hit by an approaching trolley.

All through this experience, Massaguchi Moriyama did not say a word. He just sat in the car when the rest of us got out to push, and when we got back to the hotel to finish our stories, he retired to a corner and put his head in his hands. Usually, he was eager to run copy from the sixth-floor room down to the censors in the lobby.

"What's the matter, Massa?" I pressed him.

When he looked up, I saw he had been crying. "I just can't get over it," he said. "There was Tojo dying and the Americans were so cruel to him, so indifferent. I know you hate him. I hated him, too, until today, but a dying man is different. When he was premier I shouted at him one day at a mass meeting in Hibiya Park that he should kill himself. But he is a human being, after all, and you acted as if he were worse than a dog. I just never thought Americans were that cruel."

There was no use telling him that, first of all, our indifference and callousness had been only skin-deep and, secondly, that, sure, Americans and Englishmen and Frenchmen could be just as cruel

114

as Japanese. The difference is that you don't admit it in wartime, and the bigger difference is that the acts of cruelty we committed in the war were not a part of national policy, not the product of centuries of training in systematized brutality, but the deeds of frightened men temporarily brutalized by the savagery of conflict.

In this war, we did everything to the Japanese that they did to us, except eat them. At times, their hungry soldiers ate the flesh of our dead. We did not do that. We did murder unarmed prisoners. We did on occasion, so numerous soldiers told me, cut them up into little pieces, slowly, piece by piece. Those things happened in or just behind the front lines, in the midst of the fighting, and were not common occurrences. We did not have a policy of mass starvation of prisoners, as the Japs did at Santo Tomas and Bilibid, Nichols Field and Singapore.

The Japs did not think those things were wrong. They believed that the victor had the right to do whatever he wished. We knew the things were wrong, but on occasion we did them anyway.

One day in Sicily I witnessed the mass murder by Americans of seventy Italians and one German. That was about the third day after our landing, when we were fighting to get the Biscari airfield. Driving in a jeep with an Intelligence captain named Minor, I heard the sudden spurt of tommy-gun fire from an olive grove beside the road. We jumped out and ran over.

Thirty-six Italians were lying there in a double line. One was still conscious, flopping around like a chicken who has just been hit by a badly aimed axe blow. Blood was pouring from his throat. "*Mama mia*," he screamed. "Sweet tears of Jesus. Kill me! Kill me!" Minor calmed him down and put a dressing on his throat. The Italian changed his scream, "Take me to a hospital! Save me! Save me!" We went down the line of bodies and found three men still breathing faintly. The captain shouted to a Red Cross man, an American who stood just below us on the hillside.

"Help these men! Take them to a hospital."

"Nuts," the aid man said, walking over. "They shot at my buddy."

And he refused to obey the order. We checked up and found that while the prisoners were being led from the front lines—which we could see on the hillside opposite us—a sniper had fired a shot from the olive grove. The Americans had then lined up the prisoners and cut loose with tommy guns.

Later the same afternoon, after the airfield had been captured

115

under fire from German tanks, Captain Minor and I again heard the sound of tommy guns from across the gravel roadway. We sprinted over and saw the same scene. But this time the American sergeant and private who had done the murders were still standing there. We went over the bodies, and all thirty-six were dead. One was German, the rest Italians.

"Why did you shoot these guys?" Minor asked.

"Patton told us to," said the sergeant.

"Nuts! I don't believe that."

"Well, he sure did. He talked to us in Africa before we came over here and he said, 'if any of those bastards takes a shot at you, and then throws down his gun and comes out with his hands up, you have a right to take one shot back at the son of a bitch.' We were marching these prisoners back when somebody fired from behind the hill, so we let these guys have it."

I talked to the captain who commanded the company. (He came from Oklahoma City and I still remember his name.) He said, "That's right. Patton told us not to take any prisoners."

Our policy then was to try to get the Italians to surrender without fighting, something they wouldn't do if they knew they would be shot on giving up, and I went at once to the division commander, Major General Troy Middleton. "No," said the general, "Patton didn't say exactly that. But I can understand how these boys could have taken it that way." He gave orders designed to prevent any further massacres by his 45th Division.

Such incidents did not occur every day, but neither were they unique. Friends who fought at Malmédy where American prisoners were shot down by the SS in the Battle of the Bulge, told me that our side had done the same thing first. The Germans had been so angry that they had turned their guns on our men.

Fear was the underlying cause of such acts, regardless of which side committed them. A soldier under fire, half crazed by the killing, knows that the man in the other side's uniform cannot kill him if he is dead. So he disregards the upraised hands and even after the enemy has ceased to breathe he pours shots into the inert body. It is like whaling a rattlesnake for hours after he has been dead and harmless.

I remember how shocked was Lee Miller, who was Ernie Pyle's friend, when he got his first glimpse of war in the Walled City of Manila in February of 1945. A Jap stripped to his G-string, unarmed,

116

hands over his head, walked toward a group of GIs at the corner of a ruined building. They let him get about thirty feet away and then an American soldier pumped a couple of M–1 bullets into his belly.

A few days later I watched an American sergeant fire at least twelve shots into the back of a helplessly wounded Jap and then, deliberately reloading his gun, do the same thing to four others.

One Japanese who had been a close pre-war acquaintance died in the same way in Manila. He was Colonel Jiro Saito, the man who pulled the trigger on World War II by transmitting the orders for the Japanese to take Mukden back in September of 1931. I wrote a story about him for *Collier's* during the war and somehow or other the magazine reached him in Manila. He summoned the Jap newspapermen and gave an interview in which he expressed regret at my attitude and hoped that we would "have many drinks together after the war." When they picked him up in Manila, his belly wouldn't have held even one drink. It had a big hole in it. He had come out of a house with his hands over his head, unarmed, and a GI stuck him with a bayonet. He took five hours to die.

Sure, Americans do things like that. The difference this time is that we won and we don't have to be tried for them. Imagine what would have happened in a war-crimes court—if we had lost—to the Americans who invented the atom bomb and the Americans who dropped it!

Chapter Eleven

He Was Kind to the Jews

THE C.I.C. WAS RUNNING A BAD SECOND IN THE RACE to catch up with newsworthy figures in Japan. Things might have gone on this way if I had not made the mistake of confiding some of our reportorial plans to an Army officer. The officer was Colonel Fred Munson, whom I had known for some years as an Army career man, host, and perennial bachelor around Tokyo, Peiping, and Shanghai. He was now on MacArthur's liaison staff after having served for a long time before the war as an Intelligence courier in the Orient. I met him in the grill of the Imperial in Tokyo one evening, when the city was still out of bounds to correspondents, and he invited me to ride down to Yokohama with him.

Knowing Freddy's previous interest in Intelligence, I talked freely in the car about the stories we had written and were working on. Indeed, as it turned out, I talked too damn much. Names rolled out, "Tokyo Rose, Black Dragon Society, Tojo, Togo, Suzuki, Konoye."

"We found Tokyo Rose," I said, this being several days after publication of her life story.

"She's a Canadian girl," Freddy said.

"Sorry," I insisted, "but she's from Los Angeles."

"You're wrong. She's a Canadian."

I changed the subject. "There's a bird named Tanaka up in the Imperial who's making a monkey out of the Americans. He's an Army major, and a national hero for his fight against the Russians at Nomonhan back in 1939—a slick, long-haired guy who looks full of dope. He wants to open some night clubs and he's getting in good with the Americans by passing out beer and steaks, and silk flags. The bad part is that he's widely known to the Japs as a fire-

118

brand militarist and a hothead, and it doesn't do any good to have him seen around on pally terms with American officers."

"You're imagining things," said Freddy.

Another change of subject was indicated. "We're going out tomorrow to bring in Colonel Meisinger, the Butcher of Warsaw and the Number One Gestapo man in the Orient." I had known about the Butcher ever since Hitler sent him to the Orient in 1941 and I had been tipped off that he was now in Japan.

Colonel Munson said, "I never heard of any Meisinger."

"Well," I promised, "I'll introduce you."

I went back into Tokyo that night and through our interpreter summoned the Jap secret police officer, Captain Muto, to the Imperial.

"Captain," I asked, "where's My-sin-ga of the Nazi Embassy?" He understood English when the questions weren't embarrassing.

"Choto, just a minute pureesu," he answered, jumping for the telephone.

The captain's alacrity in responding to this request—as he had to our request for help in finding Tojo—was as striking an indication as could be imagined of what was taking place in Japan. Before the war, members of the Japanese gendarmerie, the Kempei, were universally dreaded and hated by foreigners and Japanese alike. Their methods were brutally stupid, persistently annoying; their manners intrusive and loud. Nearly everyone in the Japanese Empire had unpleasant sessions with them.

And now a member of this Jap Gestapo was jumping to obey our orders. He was one hundred per cent for helping the Americans.

In five minutes, the phone in Harry Brundidge's room rang for the captain; he took the call, and then turned away from it with a sneer, which he imagined to be a smile.

My-sin-ga-san, he informed us, was at Kawaguchi, near Mount Fuji. Contrary to rumors, he had not yet committed suicide but was living with about a hundred other Germans somewhere around the shores of Lake Kawaguchi. The captain knew of Meisinger's reputation. "Ah," he said, "be bery carefur, prees. I think so this bery bad man, Butcha of Warsah."

Meisinger was not only a very bad man, but a very dangerous one, a key figure in the Nazi-Tokyo setup.

He had been ordered to the Far East by Hitler in 1941 as Gestapo chief with the duty of keeping a check on the loyalty of the thousands

119

of Germans spotted in Japan, North China, Manchuria, and Siam. These men were hand-picked industrial, economic, diplomatic, and military experts who were sent out after Japan joined the Axis in 1940, and their job was to help Japan get ready for war. The war that they wanted Japan to fight, as has since been shown in the Nürnberg trials, was not against the United States. They tried to urge Japan to seize Singapore, hoping thereby to "frighten" the United States into staying out of the Atlantic and concentrating in the Pacific, but not actually entering the conflict in either area. The Japs just accepted the German assistance and went ahead with their own plans per schedule, a schedule which, it cannot be repeated too often, did *not* count on the secret connivance or assistance of Franklin D. Roosevelt.

Meisinger's principal job was spying on his fellow German spies, and he performed it so effectively that a good many of the Nazi envoys were terrified of him.

We were a bit nervous ourselves when we went out to capture the Butcher of Warsaw. There were six of us in the party: veteran John R. Bockhorst, with his movie camera; Bob Brumby, of Georgia and the Mutual Broadcasting Company; two capable veteran Army combat photographers, Fred Mallwitz and Dutch Glasser, both of whom spoke German; Sergeant Kodomo, our Nisei interpreter; and myself.

Driving away from Atsugi airfield and through the nearby village, we bluffed our way past two American sentries and turned the jeep west into unoccupied country. No other Americans had been there, and we didn't know whether we'd find the Japs still armed and full of the Kamikaze spirit, or whether the same docile acceptance of the surrender that we had discovered elsewhere would also prevail in this area. It was a wonderful morning, with the sun shining on the rich-green, nearly ripe fields of rice and lighting up the snow on distant Fuji-san.

We were nervous as we approached our first Japanese soldier, but he saluted and pointed out the road. There were more and more soldiers as we went on, riding in trucks which they were assembling at various points preparatory to turning them over to our forces. After their first amazed glances, they saluted and we quickly saluted back. We passed through a mountain tunnel piled high with crated military stores, and just outside it were a dozen mobile one-five-five field artillery pieces.

120

"Sure a lot of headaches for us in that tunnel," Brumby drawled.

And indeed, the whole area around Fuji, if the Japs had elected to defend it with their usual fanaticism and customary digging-in tactics, would have presented an almost unconquerable fortress—atomic bomb or no atomic bomb. To fight up those tremendous, sheer hills; through the valleys with their swift streams of cold green water racing over tumbled boulders; to have battled not only an army but women and children who knew every foot of the country and were armed with grenades and rifles—would have been the most costly and lengthy series of operations in military history. A staggering amount of America's best blood would have been shed on those hills.

We saw that the Japs had planned to defend this area, although the actual digging in had not yet started. Thirty miles from the seashore we came across new, fast-looking amphibious vehicles. And everywhere, as we bounced over the narrowing roads through the town of Gotemba and up the flank of Fuji, we saw evidences of Japan's demobilization. Soldiers toiled up the roads, bent over under the weight of their heavy packs; headed home to their mountain villages and to the job of trying to explain to their families that they had stopped fighting only because the Emperor issued the order.

But as we neared the end of the four-hour drive, our thoughts were on Meisinger. "Let's go into Kawaguchi like casual American soldier-tourists," I suggested. "We'll get lunch, find out where Meisinger is, and then send word that he can either surrender or fight it out."

We wasted a half hour by taking the wrong road around the shores of Lake Kawaguchi, and then located Japanese police headquarters in the area. In answer to our inquiries for "My-sin-ga" they told us that German Embassy headquarters were in the Fujiview Hotel, and the Nazis there could tell us the Gestapo colonel's whereabouts.

Through Kodomo, we told them we had come to take Meisinger, and hearing ourselves say it, we began to get scared. "Are the Germans armed?" Kodomo asked. Yes, said the gendarmes, they had pistols and light automatic weapons. "Would you care to send a gendarme with us?"

"Ah," they hissed, "so sorry. We have onry ritter pistors. Germans have machine guns."

"Okay," we answered. "If you hear any shooting, don't think the war's started all over. It will be us."

121

"Yeah," said Bocky, "us and the Krauts."

The Fujiview is an ideal hotel for a mountain resort, luxurious by any standards with its large paneled rooms, its modern but comfortable furniture, and the wide windows that open on the gemlike lake to the west; and to the east on snowcapped Fuji a few miles away. As we drove under the circular portico, the hotel seemed deserted. Then I caught a glimpse of two startled faces peering through a second-floor window. As I looked up, the faces drew back and the curtains were drawn hastily and tightly together. The two men must have seen our revolvers, but they probably saw our cameras, too. We were trying to make the cameras more conspicuous than the guns.

The lobby was deserted except for the Jap assistant manager behind the desk. He was polite enough, on the surface, but none too cordial to our request for food: "Ah, you see, this is German Embassy now, not hotel." It was the first time we had gotten really tough with a Jap. "And this is the American Army now. Get us what you can to eat."

After he disappeared toward the kitchen, there was no one in sight, but we sensed that somehow word of our arrival had spread and the hotel was already buzzing with excitement behind closed doors. Lights were flicking on the telephone switchboard, but there was no one to answer. The assistant manager reappeared with an elderly German woman. She stuck out a limp hand and introduced herself. "I am housekeeper. We do not have much food but I will try to get some sandwiches, if that is satisfactory." She and the Jap disappeared once more.

We strolled around the lobby, making enthusiastic remarks about the scenery and waiting for something to happen. In a few minutes, a German appeared on a long porch outside, walked hurriedly across and down into the grounds, headed for a corner of the building. His agitation was apparent in his walk.

I nudged Brumby. "Maybe that's Meisinger." Bob overtook the German, stopped him, and began a conversation, while we kept our hands close to our revolver holsters. Then I saw Brumby pull a pack of cigarettes from his pocket with shaking hands, and offer one to the German. "His hands were shaking twice as hard as mine," Brumby said later. "When I saw that, I knew we had him."

The German and Brumby came back to the porch, talking, and I walked over to join them. The Nazi had a very severe case of jitters.

122

He thrust his hands into the pockets of his white shorts to keep them from trembling, but his shoulders continued to jerk grotesquely. Another German, also in shorts and a clean white shirt and white shoes, stumbled swiftly across the lobby behind us and I followed him rapidly. He walked into a big room, apparently Embassy head-quarters, looked around aimlessly at the chairs, desks, and typewriters and then walked out. He, too, was shaking as he joined Brumby and the other German, who was a middle-aged man with white hair and a not unpleasant face. The younger one's jaw was split by two dueling scars. "Heidelberg," he explained, in answer to an unasked question.

At the table, the two Germans introduced themselves: the elder, Dr. Boltze, councilor of the embassy in charge of the seventy officials at Kawaguchi; and Hans Wolters, the first secretary.

The housekeeper beamed as she saw them join us. "Please excuse this poor food," she said. But there was no need to apologize. They even brought out some Japanese wine—not sake, but a grape wine that was too thin and too young. Drinking it had a sedative effect on the nerves of the two Germans, and their tension lessened as we carefully steered the conversation away from our mission. In contrast to the Japanese who could laugh at their misfortunes, the two Krauts felt very sorry for themselves. "We hear that the destruction of Germany is terrible, the Russians are very cruel, and there is no food. We hope the Americans will allow the three thousand Germans now in Japan to remain here for the winter."

"I told Dr. Boltze that we were wise to choose this place for our embassy, after being bombed out of Tokyo," Hans put in. He smiled ingratiatingly. "Certainly we will be permitted to remain here, because nobody will want to take this place, so far from everywhere."

By the time we had coffee and the last bit of wine had disappeared, the Germans were fairly well reassured that we were harmless, and slightly stupid, sightseers. They even invited us to come back to spend the next weekend. We asked for a check, but they said there was no charge. "We are happy to have you, and hope you will put in a good word for us at headquarters."

Thus disarmed, Boltze was only slightly surprised a few minutes later when I asked him to step over to another table. It was time to end the party and get on with our business.

Without preliminaries, I said, "Thanks for the food, but we didn't

123

come here for amusement." Fear leaped into his eyes. "We came for Meisinger."

Boltze's face blanched. His teeth chattered and his hands fluttered in helpless circles. He fell back, grabbing at the table for support.

"It's only Meisinger we want," I said. "Is he here?"

Boltze nodded.

"In the hotel?"

"Yes. In his room downstairs."

The German sat down, sagging into the chair. For nearly a minute he was unable to speak. Then he asked, "May I consult Hans?"

"Certainly, I'll call him over."

I explained the situation to Hans. He too was sweating in terror, but he was more in control of his nerves than was Boltze. "We came to get Meisinger," I said. "What's the best way to do it?"

"Do you think . . . ?" Boltze began, his eyes on his colleague. The scar-faced man's lips formed the word "Suicide." Then they both shook their heads negatively, and Boltze said, "I don't think he will."

We were in too deep now to back out, so I followed up like a hard-boiled fictional private detective. It wasn't the wine talking, because we had drunk very little of that. But I will confess to having read several detective stories on a recent trip around the world. The vocabulary came in handy now.

"This is a very beautiful hotel, as we agreed during lunch," I said. "Unless it's necessary, we don't want to bloody it up. But we're going to take Meisinger. He can have it any way he wants it. If he wants to play it smart and come peacefully, fine. If he wants to shoot it out, he'll get it that way."

Brumby and Bocky walked over to join the consultation. The Germans talked, mostly to each other, in half-finished phrases: "He won't shoot. . . . He'll shoot us. . . . He may commit suicide. . . . Probably not. . . ."

We cut in. "Has he got a gun?"

"Yes. But I don't think he will shoot."

"He has been saying different things in these last days," Hans went on. "He said that if the Russians came here, he would kill himself at their approach, but if the Americans came he would shoot five of us and then himself with his last bullet. Then he said later that he would surrender to the Americans as he believed he could clear himself in an American court. He knows he is on the Russian

124

and Polish lists of war criminals, and he's been expecting this. So have we, but you fooled us at lunch."

We discussed the best way of delivering our ultimatum. I decided to write a note. "I will not take it down," Boltze objected. "He has threatened to kill me. He has known for some time that you would be coming for him, and has made his plans." We decided to have a Japanese roomboy take the note to Meisinger's room on the floor below. In my notebook, I wrote:

Colonel of the Police Josef Meisinger: We have come to take you to the American Army authorities. We will guarantee you safe conduct to Yokohama headquarters. We assure you of protection on the route and that the American authorities will see to it that you have full opportunity to speak for yourself.

Mr. Boltze points out that it might be more advisable for you to be in American than in Russian hands.

Come up to the dining room unarmed and with your hands over your head.

You will be absolutely safe.

Clark Lee, War Correspondent.

While Hans translated the note into German—Boltze tried it but his hands were still shaking too hard to hold a pen—we deployed our forces. Sergeant Kodomo squatted by the bar, covering the top of the stairway where it made the last turn up from the ground floor. Fred Mallwitz got behind a pillar on the porch roof, covering the upper hallway. Brumby took his .38 and I my .45 and went to the far end of the dining room. Bockhorst and Dutch Dressler unlimbered their cameras and stood at opposite sides of the dining room, ready to shoot with either cameras or guns. We figured that if Meisinger opened fire he would have time to aim at only one of us.

The Jap roomboy took both notes, English and German, and padded softly down the polished stairway. Boltze and Hans faded into the kitchen, outside of the line of fire if Meisinger should come into the dining room.

I took a quick look around to inspect our positions. Outside, in front of the upstairs bar, there was a German kid two or three years old, a beautiful little boy. We shooed him away. A German woman walked into the upstairs lobby, took one look at the Americans with guns in hand, and ran back into the corridor, her hand over a mouth that was opened to scream but from which no sound came.

The clock on the dining-room wall crawled from 3:55 to 4 o'clock and on to 4:05. Suddenly a German woman walked into the room, quickly but unobtrusively. She was a powerful-looking female of about thirty, dressed in a none-too-white nurse's uniform which you suspected, without any visible evidence to support the suspicion, she had hastily donned over nothing at all. Perhaps it was her bare legs that gave that impression.

Boltze and Hans ghosted out of the kitchen and confronted her as she approached Bocky. They translated a brief sentence.

"Herr Meisinger asks if he has time to pack a suitcase?"

This was, dramatically, a first-rate bit of anticlimax. But we were tremendously relieved. We knew now—or thought we knew—what we hadn't a moment before: The Butcher would quit without fighting. Our apprehension up to that moment had been based on two possibilities: First, that the Butcher would kill us and, second, that we would kill him. In the latter case we, and especially myself as organizer of the expedition, would be in for a rough time from the Army.

So I was smiling when I answered the woman. "Why, certainly he can pack a suitcase. But tell him to hurry."

She disappeared down the stairs. A few minutes later she was back. "Can he have a half hour?"

"No," I said, "fifteen minutes is plenty. It's getting dark and we have a long drive."

The blonde was persistent. "Can he take two suitcases, or only one?"

"Tell him to bring what he likes. But you better pack for him. He must come up now."

As she went out, Hans whispered, "She's his girl-friend. They want to say good-bye for a half hour."

Five minutes later, the woman reappeared once more. "He asks," she said, "if he can come with his hands stretched out sideways instead of over his head."

It was a strange form of face-saving, but we agreed.

Then two minutes later, so suddenly that we were all surprised, Meisinger walked into the dining room. Mallwitz had already searched him at the top of the stairs, but we didn't know that and I kept my .45 pointed at his belly as I motioned him to come toward me and ran my hands over his pockets, and patted him for concealed weapons. He tried to grin, blinking his eyes as the sweat ran down

126

trom his forehead. In heavily accented but intelligible English he said, "I am not armed."

He was a giant of a man. "Pig!" was your first reaction. But no pig ever looked so dangerous. He stood well over six feet from the top of his bullet-shaped head through his short, bulky neck and massive shoulders and then down through a bulging but solid stomach to tremendous feet. Hands like clubs hung out of the sleeves of a belted, heavy tweed suit coat. His white sport shirt was held together by a grayish tie, in harmony with his suit. A ring surrounded his little finger like a barrel stave. Flattened ears and a hooked nose showed that he had not been on the handing-out end of all the beatings in which he had been involved. He was smoking a thick cigar, and others stuck from a small forest of pencils and pens in his coat pocket. His smile was a mockery of gold and tobacco stains. A little trickle of saliva ran from his mouth.

Looking at him, you saw not a sunlit room in Japan but a gas chamber at Dachau; the crippled, starved bodies at Buchenwald; you heard the screams of a young Jewish woman as she died in horror and pain in the ghetto of Warsaw. Some of the Nazi hangmen who have fallen into our hands photograph like human beings; but wickedness and cruelty were written in this face. Beside Meisinger, the Neanderthal man would look like the highest product of evolution.

The Butcher was pretty well in control of himself as we walked him over to a table and sat him down. He preened as Bocky and Dutch took close-ups, and we questioned him quickly.

"You know that you are called the Butcher of Warsaw?"

"Yes, I know, but—"

"You were head of the Gestapo in Warsaw?"

"I headed all the criminal police dealing with the German people only."

"How long did you work with Hitler?"

"Since 1922. But I was not in the Munich Putsch."

"Who was your boss?"

"Himmler."

Then, without questioning, came the denials: "I was never unkind to Jews. . . . In fact, I assisted them. . . . It was General Fisher and Governor Frank who killed the Jews in Warsaw. . . . How many? I do not know. I heard that a few were killed."

He signed a note saying, "I have surrendered today to Lee, Brumby, Bockhorst, and a party of Americans."

At the time, the Army men with us did not want their names to be known because they were afraid of reprisals—not at the hands of a future, reborn Nazi party—but of their own Army. As it turned out, they were wise in making this decision.

We kept a wary eye on Meisinger's every move as we escorted him down the stairs. Getting him loaded into the jeep consumed some time. When he climbed into the back, taking up the whole seat with his vast bulk, one of the tires went flat. He worked his way out laboriously, while we borrowed a pump from a Japanese and fixed the tire. Meisinger had brought two suitcases and a brief case, and we strapped them onto the hood. As we left, Meisinger shook hands with Boltze and Hans, and the two Germans thanked us for taking him away before he could shoot them; and a bunch of Japanese cheered and smiled happily at seeing the last of the man who had terrorized them as well as bullied the fellow members of his embassy.

We headed down the mountain road, now shrouded in fog and low-lying clouds. Finally we broke beneath the clouds at about 3,000 feet above sea level, and Fred Mallwitz skillfully guided the jeep over bumps that made progress painfully slow. We had Meisinger in the back, where he couldn't yield to any suicidal whim and send all of us off the road's sheer edge by grabbing the steering wheel.

Meisinger was making a fine effort to be chatty and good-fellowish. When he heard someone say, "I wish I had a drink," he put in eagerly, "Ach schnapps. I haf too much in my room. Here I haf a small bottle." We stopped while he produced a half-pint, silver flask from his brief case, announcing it was "Goot branty." I accepted it with mixed feelings. Riding beside him, smelling him and feeling the touch of his shoulder, I was getting a little sick. My stomach was turning over. To take anything from him was completely disgusting. But it was cold as hell.

"Poison!" I thought. "Has this rat poisoned this flask?" Brumby and Bocky had already taken drinks, and I took one and handed the container back to the Butcher, to see if he would drink. He fingered the flask lovingly, then he turned it upside down and shook out the last few drops on the floor of the jeep. He smiled, screwed on the top, and put the flask back in his pocket. For ten jolting minutes I kept from swallowing. Then I said the hell with it, and let the warm liquid flow down my throat. It was goot branty.

There were no deadly pains in my stomach. My only reaction was

128

increased disgust at having to ride with Meisinger, and I asked Fred to stop the jeep while I got out and perched on the hood, on top of Meisinger's inexpensive-looking suitcases. It was rougher there, but all-in-all more comfortable.

As time went on, Meisinger was alternately silent for long spells and then chatty. He worried about his nine-year-old son in Munich and we got satisfaction from telling him that the city had been beaten to hell by American bombers. He mentioned that his wife—God help her—was in Shanghai, but he didn't seem very concerned about her welfare.

"My cigars," he said, "are of the best." He smoked cigars incessantly all the time he was with us. "Since the Japanese captured Manila, I have been getting them from there." We told him, "Well, there are plenty of fine Manila cigars in Yokohama."

"Yes," he agreed, with a brief flash of humor, "but I think not for me."

That's right, we said, not for you.

He welcomed his anticipated opportunity of "proving my innocence before an American jury. I am glad to face American justice." He was talking now through Dutch Dressler, who interpreted for us.

"Yeah," we said, "we'll see to it that you get a jury of New York cloak-and-suiters, or Hollywood tycoons. They'd sure like to hear your story of how you helped the Jews in the Warsaw ghetto."

We got Meisinger back to Atsugi without incident and Dutch Dressler drove him into Yokohama where the C.I.C. placed him in fairly comfortable detention quarters. A little later, we heard that he was shouting for sympathy. He got it from an entirely unexpected quarter, a general in the U. S. Army. That general, at the request of another general, arrested me for arresting Meisinger.

There was another sequel that made me wish I hadn't described the Butcher as such an evil-looking brute. When I got back home people said, "Gee, that was exciting. I saw it in the newsreels. But which was you and which was Meisinger?"

Chapter Twelve

The Rights of Nazi War Criminals in Japan

Even with the bulky person of the Gestapo killer in their safe-keeping, the C.I.C. still found it difficult to believe that there was such a man as Meisinger. Before we arrested the Nazi, Colonel Munson had made a report of my conversation with him to General Diller of MacArthur's public-relations staff, and it was Diller's decision that my "babbling about Nazi war criminals" in Japan justified my being placed under observation. Diller gave orders to the C.I.C. to that effect.

When we actually delivered Meisinger, the C.I.C. was still not satisfied that all was well and I was arrested on a charge of "violating the rights of a Nazi war criminal." Being arrested is merely an incident in a reportorial career, but this incident is worth recording as a sidelight on the inner workings of the C.I.C. which in Japan had and still has the ticklish job of outwitting the Black Dragon Society, the former military gendarmerie, and other nationalistic, anti-democratic, terroristic organizations whose members are veterans of plot and counterplot. We had assumed, also, that the C.I.C. would be interested in tracking down members of Hitler's Far Eastern organization, but we may have been mistaken as to the scope of the C.I.C.'s duties in this connection. At any rate, some known Nazi agents were still walking around Japan a year after the surrender.

The agents detailed to arrest me wasted three days asking mysterious questions of other correspondents before finally catching up with me at the Dai Itchi Hotel in Tokyo, to which press headquar-

130

ters had been moved. There were four of them, a tough major named McCall, another major and a lieutenant, both quite reasonable men, and a young foreigner of indeterminate nationality and antecedents whom McCall had acquired as a Jap-speaking stooge. The three Americans were conspicuously armed as they stopped our jeep outside the hotel.

"General Thorpe wants to see you," McCall said.

I'd never heard of the general, and said so. Also that I had come to Tokyo to do business which would require several hours and had to be completed so that I could leave for Korea in the morning; and that if Thorpe wanted a social visit I'd go down to Yokohama later in the evening.

"You don't ignore invitations from General Elliott Thorpe," McCall said pointedly.

"Do you mean I am under arrest? And if so, what is the charge?"

McCall answered, "They told me to bring you back, and I'm bringing you back."

Other correspondents crowded around, beginning to get angry, and a lot of heated words were exchanged before we calmed down and McCall said I was wanted in connection with the capture of Meisinger. Bob Brumby spoke up: "I was there and so were four others. Don't you want us?" McCall answered that it was Lee alone that he wanted. Even though he wasn't "wanted," Bob Brumby crowded into the jeep for the bumpy ride back to Yokohama; and in the New Grand Hotel, where GHQ officers had their mess, Thorpe was summoned from the dining room. He looked so pleased that I expected him to pin a Congressional Medal on McCall on the spot. Thorpe was a buck general, Regular Army, a tall, white-haired harassed-looking man. His was the vital job of rounding up enemy war criminals, of breaking up the Japanese military police machine and of preventing the formation of an underground movement that might give us serious trouble in the future. A good many of the badly wanted war criminals committed suicide before the C.I.C. caught up with them, which was not surprising in view of the fact that many of the Army's Japanese experts were in other theatres at the time of the surrender. Later, MacArthur obtained the services of some police and intelligence experts with experience in Japanese methods and prior acquaintance with the individuals sought for trial or examination.

Thorpe ordered me to follow him to his room. At the foot of the

131

stairs, I balked. "Before we go anywhere, I want to protest against being arrested and brought here and I want it understood that I am accompanying you under protest."

"That's okay," Thorpe answered, "everybody who is arrested always protests." Which I must admit was not a bad line.

Upstairs, Thorpe set the scene carefully. The tail end of a typhoon was whirling the window curtains around and blowing papers all over the place, but Thorpe hooked the door back about nine inches with the remark, "We'll just leave it open so we can get a breeze in the room." Since the last thing in the world that we needed was a breeze, I suspected some other motive and a glance at the door justified those suspicions. In the hallway I could see part of one big Army shoe. It belonged to McCall, who had been stationed there to listen in on the conversation.

In the months since our interview, I have come to feel a bit sympathetic toward Thorpe because of his admitted inexperience in the job to which he was assigned. During the whole war, the only feats by which he attracted newspaper attention were the arrest of 3,000 "collaborators" in New Guinea—fuzzywuzzies who had done manual labor for the Japs—and the arrest of the two allegedly pro-Jap sons of President Osmena in the Philippines; later, in Japan, he earned some headlines by his adverse "loyalty" report on two *Stars and Stripes* writers who were dismissed from that publication.

That night in his room in Yokohama, he sat down at a small table, placed me opposite and took out a leather-bound notebook whose contents he hid from my eyes. We were both a little tense.

"You know that you are subject to military discipline and court-martial."

"Yes," I said, "provided I have done something wrong. That is our understanding with the War Department. But what is this all about?"

"You may refuse to answer any questions. I must remind you that anything you say may be used against you in court-martial proceedings."

"What is the charge?"

"Did you write a note?"

"I've written lots of notes. It's part of my business. I assume that you are asking whether I wrote one to Meisinger to induce him to surrender. I did."

"Is this the note?"

"I can't say unless I see it." The note to the Butcher was, in fact,

132

in my wallet and it seemed to be burning a hole in my pocket. Both the original note and the translation were returned by Meisinger so they could be photographed.

"Now, answer yes or no! Is this the note you wrote to a German army officer?"

"I've never written a note to any German army officer. I did write one to a Gestapo colonel. I cannot identify that note without seeing it. And with what am I charged?"

"You realize," Thorpe said, "that you have gotten us into serious trouble. You have violated the rights of a German army officer to be protected against arrest by American civilians."

That sounded very silly, because correspondents had accepted the surrender of hundreds of Germans and Italians in Africa and Europe. I had captured a few Germans myself. Nobody had ever done anything before except congratulate us. We had worked closely with the C.I.C. in Europe, exchanging mutually valuable information. I said so.

"Yes," Thorpe agreed, "but you never got a hot potato like this before."

"We were never this lucky before."

"Lucky!" He got angry. "The Government of the United States is in serious trouble. You should know that we are still at war with Germany. The German embassy people here have rights. So do the German army people. I am going to protect those rights."

"I fail to see what rights a German war criminal has. Isn't Meisinger on the list of people to be captured?"

"A German war criminal has just as much right as you or any other American," Thorpe reiterated. "And I am here to protect them. You may not know it, but there are two German army generals here and they and the German ambassador protested this morning. The State Department is in serious trouble because of what you've done."

"To hell with their protest. Why do you love Nazis so much?"

Thorpe changed his tactics. "I can see why they say you are hard to get along with. You are certainly very jealous of anything having to do with your rights as an American."

"That's right, I am."

"You seem to be pretty tired. Are you feeling okay? Do you find yourself mistrusting your judgment? Are your nerves in good shape?"

I recalled that Diller had told one officer, who relayed the information to me, that the remarks I had made about Nazis, and Tojo,

133

and Tokyo Rose indicated that I was near a nervous breakdown, a matter with which Diller is not unfamiliar.

I couldn't help snapping to Thorpe, "I'm fine, old boy. And how is your health?"

Thorpe changed the subject and said, "Let's go on from there."

"Let's go back," I said, "to the German protest. I just can't understand who protested. Meisinger expressed his thanks to us for capturing him, and said he would have killed himself if the Russians had come for him. The German embassy officials also thanked us. They were afraid he would kill them."

"They did?" Thorpe inquired.

"Yes. And I can't understand the mechanics of the protest. Who made it and who brought it to you? Most of the Germans are far up in the hills, and I don't see how they got word through to you. In fact, I don't believe it."

"I never said there was any protest," Thorpe replied.

"You said it less than ten minutes ago. Now, who did protest?"

"Meisinger is protesting now."

"Have you seen him?"

"I won't say whether I have or not."

Again he changed the subject. He lit a cigarette, having trouble getting it going in the miniature gale whipping through the room.

"Did you beat this man up?" he asked.

"Hell no. We never touched him except to search him for a gun."

"Didn't you take anything out of his pocket?"

"Nothing at all. This was an arrest. Not a stick-up. Bockhorst has pictures of the whole thing. And there are plenty of witnesses, one of them downstairs now."

"Will you call him?"

I got up to go after Brumby, but just then McCall, forgetting that he was in hiding, called out through the partially opened door, "I'll go get him, General." Brumby came up and sat on the edge of the bed and Thorpe asked him, "Did Lee mistreat Colonel Meisinger?"

"Gosh no, sir! Nobody touched him. He came with us willingly and even thanked us."

"I am certainly relieved to hear that," the general said.

"Were there any marks on his ugly mug?" Brumby wanted to know.

"No," Thorpe answered. "But you know how it is about such

things. If he comes to trial three months from now, he may claim he was beaten up."

"Once again, General," I said, wanting to have Brumby hear Thorpe repeat his previous statement, "I fail to see why you are so solicitous about this man's rights."

"Well," Thorpe repeated, "I am. And you might as well understand it."

I asked, "What are you doing about arresting the war criminals on General MacArthur's list?"

"Nothing yet. I have orders not to go after them. And I don't have enough agents."

"The four guys that spent three days looking for me might have put in their time better by rounding up some of the Germans and Japs."

"Never mind about that," Thorpe answered, shaking his hand at me. "And don't go putting the finger on any more Japanese generals or admirals. You'll get me into serious trouble."

That about ended the conversation. Thorpe told me he wouldn't hold me for the time being, but might recall me for interrogation if "the State Department or Army got into any worse trouble with the German government." I protested against McCall's "Gestapo methods and threats," and Thorpe shrugged it off with the remark, "You're really not easy to push around."

But the incident wasn't over. When Brumby and I returned to the jeep, meeting four other correspondents who had followed us down from Tokyo, they got so indignant that they insisted on turning around after we had driven a couple of miles out toward our quarters at Atsugi. Already angry over McCall's attitude that afternoon, four reporters, Bill Downs, Homer Bigart, Jim McGlincy, and Fritz Opper steamed up to Thorpe's room, after first taking the precaution of hiding Brumby and myself around the corner of the block in case Thorpe should retaliate by having me arrested again.

Opper made a partial record of the conversation. This time Thorpe was answering the questions.

"Why did you arrest Lee?"

"Because he arrested and searched a German army officer."

"Wasn't Meisinger a Gestapo officer, not army?"

"I don't know."

"Is it a crime to arrest him, regardless of which he was?"

"Yes, it is."

"What crime?"

"I don't know. I'll have to look it up. Lee's a civilian and he went out and did what he should not have done. I don't want him to get the Army in trouble."

"Trouble with whom?" Opper asked.

"With the State Department," said Thorpe. "We haven't signed a peace with Germany. We are still at war with them and they have rights."

"Was Lee actually arrested?"

"Well, if you want to call it that. He was brought here for me to question."

"How did you know he had caught Meisinger?"

Thorpe ignored the question, but said, "The facts are these. This chap arrested a German officer and I arrested him while I investigated him. I take full responsibility."

Answering other questions, Thorpe said he had intended to arrest Meisinger when he got around to it; and also intended to arrest the Japanese war criminals some time. He wasn't quite sure about who Meisinger was; Major McCall hadn't ever heard of him and the major was one of Thorpe's best men. He hadn't had time yet to make a full study of the war criminals whom he was supposed to take into custody.

The conversation took an even more ludicrous turn when Jim McGlincy, who was very indignant, declared, "General MacArthur raised the American flag over Tokyo today. We are here to see that it is not torn down. We've heard a lot about Jap military gendarmes, but I can't see much difference between their methods and yours." Thorpe was aggrieved, but belligerent. "I've fought for the flag more times than you have!"

McGlincy cracked back, "You've been around longer."

Like a kid saying to another kid, "My old man's got more money than yours," Thorpe came back, "I've been wounded more times than you have!"

"I ducked, General," McGlincy answered.

Everybody had to laugh at that and the situation eased a bit. Thorpe said, "I suppose you fellows think somebody put me up to this." Nobody made any comment and the general went on talking. "Now, I don't care what happens to me. I'm just a country boy and this stuff is over my head and all I want to do is go home."

A few months later, MacArthur granted Thorpe's request and the general returned to the United States. McCall had gotten home even before him, by a lucky break. He was assigned the task of guarding Meisinger on his flight to the United States, en route to trial, and four months after he had arrested me in Tokyo I saw the vacationing major in the Reforma Hotel in Mexico, where I made the mistake of shaking hands with him before realizing his identity.

Chapter Thirteen

The Man behind MacArthur

Iᴛ ᴍᴀʏ ᴏʀ ᴍᴀʏ ɴᴏᴛ ʜᴀᴠᴇ ʙᴇᴇɴ "ꜱᴏᴍᴇʙᴏᴅʏ ɴᴀᴍᴇᴅ Diller" who caused my arrest by the C.I.C. in Japan.

But it definitely was, reader, somebody named Diller who is responsible for a lot of the ideas that you have about our war in the Pacific and for a share of your opinions about MacArthur, for it was Diller who controlled every word that came out of MacArthur's area from the Bataan days until after the surrender of Japan.

LeGrande A. Diller was Douglas MacArthur's public-relations man throughout the war and at one time held the lofty rank of a general officer, this temporary promotion being rescinded after the shooting stopped. Diller was likewise head of the self-constituted, non-official but all-potent, "Protect MacArthur Society," whose workings will be partially examined in this chapter. Scores of thousands of Americans, by guess, seem to be convinced that MacArthur is essentially a publicity seeker. They believe that his communiqués (MacArthur calls them "communeeks") never gave enough credit to the Navy or the Marines in his command. They think that reporters sent to MacArthur's area immediately lost all critical sense and the global viewpoint and jumped wholeheartedly on the general's bandwagon. These conclusions may or may not be partially correct. But what is essential to a fuller understanding of the entire picture is some knowledge of Diller's role in the MacArthur set-up.

The ex-public-relations officer is a slight, nervous West Pointer who started the war as a major and ended it as a brigadier general in command of a strangely assorted army consisting of some communications officers and equipment, a couple of cooks, a few jeep drivers, a handful of censors and several score hard-to-handle correspondents who were dependent on Diller's organization for trans-

138

portation, food, lodging, and communications facilities, and to a great extent for news—inasmuch as the independent gathering of news was not encouraged in MacArthur's area where it was preferred that reporters get their "facts" through official channels and communiqués. That Diller should undergo rapid promotions to general was accepted as natural by those who know that MacArthur always rewards those who are loyal to him.

Relations between correspondents and Diller's organization were not always of the most cordial nature. There was at least one flurry of fisticuffs, although slugging matches are severely frowned on in army regulations. Members of Diller's staff on occasion referred to newsmen as "shoe clerks," "sports writers," and "police reporters," the plain inference being that they had no business around a big-time war. Some of the correspondents held equally uncomplimentary opinions about Diller and his cohorts. I myself had the opportunity to see censorship at work in all theatres of the war, and, having been under Diller's control at both the beginning and end of hostilities, I feel competent to pronounce his censorship the worst that existed anywhere. It was a perfect example of what Fletcher Pratt has called the "technique of suppressing any facts but those they [the censors] want people to believe."

In most areas of the war, censorship paid at least occasional lip service to the idea that the American public was entitled to the news. In MacArthur's area, however, and despite the Supreme Commander's own statements to the contrary, I never once heard a public-relations officer express the thought that the public had any vested interest in the news of the war. From the military standpoint, MacArthur's censorship was notably more liberal than that in most other theatres; units in combat could be named and other morale-building information published. But above and beyond strictly military censorship, there was one principle that guided MacArthur's public-relations officers from the early days of the war and on through Melbourne, Brisbane, Port Moresby, Hollandia, back to Manila, and finally in Tokyo.

This principle was expressed in three words which had a potent effect on American public opinion throughout the war. The words were: "Protect the general!"

This unprecedented concept of the function of public relations was a natural offspring of the idea prevailing among the men around MacArthur that World War II consisted of two fronts. On one of them, MacArthur faced Japan, and on the other he was embattled against his "enemies" in the United States whose sole aim was to prevent the general from getting at the Japs. Likewise, the protective wall had two faces. It served—by suppressing all news unfavorable to the general—to keep his enemies from getting ammunition to use against him; and at the same time it kept from MacArthur's eyes and ears any disturbing stories about the "other side's" foul tactics. To this latter end, MacArthur's aides and public-relations officers carefully combed his incoming mail and destroyed letters or newspaper clippings that would have upset the Supreme Commander.

Ex-Brigadier General Diller was the member of MacArthur's staff who put into concrete form this idea of censorship and who enforced it until the blue-penciling was finally terminated in October of 1945 after repeated hints from Washington and in the American press that the shooting had at last ended. Of course, this censorship was not the result of a deliberate plot by Diller. Rather, he fell into a way of thinking that was common to those serving with MacArthur —a state of mind that took shape during the Bataan days when MacArthur's men were left alone to face an overwhelming foe. A persecution complex was born, and with it the determination that no word should be written or broadcast from MacArthur's area that would in any way injure the general.

For Diller—the man who determined what the American people should and should not read about the war in the Far Pacific—the world consisted of two classes of people: those on MacArthur's side and those against him. He had two loyalties, to his country and to MacArthur, a condition that is common among those who live close to the general and who fall under the spell of his magnetic personality and the logical, convincing arguments with which he expounds his views and opinions.

Outside of any military considerations, an additional criterion was applied by Diller and his censors to every story that they reviewed: "Will it hurt the general?" If so, kill it; or change the context. If a writer's stories were consistently favorable to MacArthur, Diller came to regard him and refer to him as "on our side." Every correspondent heard the words, "Protect the General," repeated or paraphrased scores of times in the war years.

I happened to be in at the start of Diller's political censorship which was based on the "policy" of MacArthur's headquarters as interpreted by Diller, who was the general's aide in Manila at the outbreak of hostilities. We soon learned that our function as correspondents on Bataan and Corregidor—as seen by Diller—was not to report the news as we saw it, but to try to play on the sympathies of the people of the United States so that they would bring pressure on Washington to get men and supplies to MacArthur.

I ran afoul of Diller in one of my first dispatches which reported my sharing a good meal with an aircraft detection outfit on Bataan. The item was cut and Diller warned me not to "give them an idea back home that there is plenty to eat here." Of course, it would encourage the Japs to know that our food and supplies were low, but Diller disregarded that angle in his effort to arouse pity for Bataan. In another story I was asked to insert the words "chewing on a mule steak sandwich."

During an interview with Captain Arthur Wermuth which resulted in my dubbing him "One Man Army of Bataan," I told of eating carabao steak and was warmly commended by Diller for "playing up the hunger angle." Similarly, the late Melville Jacoby was praised for coining the jingle: "We're the Battling Bastards of Bataan—No Papa No Mama No Uncle Sam"; as was the writer for reporting the organization of a subscription fund with the slogan: "Better Buy a Bomber Than Be Buried in Bataan." The purpose of these stories was to rouse public sympathy for Bataan's defenders in the United States.

Of course, there soon was a food shortage in Bataan; our airplanes soon ran out; there was bitterness among the men who felt their country was letting them down. I believed as did others, that it was necessary to get after the Japs before they had time to dig in and consolidate. On returning to Washington after Bataan fell, the War Department freely permitted me to express my opinion on the subject of "Fight Japan First." Other writers were similarly allowed to assert that Hitler was enemy number one and should be beaten first. But from MacArthur's area you were not able to admit that there were two sides to the question. Stories either stressed the Pacific war, or they were killed. Thus, Diller's censorship became one of propaganda and special pleading for one area of the global war.

Little by little as radio reports from the United States began to show that our Bataan stories were being widely read, MacArthur's officers took us into their confidence. They began to speak of "Washington" as an enemy of MacArthur and then to mention names of those they felt responsible for the failure to reinforce Bataan—"Marshall," "Eisenhower—who is jealous of the general," "Roosevelt, who fears him politically." Through our dispatches they tried to go over the heads of these "enemies" and get to the people. Very shortly, Bataan had become a political hot-potato back home. The McCormick-Patterson press lambasted Roosevelt for not helping MacArthur; they nominated the general for President. I am not going to say that Diller forced me to slant all my dispatches, which quite naturally reflected some of the bitterness of Bataan's defenders. I am no hero, and I did not want to get killed there, or anywhere else. Until I learned what had really happened at Pearl Harbor and how little advanced was our military program, I kept hoping that Bataan could be reinforced.

On one occasion, I voluntarily participated in a bit of extra-official special pleading to which Diller lent the facilities of the Army.

It was in February, 1942, that the War Department finally notified MacArthur that no major effort could be made to reinforce Bataan. Diller refused to accept this as final and urged the correspondents to think of a way to appeal directly to the people. A few days before, Senator Millard Tydings of Maryland had made a speech urging assistance for the "gallant men in the Philippines." We knew that the War Department probably would not forward any message to Tydings, and I suggested attempting to communicate with him through his great friend, the late Princess Kawananakoa of Honolulu. Accordingly, we worked up a roundabout message to the princess asking her to "tell Eleanor's husband that Millard's good tidings joyously received here please keep up good work hopes prayers of thousands of men rest on your efforts." Eleanor is Mrs. Tydings.

Diller gave the message top priority on the signal-corps radio and it was sent to Honolulu where the princess immediately understood its import. The Army commander in Hawaii, Lt. Gen. DeLos C. Emmons, refused at first to allow it to be retransmitted but eventually it was cleared and relayed to Tydings. By the time it reached him, however, he knew that it was the government's decision that nothing much could be done to relieve the Philippines and all he could do was reply noncommittally that Washington was praying for us too, and "God bless you."

By the time MacArthur escaped to Australia, taking Diller with him, the policy of dividing everybody on earth into those "on our side" and "our enemies" was firmly fixed. By that time, it was the firm conviction of Diller and many others on MacArthur's staff that the President feared the general as a rival and consequently would not give him supplies and men to fight the Japs. Accordingly, Roosevelt was promoted to top position on the list of "enemies," while, on the other hand, correspondents of anti-New Deal papers became the fair-haired boys at press headquarters in Melbourne and Brisbane. The New York *Daily News* and Chicago *Tribune* were furnished many newsbreaks by Diller and became mouthpieces in the campaign to get more material for the Pacific. In partial support of Diller's point of view in this case, there seems to be little doubt that some New Dealers took MacArthur's proposed candidacy seriously. In the home of Secretary of War Stimson in Washington, the writer expressed surprise at having discovered, on returning to the United States, that "The opinion was widely held that MacArthur is not receiving supplies because he is a political threat." Stimson did not comment but Major General Surles, chief of the War Department's public relations, answered, "The worst day in MacArthur's life was the day the Patterson-McCormick press named him as a presidential possibility." He did not elaborate on this very interesting statement. But I doubt that anyone can produce evidence to prove that President Roosevelt, against the best interest of his country, decided to fight Hitler first for political reasons and deliberately denied MacArthur supplies.

However, Diller was strongly convinced that such was the case and directed his censorship accordingly. To prove his point, he cited the sudden recall from Australia of General Pat Hurley and his appointment as Minister to New Zealand. Hurley, it was believed at GHQ, was regarded in Washington as a possible Republican running mate of the general and the New Dealers wanted him as far as possible from MacArthur. The addition of Colonel Phillip La Follette, former governor of Wisconsin, to MacArthur's staff was also considered to have caused a great amount of worry in Washington.

After his early experiences, Diller rapidly expanded his activities. From the European theatre, Ernie Pyle and Hal Boyle and others were able, within the limitations of family publications, to report fairly accurately how the soldiers talked and felt. Diller and his censors eliminated all profanity, and the general himself once cut a reference to "Jesus shoes" on the grounds that it wasn't nice. This was in one of my Bataan stories. About all we had to live on in those days were optimistic rumors, and one of them was that—"They're building a bridge from San Francisco to Manila and 100,000,000 men are coming across it to give us a hand here." The soldiers said, "While they're building it, we sure wish they'd put Jesus shoes on a couple of divisions and walk them out here across the water."

Because of Diller's censorship, many American newspaper readers have the impression that MacArthur's troops went ashore bloodlessly on unopposed beach after beach. In fact, MacArthur repeatedly did outguess the Japs brilliantly and make landings without opposition. Unlike the marines, MacArthur didn't believe in storming beaches head-on if there was a back door. But his troops talked like any other GIs and they had their bloody battles. Buna was nearly as bad as Tarawa or Guadalcanal, though on a smaller scale than the latter, but Buna is already a nearly forgotten name in the American public mind. It is my conviction that Diller's censorship is partially to blame.

Under the circumstances, it is very ironic that General MacArthur himself shares the opinion of Henry L. Mencken, who considers World War II the "worst reported" in history. He expressed that point of view one evening when three correspondents called at his headquarters in Tarlac. "What a pity," MacArthur said, "that there are no more great correspondents like Churchill and Richard Harding Davis and the others! They got their stories of the fighting from the men who knew what was going on. I know, perhaps better than anyone, what is taking place in this battle yet no correspondent comes to see me. You men are not to blame. The trouble is censorship. I am strongly opposed to all censorship, but the War Department insists on it." As an admirer of much that the general has done, I am at a loss to reconcile that last statement with the fact that a member of his staff was responsible for the most rigid and dangerous censorship in American history. Nor will I insult your intelligence by claiming that MacArthur did not know, in general, what Diller did.

The occasion for that meeting at Tarlac was to protest to MacArthur against Diller's censorship. Three or four days after our troops entered Manila from the north in February, 1945, MacArthur announced in a communiqué that the city had fallen, proclaimed "On to Tokyo" as his battle cry and announced, "We are ready with this tried and tested command when called upon. May God speed the day!" At that time, the question of who would be supreme commander for the attack on Japan had not been decided, and MacArthur was making it clear that he was all set to take over. Another communiqué also announced that there was no starvation in Manila.

144

The truth was that Manila had *not* fallen—we were in one part of it north of Pasig River and the Japs held the rest. No food was coming in; and the living skeletons of the Americans liberated at Santo Tomas—but still under shellfire—were proof of the fact that they had been starved.

As a result of the general's communiqué, we were not allowed to write the truth about Manila. There could be no starvation, no fighting, no rape, no shooting down of Filipinos with hands tied behind their backs, no murder of priests and nuns, no burning of the city. How could those things happen, the censors argued, in a city that the general had declared "fallen." After protesting in vain for a week, we went to MacArthur as a last resort.

"General," I said, "here is one of the most terrible stories of all time and we cannot write a word of it. It is the rape of Nanking and the battle of Stalingrad in reverse. It is the death of a city."

MacArthur had tears in his eyes as he interrupted. "No, no. You're being too dramatic. I understand how poignant your feelings are. But, nonsense, this city is not dead. Manila will be my great base for attacking Japan." Actually, the whole terrible truth about the rape of Manila never came out until Yamashita's trial. And although at war's end Manila was indeed a mighty base, it was no longer a city.

As he got more experience, Diller perfected his technique of protecting the general. MacArthur himself insists that a study of his "communeeks" will show that he gave due credit to the marines, the Navy, and the Air Forces in his operational reports. I don't believe that the general will know until he reads these next two paragraphs to what extremes Diller went in focusing the spotlight solely on MacArthur. In this regard, Diller's most notable dictum was issued on the October day in 1944 when American troops splashed ashore on Leyte's beaches and raised the flag over the Philippines once more. Some radio broadcasters had prepared a canned interview with Admiral Kinkaid, the tough and able commander of naval forces in the landing, and they took the record to Diller's censors. The matter was referred to Diller and he refused flatly to allow the broadcast. "Why?" the broadcasters demanded.

"On this great day," Diller replied sternly, "nothing shall be said or done that will detract in any way from the personal publicity or glorification of the commander-in-chief." Period.

A few weeks later, MacArthur announced the victory of American forces on Leyte and declared the campaign had reached the mop-ping-up stages. Protesting, the correspondents went to Diller. They pointed out that there were still some 80,000 to 100,000 Japs on the island, that our forces were making only slow progress over the tough mountains, and that the hardest battling was still ahead—as indeed it proved to be.

"I know," declared Diller, "but the elections in the United States are coming up in a few days and the Philippines *must* be kept on the front pages."

Life with Diller during the war was very trying to a correspondent, but when you look back you can see that it had its lighter side. There was, for instance, the PRO officer who was inordinately fond of alcoholic refreshment and who heartily disliked enlisted men. In this latter inclination he was hewing to the policy of strict segregation of "gentleman and officer" civilian correspondents and enlisted personnel attached to PRO. Thus, when for a short time after the occupation of Tokyo it was necessary for PROs and civilian correspondents to eat in the same dining room with enlisted men, a set of screens was placed around the enlisted men's tables and the gentlemen were spared the sight of such talented men as Sergeant Joe McCarthy and Corporal George Burns of *Yank* digging into their C-rations. In the days of the reoccupation of Manila, the alcoholic officer's pet target was Sergeant Jack Slocum of the U. S. Marine Corps.

Daily, this officer would work out on Jack. With his head still in a whirl from the night before, he would roar out from breakfast and sight Jack walking down the street from the Filipino home where, not being permitted to live with the civilian correspondents or PRO officers, he had found shelter.

"Shlocum," the officer shouted, "come here!"

Jack walked over and threw a salute.

"Shlocum! I'm short of food."

"I'm sorry about that, sir, but I'm not eating in your mess and I'm not responsible."

"Shlocum. I haven't got enough beds."

"I'm not sleeping there, sir."

Slocum got the rap for everything from the temperature to the Jap shells that fell within a few miles. One day, I heard the officer accost him and stopped to listen to Jack's latest crime.

"Slocum," the officer roared, "I'm short of gasoline."

Jack winked at me. "Well, sir," he replied, "I haven't got a jeep

146

and gasoline is the one thing I don't drink, so you can't very well blame me."

Another day, the officer called Jack into his office. "Slocum," he said, "you're giving me a bad time. Let's not talk this over as officer to sergeant but as man to man."

Jack jumped at the chance. "Listen," he said, shaking his finger, "that's where you made your big mistake." And he proceeded to give the officer a really rough time that partly paid back for all the punishment he had taken.

When the end of censorship came in the fall of 1945, Diller took it in stride. He warned correspondents, "Now, don't think this means you are going to get away with anything. Remember, the Army is still in control here!"

Diller and all GHQ were greatly upset by the criticism of MacArthur's supposed leniency toward the Japs in the early days on the occupation of Tokyo. Turning down a story submitted for censorship, Diller announced, "You can't print that. I can stop this story —and I am doing so." The story, which was critical of MacArthur's policies, never got through.

Although MacArthur removed Diller as public-relations chief after Diller was criticized in the American press, an examination of current dispatches from Tokyo will show that the Supreme Commander's staff is still very thin-skinned and sensitive to fault-finding. If any act of the general's calls forth criticism in American newspapers, the following day's papers will carry a dispatch from GHQ in Tokyo pointing out that MacArthur was acting on a "directive" from higher headquarters. Negatively, when MacArthur's actions or policies are praised back home, there is never any suggestion that they were anything but MacArthur's brain children.

Before Diller's demise as PRO, some of the "old group" of trusted correspondents went to see Diller in Tokyo to ask if MacArthur had been invited home to share in the celebrations already enjoyed by many leading generals and admirals. One of them suggested a press campaign to get the general back to the United States.

"Yes," said Diller seriously, "I would like to see such a campaign if it was put out as a spontaneous one and not as an inspired campaign. But there's another factor involved which makes me hesitant to start such a campaign at this time. Right now there are still a lot of correspondents from the other side of the fence [correspondents attached to the Navy] here in Tokyo. They'll be going back soon, though. When they do, and we have the old gang we know and who understand the whole picture, then I'd welcome such a campaign."

A reporter asked how President Truman felt about the situation. "Truman was always friendly to MacArthur until he became President," Diller answered. "Then apparently somebody from the old gang [Roosevelt's] whispered in his ear and told him MacArthur was the only man who was a danger to him—that he could be President in 1948 if he could beat one man—General MacArthur. So he hasn't even sent a message of congratulations and hasn't invited MacArthur to come home for a welcome. Let me check, though. He may have sent congratulations. There is one message I haven't seen. But the strategy back there is to let the general die on the vine, let him come home when all the steam is off. The Navy is making a big splash on Navy Day. Maybe the people in Washington will try to pass off the Wainwright reception as the official reception for the Army. But the people want MacArthur and the other side's strategy won't stop that."

Diller didn't make it clear whether he thought the people "wanted the general" for president or to come home for a much deserved welcome. In discussions of MacArthur as a presidential possibility, Diller never denied that he would like the post of White House press secretary. Other members of MacArthur's staff have similarly speculated on what jobs they would hold if MacArthur became president.

One of Diller's remarks became a password around Tokyo. A reporter protested against censorship of his factual account of Diller's orders to the guards around the American Embassy to keep newsmen away during the Emperor's first visit to MacArthur. One correspondent asked a guard, "How far are we ordered to stay away?" The GI fingered the trigger of his rifle and replied, "This'll shoot pretty far."

"No," said Diller, in turning down the story, "I will not let you send that."

"Why not? There's no security involved."

Diller sat back in his chair, and, after a few minutes' thought, summed up what took place for four years under his reign. "Well," he said, not smiling, "you can call it whimsy if you like!"

148

Chapter Fourteen

Case of the Letter

THIS IS PROBABLY AN OPPORTUNE TIME FOR A BRIEF detour to discuss some features of U. S. Navy wartime public relations.

Like MacArthur's, the Navy's setup had a double mission—that of protecting and glorifying the members of the Annapolis Admiral's Association and, secondly, assisting the correspondents in giving the American people the Navy's version of how it was winning the war.

Certainly, I agree that certain things were quite rightfully withheld from publication during hostilities, because possession of the information would have aided the Japs. It is also true that the Navy had plenty of reason for self-glorification as it came back from the beaten, demoralized organization of Pearl Harbor and, after eliminating most of its poor leaders, developed and grew into a mighty, aggressive fighting force. Along the way, the Navy naturally made some mistakes and did some things which were withheld, disguised, or concealed solely to protect the admirals. In the latter category were:

The turning back of a task force en route to relieve the marines on Wake Island.

The fact that our own ships fired on each other following the "surprise" Japanese attack in the first battle of Savo Island, off Guadalcanal. Three American and one Australian cruisers were lost. An officer of an American cruiser told me that his ship sunk a sister cruiser.

The fact that on the day following that battle, the American Navy withdrew in unseemly haste from Guadalcanal, taking away not only combat ships but the still unloaded vessels with marines' supplies aboard.

The failure to follow up the victories at Midway and in the First Philippines Sea Battle.

Halsey's getting decoyed out of position in the Second Battle of the Philippines Sea (or, as MacArthur renamed it so as to identify it more closely with the Philippines and thus with himself, the Battle of Leyte Gulf).

These things, if known to the Japs, would have done them no good. There was, however, one most vital secret—the most important of the war—which was in the Navy's possession. It was the fact that we had cracked the Japanese navy's code. And in this case, instead of covering up, our Navy did its asinine best to let the Japs know all about it.

This famous case involved a reporter for the *Chicago Tribune,* Stanley Johnston. Johnston had been a witness of the dramatic sinking of the aircraft carrier "Lexington" in the battle of the Coral Sea and had described it brilliantly and exclusively for the American press. At the time of the Battle of Midway, a few weeks later, Johnston did a stupid thing, a dangerous thing. He revealed in the *Tribune* that the American Navy had been all set for the Japs at Midway because our experts had broken the enemy's ultra-secret code and hence knew well ahead of time their plans for the battle. This was the same information that Governor Thomas E. Dewey kept to himself in the 1944 presidential elections. Dewey's supporters, notably *Life* magazine which never missed a chance to make Roosevelt look bad, alleged post-facto that if Dewey had disclosed what he knew, he would have been elected; that Dewey performed a magnificent public service by keeping silent, and that Roosevelt had taken unfair political advantage of his opponent. The fact is, of course, that if he had done so he should have been stood up against a wall and shot. Nor can there be any excuse for reporter Johnston's stupidity.

But the Navy compounded his foolishness. They would have been wise to let the story slide by without comment, hoping against hope that it would not reach the Japanese through their sources in America and neutral countries. They should have done everything possible to distract attention from the story. Any furore over the Johnston articles would tend, of course, to cause the Japs to change their secret communications code immediately and to substitute a new one which would remain a mystery for months or years until our experts could untangle it.

Instead of playing mum, the Navy promptly set about creating a grand hullabaloo. They had Johnston indicted by a Chicago grand jury. They gave the widest possible publicity to the case for several weeks. Then they suddenly woke up, dropped the whole matter, and clamped a lid of silence on the affair. Only the fact that the Japs were even more stupid saved us from a very severe setback. They did not change their code, neither then nor after a group of dopes in the O.S.S. broke into the Jap Embassy in Lisbon and stole the military attache's code books, a highly unnecessary stunt calculated to call Tokyo's attention to the fact that we were divining their battle intentions with surprising accuracy.

On the whole, though, the Navy's public relations did a pretty thorough job of hushing things up. This policy was eventually to backfire and bring about a shake-up in which Rear Admiral Harold Miller took charge. Captain Waldo Drake, who had been Admiral Nimitz's PRO at Pearl Harbor, was removed. After the war, Waldo proved himself a first-rate and liberal newspaperman with his dispatches from southeastern Asia to the *Los Angeles Times.* But during his tenure at Pearl Harbor he supervised a highly screwball outfit which devoted more of its time to hounding correspondents than it did to assisting them in their work. Waldo was more concerned about "security" in trifling matters than with news.

My own first contacts with Navy Public Relations were at long distance. In the early days of January, 1942, Lt. John Bulkeley of the famed Bataan P–T boat squadron came back from a raid into Jap-held Subic Bay. I met him on the Corregidor dock and asked the bearded naval officer, "What did you hit, Charlie Chan?" That had been his nickname when he served on the U.S.S. "Saratoga," and was traceable to his interest in China.

"I sure as hell don't know," Buck said. "We got a shot at something or other and there was a splash. As I guess, I'd say it might have been about a five-thousand-ton freighter, but you can't see much in the dark."

Now, like all the other ships that the P–Ts were to attack, "this might have been five-thousand-ton freighter" was destined to grow and the "might have been sunk or hit" to become almost always a certainly sunk enemy vessel. Listening to the radio reports based on the Navy Departments' announcements, as they came back to us from San Francisco, we found it almost impossible to identify the supposed enemy target as the same one that Buck had described to us on his return from patrol a few hours earlier.

I have forgotten exactly how big the Navy made the "might have been five-thousand-ton freighter," but in *They Were Expendable,* which was approved by Navy Public Relations, it had become a six-inch-gun auxiliary cruiser which was definitely sunk and Bulkeley was quoted as saying, "We saw the red fires rising and presently two more explosions which might have been her magazines."

A little while after his first attack, Buck came back another morning and told me he had hit a ship. "It looked like a three-thousand-ton freighter." But in *Expendable* it comes out a "modern, streamlined, six-thousand-ton auxiliary aircraft carrier." Whatever that is.

Two of my own experiences with Navy Public Relations are nearly enough typical to be included in this story. One involved a crap game at Tonga Tabu one Sunday afternoon, a game which for six months caused me more worry than any dangers in battle. For that period I was afoul of Navy Intelligence—or Gestapo, if you prefer—in an encounter which might easily have cost two officers their careers and reputations and ended my own work as a correspondent.

We limped into Tonga in September, 1942, on the "Saratoga," after picking up a Jap torpedo off the eastern Solomons. It was no surprise to any one, except possibly the admiral in command and the captain of the ship, when we were torpedoed. Off and on for three weeks we had been circling with a big task force in a 200-mile stretch of ocean between the Solomons and the islands to the east. Four Jap subs could easily have patrolled those narrow waters every day. In fact, they did. On the morning of August 31st one of them approached our task force on the surface and was picked up by radar. There was a brief alert and then everybody went back to sleep until the usual sunrise general quarters, which was followed by a relaxation of battle conditions. A little before eight o'clock, the sub commander let fly with four fish. We were going at about ten knots and not zigzagging and one of the four hit the "Saratoga."

Luckily, no one was killed and the "Sara" got away under her own power. A short time later the "Wasp" was torpedoed and blown up under almost identical circumstances in nearby waters. But these torpedoings happened during the war and the Navy not only could but did suppress the circumstances of the "Saratoga" and "Wasp" attacks, whereas, when the "Indianapolis" was lost to a Jap sub, the torpedoing happened so near the end of hostilities that public clamor for an inquiry had to be heeded.

There was nothing unusual about the crap game on the day the "Saratoga" made it into Tonga with a hole in her belly. I lost all my cash and borrowed thirty-five dollars from Lt. "Acey" Stark, a fighter pilot off the ship. Then I hitchhiked an airplane ride back to Pearl Harbor, where I wrote out a check for Stark and left it for him at the fleet post office. There were headaches for me at Pearl. My stories on Guadalcanal and subsequent actions had been so badly cut as to be nearly unusable, the censor at that time being an officer who had been relieved of his submarine command for "lack of initiative," but who was considered amply fitted for a key job in keeping the news from the public. Vigorous protests brought me an interview with Nimitz's chief of staff, a captain, who agreed that the censorship had been lamentably unfair. "There is no way to make it up to you now," he said, "but is there some story you would like to write?" "Well, sir," I said, "with the present limited range of airplanes it seems to me that aircraft carriers are the most important factor in naval warfare and I'd like to write about Japan's carrier strength."

The chief of staff said to go ahead. I wrote the story and took it out to Pearl. The censor read it and passed it. Waldo Drake read it and approved. The chief of staff personally put his okay on the copy. The story was sent and, I thought, forgotten. Three days later I got a telephone call from Drake. "Shhh," he said, "don't tell anybody where you are going, but come out here to Pearl. The chief of staff wants you. It is very important that no one knows where you are going." Considerably mystified, I drove out to naval headquarters where Drake met me and escorted me in silence to the office of the chief of staff. One look at the room gave the impression of a stage-set. A chair was carefully placed for me in front of the captain's desk, so that when I sat down the sun was shining in my eyes. The captain's chair was backed into the corner, in the shadow, and on another chair between the two windows and facing me was Commander (later Captain) Edwin Layton, Nimitz's chief Intelligence officer. Still not knowing what it was all about, I sat down at a signal from the chief of staff.

He leaned forward, glaring at me, and asked:

"Which officer did it?"

"Did what, Captain?"

"You know very well what. Which officer sold you that information?"

All I could do was stare.

"Some officer on the 'Saratoga,'" the captain went on, "sold you the information on which you based that story about the Jap carriers. It was contained in a confidential bulletin restricted to officers alone."

"That isn't where I got it," I protested.

"I think," said the captain, "that you paid thirty-five dollars or fifty dollars for it. That officer is guilty of treason. He may be shot. Tell me his name."

With a sinking feeling, I suddenly remembered the crap game and the thirty-five-dollar check made out to Stark. The captain and Layton were in no mood to believe me, as was obvious.

"Look, Captain," I stalled, "you yourself okayed the story. So did the censor, and so did Drake. Why this kickback?"

"We got a severe rebuke from the Navy Department for releasing the information."

"Well," I said, "you have things all wrong. I did not buy the information from any officer. I did not try to evade censorship. I got the dope about the Jap carriers from diagrams and pictures posted on the bulletin board in the officers' mess on the 'Saratoga.' If there was any reason not to release it, you should have said so the other day."

The captain thought it over. "You claim you got it from the bulletin board. I'll check up to see if it was posted there. I still believe you bought it from an officer." He got up and left the room and I turned to Layton.

"Are you guys nuts, Eddie?" I asked. "You must have been seeing too many spy movies. All you need in this room is a blackjack and some thumbscrews. I'm telling you the truth."

But the thought of that thirty-five-dollar check was very disturbing. Layton came over and put his arm around my shoulder. "Look, Clark," he said confidentially, "we've known each other for some years in Tokyo and here. Now, just whisper to me the name of the officer and I won't tell a soul where I learned it. Just tell it to me, huh, kid! Tell me who he was."

I couldn't help laughing. "You jackass. I got it off the bulletin board."

Then, apparently to win my confidence, Layton let me in on what

I have already described as the biggest secret of the war—our possession of the Jap code. He told me how he had been able to predict to Admiral Nimitz on May 4, 1942, that the Jap fleet would be in a certain position off Midway a month later. He was right within five miles and one hour. But I still couldn't confess.

In a few minutes, the chief of staff came back and invited me into Nimitz's office across the hall. No mention was made of the "officer traitor." The admiral talked about the naval situation and his problems. "One difficulty," he said, "is getting some of my subordinate officers to mix it with the enemy. They are too cautious. In fact, I recently had to put out an order telling them to close in and slug it out, and saying that we had to risk ships and lives to win the war."

"Admiral," I said, "I saw that order. It seemed to me a milestone in American history; first, because it was necessary to tell your admirals to get in and fight and, second, because your having done so means that we are going to start winning the war. In fact, I thought so much of that order that I have a copy in my wallet."

Like a flash, the chief of staff was on his feet. "Where did you get that?" he demanded. "It was passed out to all hands on the 'Saratoga,'" I answered.

"I'll check on that, Admiral," the captain said, and darted out of the room. In about fifteen minutes he was back. "That's right, Admiral," he reported. With that, the atmosphere cleared and we all went up to Nimitz's house for a friendly lunch which I was able to enjoy knowing that Stark seemed in no immediate danger of being shot by a firing squad.

The incident apparently was forgotten—but some two months later, in New York, I received an urgent telegram one night from the commander of the 12th Naval District, San Francisco, directing me to turn over at once any fleet credentials in my possession. I replied that the only one I had was an identification card that I had shown personally to the admiral in San Francisco and which he told me to retain as a souvenir.

"Return card at once," a wire came back.

"Card in scrapbook and inextricable," I answered. "Shall I airmail scrapbook?"

Then, the following day, thinking that if the Navy was in such a stew about that piece of paper as to be sending urgent telegrams, the situation must be serious, I wired, "Have succeeded in extricating card forwarding by airmail special delivery." That thirty-five-dollar check, I thought, must have turned up to plague Stark, and now me.

155

But it turned out that this was a different matter. The Associated Press summoned me to tell me that the Navy Department had rescinded my credentials. They showed me a letter supposedly written by me. In fact, it was a reply to a letter some months before in which a friend had accused the admirals of clinging to their battleship mentality and refusing to recognize the importance of airpower. On the basis of the Navy's performance at Midway, I had defended the admirals. In this letter I apologized for having done so. "Everything you said is more than true," my letter said in part. "The only wonder is that even a few people survive four years in the graveyard on the Severn—Annapolis—with reasonably open minds. They catch 'em young and freeze their mentality at that age."

"Did you write this letter?" asked Alan Gould of the A.P.

"Yes," I admitted. The letter had been written in an outburst of anger immediately after the first Battle of Savo Island. Everybody on the "Saratoga," except the admiral, was burned up about it. On the afternoon of August 8th we knew on the "Saratoga" that a Jap force was coming down on Guadalcanal. We had some 180 planes available to attack the Jap vessels. But instead of attacking, the admiral had turned our task force around and headed south, away from the enemy. He was still running south the next day, after the Japs had come in and sunk our ships and escaped to the northwest. Many hundreds of our men had lost their lives. Our fliers, who would have had to risk their own lives to stop the Japs, were especially angry and I had echoed their feeling in my letter.

"Who censored that letter?" the A.P. demanded.

That was a question that I heard probably a thousand times in the next few months. I was summoned to Washington several times for questioning by the top guns in Navy Public Relations, the chief inquisitor being Commander Slim Beecher, the Navy's number-one song-writer. The charges against me, it developed, were serious. I was accused of having stolen a censor's stamp and imprinting the seal on my own envelope. Incidentally, although it bore the proper stamp, the letter had been intercepted by Waldo Drake at Honolulu and the investigation instigated by him. There is no telling how much that letter cost the Navy in dollars and in the time and effort of men who might otherwise have been concentrating on the defeat of Japan.

Beecher told me about the inquiry. "We have questioned every officer on the 'Saratoga,'" he said, "and they all deny having censored this letter."

"What's wrong with the letter?" I asked.

"Nothing," he said. "That is, you have a perfect right to your opinion about Annapolis. There is no security involved. But no naval officer would have okayed this letter."

"Why not, if it doesn't involve security?"

"They just wouldn't."

"Look," I answered, "one of them did."

"Ah," said Beecher eagerly, "that's what we want to know. What officer censored it and how much did you pay him? What is his name?"

It pained me to discover again that the Navy took such a poor view of the honor of its officers, but I replied. "You told me you talked to everybody on the 'Sara' and that every officer denied it."

"That's right. We questioned them all. None of them did it. But what was his name?"

"I can't recall."

The Navy's line of questioning was all too reminiscent of the Japanese Kempetai in pre-war Tokyo. They would show a correspondent a story he had supposedly written and ask, "Why did you write it?" "I didn't." "Yes, but when did you write it?" "Never." "Ah, so, but why did you write it?" "I did not." "What was your reason in writing it?" And so on, and on.

And now Beecher said, "Even if you can't recall his name, just tell us who he was and everything will be all right." Actually, I did not remember the name of the officer, although I did know his identity and his position on the ship. He was a flight surgeon from Oklahoma and if he is still alive I am certain he is now out of the Navy, so there is no harm in revealing that much about him at this late date. I had handed him the letter as he sat at a big table in the officers' mess on the ship, and he read it and said, "This is pretty strong, but there is no violation of censorship regulations." He stamped and initialed it, and his initials were on the envelope as Beecher questioned me.

Beecher, Captain Lovett, chief of Navy Public Relations, and the other officers began to sound more and more like the Kempetai as the inquiry progressed. No officer, they insisted, would have okayed the letter; therefore, I must have stolen the stamp. They had interrogated "all the officers on the 'Saratoga' " and from them had determined that the stamp lay on the table where I could have taken it. But at the same time they wanted to know the name of the officer who had initialed the letter. If I just told them the name of the man who couldn't have done it, all would be forgiven. No, of course, they had no intention of persecuting him—just wanted to find out so they could give him a friendly pat on the back. Meantime I was suspended as a correspondent, relieved of my credentials, and deprived of the right to go out again with the Navy, even though I was, of course, completely free to have my own opinions about Annapolis and had violated no regulations.

It became very evident that the officer in question, though of course no officer in the Navy would have passed such a letter, was in for a rough time if his identity were discovered. I refused to identify him unless they would give guarantees that he would not be punished, which they would not do. Soon the whole affair was beyond the stage of the ridiculous, and involving more and more men as the investigation was pursued in Washington, in Pearl Harbor, in San Diego, and in the distant South Pacific. At one third-degree session, I tossed a bombshell by pointing out that after the "Saratoga" was torpedoed, a good many of its flight personnel had been transferred to island bases and that it was possible that the officer who censored the letter was down there. Had they questioned all those officers? They had not. Agents were dispatched hither and yon to track down the mysterious initials.

The inquiry into The Letter went on from October until April. Eventually, I sought a hearing before Captain Lovett and demanded a trial by a Navy board. "If they insist," I told Lovett, "I will identify the officer and at the same time will make the whole story public so that if he is punished, the reason will be known. Meanwhile, I refuse to put up any longer with your accusations. You talk in circles. You say I stole the stamp but you want at the same time to know the name of the officer who censored this letter. You admit there is nothing wrong with the letter, but you insist on learning who censored it so you can persecute him."

The result was not a Navy trial but a letter which came from Captain Lovett. "Admiral Nimitz," I read with relief, "is satisfied that you have done nothing wrong and will be glad to welcome you back in his area as a correspondent."

The Navy, however, reformed long before the end of the war, although Diller never did. The Navy woke up to the mess in which its public relations were entangled and by the appointment of some first-class men had established a highly satisfactory setup by the time of Japan's surrender.

Chapter Fifteen

The Chinese Want Shanghai to
Be Chinese

BACK IN NOVEMBER, 1941, I JUMPED THE GUN IN Shanghai and got away to the Philippines on the next-to-last ship to leave before the Japanese occupied the great Chinese metropolis and imprisoned all the American inhabitants.

Four years less three months later, we again jumped the gun and this time went into Shanghai prior to Japan's surrender and while the city was still in the hands of Japanese troops. The visit was made before the events in Japan described in the foregoing pages. We didn't exactly have permission to go to Shanghai, but we became bored while waiting on Okinawa for the occupation of Japan to begin and just took off one morning for the Chinese coast. Our plane was a B–17 of the Strategic Air Forces in which we had come half-way around the world from Washington by way of Europe to Guam and Okinawa. We were scheduled that day to fly over Hiroshima—although, of course, we could not land because Japan was not yet occupied—but on the truck ride down to the runway those of us who had lived in Shanghai had been regaling the others with a barker's spiel on the city's enchantments. "It's San Francisco and Paris, Marseilles and Port Said rolled into one. Hot and cold running blondes in every room. Find out which way the trolleys run in China. See incredible Shanghai, the world's most fantastic metropolis."

So when Mark Magnam, our pilot, asked where we were going, the voices of twenty-six correspondents and crew members chorused, "Shanghai!" The pilot came back from the control tower waving a piece of paper. He was still a little doubtful about taking off, but we urged him into the plane with a promise, "You'll be dancing with

159

a lovely, blonde White Russian tonight." I was one of the main urgers, because I wanted badly to see Shanghai. The city had been my home for three years just before the war and since December 8, 1941, we had heard almost nothing from there except Japanese dispatches and the stories of those few Americans lucky enough to be exchanged and repatriated. There had been only brief postcards from the American and other civilians in internment camps; no word from friends among the 27,000 Jewish refugees from Hitler's Europe who found sanctuary in Shanghai in 1939; from other friends among the 30,000 White Russians who had fled from the Bolshevist terror back in 1919 and 1920 and worked their way down through Manchuria and North China into Shanghai, the only place in the world where no passports were required.

As we took off from Okinawa, I was worried about our lack of knowledge of the Japs' attitude in China toward the surrender. We had read and heard the broadcast threats of various Jap generals on the Asiatic mainland that they would never give in—although Tokyo had already announced its acceptance of the Potsdam terms—but would fight to the death with the 2,000,000 crack troops under their command. We might be running into a hotbed of fanatics who would shoot down our unarmed plane, or capture and kill us if we reached the ground safely.

Then we were flying over a vast expanse of yellow water, discolored by the silt which the swift-flowing Yangtze claws away from the good earth of China and tumbles into the sea; and soon we were over land and suddenly there was Shanghai ahead of us, a vast, semicircular mass of buildings rising out of the green rice fields beyond the twisting, yellow Whangpoo. Flying over Shanghai before the war you had been able to spot the city from miles away by a cloud of dirt and dust that hung over it, and even at 5,000 feet its stench seemed to pollute the air. But now the city looked clean and the air was fresh and clear.

The Shanghai I had left three weeks before Pearl Harbor had been a huge prison, surrounded by the Japanese and partitioned off into separate cells marked "International Settlement," "Frenchtown," "Hongkew," "Bad Lands," and "Pootung"—cells in which the Japanese warders allowed the American, British, German, French, White Russian, Jewish refugee, and Italian prisoners to carry on a macabre dance of dollars and sex—while the Emperor's troops bided their time to step in and lock the cell doors. Set off as it was by bayonets and barbed wire and foreign troops, from the rest of the country, Shanghai had been a part of China, yet not Chinese; a pleasure- and business-mad metropolis, a hotbed of espionage and counter- spying, a cradle of crime and sordid lust, of luxury and terrible suf- fering. It had been a symbol of the White Man's mastery of Asia, the stronghold of the Europeans and Americans who were not subject to China's laws but lived under an imperialistic device called "extra- territoriality" which permitted their own countries to maintain their own laws on China's soil, thus clearly proclaiming to the world that the Republic of China was not fit to govern the white men within its borders.

Shanghai was also a monument to the desire of men—white and yellow—to trade with each other and make money, and the devil take the hindmost; and the rich Chinese was just as indifferent to the lot of his fellow national as was the white man. Unless, of course, the Chinese were a relative and hence could claim and get assistance in accordance with that family system which makes blood kinship all-important and citizenship a secondary matter. The Chinese "hindmost" in Shanghai had accepted fatalistically the knowledge that they had to wear out their bodies and break their backs on starvation rations.

I recalled the office boy in the Associated Press bureau in Shang- hai, a tall, handsome, clean lad of twenty-four, who had come to me back in the summer of '41. He had asked the office manager for a raise in his salary of seven dollars monthly and had been refused. "I am quitting," he told me.

"Don't do that," I protested. "I'll make the money up to you and buy you a sack of rice each month."

"No. It's too late now. I have tuberculosis and I am going to die."

I offered to send him to a hospital, but he insisted. "It's too late. I'll be dead in a month." Three weeks later the other office boy went to the funeral, and the dead man's sister came to call and I gave her some money for rice.

Now, up in the pilot's compartment of the B–17, reporter Fritz Opper voiced my thoughts, "It's not the same old Shanghai. As of day after tomorrow, when the peace treaty is signed, it will be Chinese again—provided the Japs here give up. We've renounced our extraterritorial rights, and the British and the French have given up their concessions. Seems to me the Russians did it back in 1924. So the Chinese will have their city." The Japs, in fact, had beaten us

161

to the punch. They had made a great show of abandoning extrality and concessions shortly after attacking us in 1941.

When the Chinese historians write of the recent war, they will probably give Japan credit for achieving one of the most important contributions to China's independence by forcing abandonment of extrality. It was not until the Japs had us on the run in 1942 that we agreed to surrender this unequal bit of special privilege, and also to repeal the Exclusion Act which for years had been a strong talking point of anti-white Chinese and of the Japanese propagandists. The Japanese permitted the Chinese to set up their own governments in Shanghai and the other great coastal cities, and while it is true that these were puppet regimes subject to the Japanese military, it is also true that they were at least Chinese in personnel and thus a step in the right direction.

I watched the city growing larger ahead of us, until the individual buildings stood out. There was the big Broadway Mansions building over in Hongkew—the Japanese section which we used to enter with trepidation because Japanese sentries guarded the bridges over Soochow Creek and failure to obey their orders could get you a slap in the face to which there was no retaliation. Ahead was the tall Park Hotel, and beneath it the bright green oval of the race course. And below our left wing was the Metropole Hotel, where I had lived for two years and where I had promised to get accommodations that night for my companions—if the Japanese didn't interfere with our plans.

There were scores of Japanese fighters on the airfields both east and west of the city, and we saw Japs moving around on the runways and coming out of the hangars to stare up at our plane. We circled lower, right down on the rooftops, while I wrote out two notes addressed to Ed Arreger who had been manager of the Metropole four years before. We made two runs up Foochow Road, just missing the radio towers on the police station, while Mark—the pilot—buzzed the hotel, changing the propellers from low to high pitch to attract the attention of the people in the building. Down on the Bund, the wide street that serpentines in synchronization with the Whangpoo, I saw Chinese jumping up and down in front of the big banks and business buildings. Traffic was stopped and pretty soon all the streets and rooftops were a mass of upturned faces and waving arms and thousands of Chinese and American, British, and Russian flags. We were so low that it was almost like riding in a ricksha as we came up Foochow Road again and tossed out the message, watching it flutter downward behind a yellow cotton streamer. Once more we made the run and dropped the duplicate message. It said:

"Ed: I am in the B–17 up here. Have 26 people with me and we want to land and stay in the hotel. Please give me my old room—1001—go up on the balcony of 1001 and give us signals. The bachelors aboard want dates with blondes so round up about 20. From the look of the flags and the people in the streets, everything seems under control. If the Japs are shooting up the town or we can't get through their lines around the city, wave your hands crisscross over your head. If it's okay, hold up both thumbs. Then get some taxis, if there are such things, or have the Swiss consulate get a bus and come out to the Lungjao airdrome for us.

"Please arrange for chow for all of us, and round up my gang."

We started to circle again, watching the balcony for Arreger to appear, when somebody yelled: "Fighter at four o'clock!"

There was a fighter plane just above and behind us, coming in fast as if to make a firing pass. Then it zoomed away and, just as we recognized it as a Mustang, we heard Colonel Tex McCrary's voice over the radio: "So youse guys thought you could get away from me."

We had eluded McCrary, who was in charge of our party of correspondents, when we left Okinawa. He had learned our destination and taken off after us. Now he said over the radio, "Stop trying to knock the tops off these buildings and follow us in and land. We've found an airport where there's no Jap planes." Tex, riding piggyback behind pilot Sandy Moats, thought he had spotted an airstrip. Actually, it was a straightaway for working out racing dogs. Moats sat his P–51 down in a swirl of dust, and Mark Magnum followed him over Hongkew and landed the heavy B–17 behind him. Before we could climb out, we were surrounded by Chinese, smiling and waving and clapping. They seemed to appear from nowhere out of the fields. It was very reassuring to see that they did not fear displaying their feelings. But in a few minutes the Japs started to arrive on foot and in trucks which turned off the highway paralleling the dog track. Some were carrying swords and others guns, and to me they looked as menacing as they had four years before when it had meant risking your life to come out into this area without a Jap army pass. We stood close to the plane, joking with the Chinese and nonchalantly ignoring the Japs while they surrounded us in an

163

ever-thickening circle. Finally, a young Jap officer stepped forward and McCrary went to meet him.

"Watch McCrary," Jim McGlincy whispered. "He's going to put his foot in it."

"Yeah. He better act as if he owned China and not ask permission for anything. Our only chance is a big bluff. Be polite, but let them know we won the war." I walked over to listen, while Tex talked through a Chinese who spoke both English and Japanese.

"If it's all right with you, sir," said the American lieutenant colonel to the Jap second lieutenant, "we'd like to go to Shanghai."

That was enough for me. I signaled Opper and McGlincy and we pushed through the Chinese and Japs to a shiny Plymouth sedan parked fifty yards from the plane. It was occupied by a Jap navy commander and two civilians, and was driven by a pidgin-speaking Chinese. We instructed the chauffeur. "You speakee masta we wanchee takee cah go Shanghai chop chop." The Jap officer answered at length and the chauffeur translated. "This Japanee mastah say his mastah, Numbah One Japanee Navy, wanchee surrendah Japan soldiah man to Amelican." We should have accepted the offer, but we gestured toward McCrary and the Jap officer went over to talk to him while we piled into the car and started for Shanghai.

I didn't feel entirely safe even yet. It's a hard thing to explain, but to me the whole Hongkew area of Shanghai and the lands outside of it were filled with menace. When I lived there we had been at the mercy of brutish Japanese sentries, and the memory of the danger still clung on like mustard gas in a damp field. I imagine our soldiers will feel the same way when, years from now, they visit the battlefields where they crouched under mortar and machine-gun fire. Memories of terror will still live in the green and peaceful scenes.

As we drove into the city, surprise followed surprise. There was almost no new bomb damage and Hongkew was still much the same in some aspects as four years before. Its streets were filled with Jap soldiers, some walking, some in trucks, and some dragging long handcarts piled high with equipment. But in these narrow streets that had been choked with fear, the Chinese were walking about freely. On the corner under the now-closed "Brue Bird" cafe and the "Tiga Dance" hall, street vendors were selling Chinese, American, Soviet, and some British flags under the unseeing eyes of the once arrogant soldiers of the Emperor. I caught my breath in disbelief as

164

I saw a Jap major step into the gutter to walk around a crowd of Chinese gathered in front of a shop window which displayed a crudely tinted portrait of President Truman, obviously a picture taken years before. In pre-war times, the major would have booted the Chinese out of his way or slashed at them with his sword. We passed the Bridge House, the dreaded prison where so many men had been tortured and killed by the Jap military gendarmes and where General Doolittle's fliers were held before their execution. Today, it looked like an innocent if run-down hotel. There were not even sentries outside.

Nor were there sentries on the bridges over Soochow Creek and that, more than anything, seemed to symbolize the fact that Shanghai was about to become a single city, and a Chinese city. In the southern part of the International Settlement, Chinese flags were everywhere with pictures of Chiang Kai-shek and Sun Yat-sen, and in lesser numbers flag-draped portraits of the Big Three with America, represented sometimes by Roosevelt and sometimes by Truman. Workmen were busy tearing down the Japanese signs from the Chase Bank and the other foreign business houses. When the Chinese recognized us as Americans, their faces split into wide smiles.

We pulled up in front of the Metropole and the same Indian doorman who had called a taxi when I left to catch a boat for the Philippines four years before, opened the car door now and greeted me with a warm handshake. The turbaned Sikh pointed at the steps, and there were the same waiters, roomboys, and clerks. My wife's handsome Chinese amah rushed down and threw her arms around me: "Ah mastah come back. Where Missy stop?" Ed Arreger was there, too, and I embraced the tall Swiss in Latin fashion, and the whole gang of us had a little, joyously inarticulate celebration. It wasn't quite as frenzied as the liberation of Paris but here we were greeted as the first liberators, even though a C.I.C. party had beaten us into the city. When everybody calmed down, Arreger said:

"This is the first time I've been to the hotel in four years. The Japs threw me out right after Pearl Harbor and slammed me in the Bridge House for six months with Fred Twogood of Standard Oil [who has died since as a result of what they did to him], and MacKay of the City Bank and a bunch of others. The Metropole belonged to Sir Victor Sassoon and was considered spoils of war, so they seized it and put a Nazi in as manager."

After his release from Bridge House, where he underwent his

share of beatings and torture, Arreger had gone to work in the Swiss Consulate. The notes I had dropped from the plane had been delivered to him there almost as soon as they had been picked up from the roofs of the municipal council building and of the Hamilton House, across the street from the Metropole. The Chinese had located him immediately through that unofficial intelligence service whose functionings were always a mystery to foreigners. I saw it work hundreds of times in Shanghai. I would leave my office, telling the clerk I was going to the American Club for a haircut. In the ricksha I would change my mind and tell the boy to take me to the Cathay Hotel and, nearly there, would whimsically reverse course again and go to the Park Hotel. Walking into the Park, a bellboy would greet me, "Telephone call for you, Mr. Lee." You couldn't get away with a damn thing in Shanghai.

Now, while the Nazi manager kept himself inconspicuous, Arreger took over the hotel as if he had been away for an hour, instead of four years. He dispatched the bus to the B–17, assigned rooms, and ordered a lunch which couldn't compare to pre-war standards but seemed miraculous after Army chow. My old room, where I had many heart-to-heart talks with Jap officers just before the war, was still occupied by some Japanese civilians, but he gave me one in the tower. As a usual thing, elevators weren't running in Shanghai because no coal was coming down from North China for the power plant, but as a special event the Chinese started one up. The operator apologized for the lack of metal handles on the doors. "Japanee take everything away. Even radiator and shower handle." I had noticed that one of the city's landmarks, the bronze lions in front of the Hong Kong Shanghai bank, which over the decades had been rubbed green by superstitious people seeking virility from their touch, had also disappeared in Japan's drive for scrap metal.

Word got out through the city that the people in the plane had come to the Metropole and a crowd began to collect in my room. I received them in a sheet. In picturing my return to Shanghai, I had always seen myself in snappy slacks and a suntan shirt dripping campaign ribbons sparkling with battle stars, but I arrived in messy khaki dripping sweat. The amah bossily insisted on my taking them off so she could wash and press them. I asked the amah, "How those Japs treat you, amah?"

"All lite, mastah," she said. "But sometime he like throw me on top bed. I tell him no can do. If I do this my belly get velly big, my

166

face get velly red." But in spite of, or perhaps because of those encounters, the amah looked very healthy and well fed, and so did the other Chinese. They explained that as soon as the Japs declared war and seized all of Shanghai, they immediately relaxed the restrictions that had prevented the rice grown in the fertile fields just outside the city from reaching the starved millions inside the barricades of bayonets and barbed wire. During the war, the Chinese had more to eat than for the five years from 1937, when the Japs seized partial control of the city, until 1941 when they attacked us. Inflation had come, and the American dollar was now worth 95,000 Chinese dollars instead of the pre-war rate of 40. But nevertheless, the ricksha man and dock coolie and cotton-mill worker had been getting enough to eat, even though he paid 50,000 dollars for a fishhead instead of fifty cents. The Japanese had increased the food supply as a matter of propaganda, to prove to the Chinese that they were better off working with their fellow Asiatics than with white men. Also, the Japs had continued their public-health campaign which had done wonders since 1937 in stamping out cholera, typhus, small pox, and other deadly diseases.

"And," said a Chinese banker who dropped in to see me, "business went on as usual. Fortunes were made in speculation in gold bars—the same racket that was so popular before the war. American currency was bought and sold surreptitiously, in anticipation of final victory. Despite the bombing, there was a big race meeting this year with many millions being wagered."

The Chinese, of course, always have and always will bet on anything. When the Japs raised the big Italian liner "Conte Verdi," which had been scuttled in the Whangpoo by its Italian crew at the time of Badoglio's surrender, they tied long ropes from the ship to the Shanghai club and the Asiatic Petroleum Company building on the Bund. The Chinese were offering odds of nine to one that the buildings would topple over before the "Conte Verdi" was righted.

At the time of our capture of Okinawa, the English-speaking Chinese began saying that things were "Okay-now-a," and betting ten to three that we would land invasion forces in the Yangtze delta before autumn. They referred to the tiny air-raid shelters which they were forced to dig in the streets as "Japanese graves."

"All in all," the Chinese banker told me, "we weren't too badly off under the Japanese. The Japs had quite a few impressive talking points, especially the local self-government. And there is no use denying that the Jap propaganda was very effective in some quarters, nor that a good many Chinese were profoundly influenced by seeing how quickly the Japs defeated and humbled the white man in the early months of the war. They set an example that may be emulated some day by other peoples of Asia, unless in the meantime there is a true New Deal in our relations and we get together as equals—not as master and coolie." He ended his long discourse, turned to the roomboy, and commanded in pidgin English, "Boy run catchee mastah some ice and bottle whiskey." The boy padded off silently, accepting the fact that there will always be Chinese "master" and "coolie," even if the white master is driven out.

We drank a toast to three Austrians, Herren Basch, Basch and Buschel, who had been news photographers in Germany pre-Hitler, had fled to Austria, and thence to Shanghai with the Jewish refugees in 1939 and 1940. One of the brothers Basch, either Hans or Fritz, had been of considerable service to American Intelligence in the pre-war days of 1941. Whenever a new type Japanese vessel appeared in the Whangpoo, Major Williams of Naval Intelligence would notify me and I would send Basch down to photograph it from a sampan. It was a risky business.

"Did they ever question you after I left?" I asked.

"Nein. They're too dumb. They locked up all the Jews over in Yangtzepoo, in a kind of ghetto, but there were always ways to get out of the camp and we made out all right. A lot of the night clubs kept going through the war and are still open until blackout time."

"And what about the refugee girls who had to turn professional before the war? How did the Japs treat them?"

"Vy," said Hans, "those girls like to do business with Japs, say there is much less wear and tear on the assets than with American sailors or marines. They say that when the Japs get with a white woman they are just like wild animals. They pant and froth at the mouth and leap at the girls, and in a few seconds it is all over and the girls have fifty thousands Chinese dollars in their stockings."

The amah interrupted to announce, "Claw man come, mastah." That was her designation for Professor Robert, a one-time Viennese chiropodist who had patented a cure for athlete's foot. It consisted of an oven in which to bake socks and shoes to get rid of the fungi. The professor had never found a backer and his plans were still on paper, but he came into the room as roly-poly as ever. "Sure I'm still

168

alive," the professor said. "It's harder to kill a Jew than it is athlete's foot."

Then a group of newspapermen came in—some of them American citizens, some White Russians, and some Eurasians. They brought extras telling of the excitement caused by our arrival. "Shanghai goes wild with joy at sight of first American planes," the paper reported, adding that "some of the biggest firecrackers in the city were set off" while we were zooming overhead. One Shanghai newsman was conspicuously absent. He was Herbert Moy, a Chinese born in America who had become a Japanese radio propagandist. Herbie had hated all white men as a result of an unfortunate experience in the United States involving racial discrimination. His job with the Japs came to a sudden end. A few days after the first Japanese surrender announcement his body was found in a street outside the German school in Shanghai, where the radio station was located. The Japs announced that he had killed himself, but the Chinese said he had been guest of honor at a macabre farewell banquet, after which his throat was slit and the body tossed out the window.

I knew many Chinese like Moy whose whole lives had been changed by a physical, or spiritual, slap in the face. For instance, the leader of the anti-white movement in the Japanese puppet regime at Nanking was a Java-born Chinese, Tang Liang-li, whose hatred was the aftermath of his expulsion from "a third-rate night club" in New York where men with yellow skins were not welcomed. Tang had been embittered to such a fanatical degree that he deserted his nation's government and offered his services to the Japs. I asked after Tang now, and the reporters said he had disappeared, probably a victim of assassination by Chinese patriots.

We rode through the streets in a contraption called a pedicab, a combination of bicycle and ricksha, with the great advantage—to the Chinese—that the coolie who operates it will have some chance of living longer than the thirty-five-year span which, for a consumptive ricksha puller, constituted his normal "three score and ten."

I was amazed at the discipline of the Japanese, as they walked quietly through streets where victory arches were being constructed, or stood side by side with Chinese police to direct traffic. A Japanese truck drove past a line of 200 Chinese women bent over sewing machines in a contest to turn out Allied flags, and not a soldier looked at them.

169

"We expected everything to explode in an orgy of rape, looting, and hara-kiri," my friends said. "The Japs have done some looting, but otherwise their discipline has been perfect—with one understandable exception. The day after Tokyo announced its willingness to accept the Potsdam terms, the Russians and Chinese went wild. Out by Jap headquarters in the French club, they went up to the sentries and kicked them and spit in their faces. The Japs just stood without moving, holding on tighter to their rifles. A day later, reports came through that this did not mean final surrender as yet, and the Japs retaliated by forcing every white man of any nationality to kneel on the street for a half hour."

Afterward, the Japs had to cooperate with the Chinese police in patrolling the city and in suppressing a premature attempt by a small group of Chinese Communists to take over Shanghai. The Reds had already gone back under cover in the city, but outside they were busily engaged in blowing up railway lines north, south, and west to obstruct the anticipated movements of Nationalist troops. In fact, in the six weeks after the Japs quit, the Chinese Reds destroyed more property, did more fighting, and dynamited more communications facilities than they had in eight years of Nipponese occupation of their country. This was to prove a galling experience to our occupation forces: to find that a China which had been crying over its weakness and begging for much-needed supplies, could suddenly produce two large and apparently well-armed armies—Nationalist and Communist—which sprang at each other's throats with more enthusiasm than they had ever shown in fighting the Japs. The Chinese Communists, claiming the right to withdraw, asserted that their troops in the area numbered 300,000 men. If that was true it had been the least warlike army in the world, for internally Manchuria had for ten years been the most peaceful and orderly part of northern Asia.

In Shanghai we visited the Soviet club, riding past the American club where Jap marines with bayonets were still on guard behind sandbagged barricades and out into Frenchtown, where a group of pre-war Russian friends poured vodka and beer for us in a noisy, friendly reunion. It was not too much of a surprise to find that one of the leading lights of the club was a former Czarist officer, a riding academy owner, who had been well known previously for his anti-Soviet pronouncements. Skipping over the fact that his attitude had been an obvious cover for his pro-Soviet activities, the Russian declared, "We are proud of the Red Army. They smashed the Germans and it took them only a week to defeat Japan after the other countries had been trying for nearly four years. Now all the White Russians who have been exiled for so long hope that Mother Russia will open her arms to them again." Mother Russia did, in China and Manchuria, and the young and old flocked to the consulates to take out Soviet citizenship. After a toast to the Red Army, I asked a Soviet newspaperman what price Moscow had demanded for coming into the war.

He looked deeply hurt as he answered. "How cynical you are, my capitalistic comrade. Nobody can buy Russia. However, since we are old friends, I believe that I can tell you that as a matter of national security for the Union of Socialist Soviet Republics, an arrangement has been made by which the Chinese Government at Chungking voluntarily agreed to give us a half-interest in the former Chinese Eastern Railway in Manchuria, which was Russian property until we sold it to Japan twelve years ago. The Chinese also, in recognition of valued Soviet aid in the struggle against world Fascism, have agreed to give us Port Arthur, which is rightfully ours, and to make Dairen an international port. It may likewise be found that the Kurile Islands are vital to the defense of Siberia."

"Isn't the Port Arthur arrangement a reversal of Soviet policy in China?" I asked. "Your government gave up all its extraterritorial rights and concessions twenty years ago to prove that it was non-imperialistic."

The Russian threw back another slug of vodka and grinned. "Times change. For the imperialist nations, the concessions in China were a means of capitalistic exploitation of the poor Chinese masses. We are the friends of the masses. And we need Port Arthur as an ice-free Pacific port and to guarantee the defenses of Siberia. Seriously, can you not see why it is more right and necessary for Russia to hold the Kuriles, just off our shores, and Port Arthur, than it was for the British to hold Hong Kong and other points more than twelve thousand miles from London?"

This Russian was a Communist with a sense of humor, but he was no less an ardent nationalist because of that. He knew China well, having studied the dialects of many regions at the Oriental Institute in Moscow before coming to China and visiting twenty-eight provinces in travels of many thousands of miles, and it is not difficult to imagine the advantage he had in discussing China with American

171

career diplomats who had not only refused bluntly to speak Chinese or to admit Chinese people to their homes, but whose travels were confined to home-consulate-American club-country club.

I asked him, "What will Russia's policy out here be now? Are you going to help the Chinese Communists overthrow the Nationalist government?"

"Absolutely not," the Tass man assured me. "Stalin has publicly and repeatedly proclaimed his recognition of the Chiang Kai-shek regime as the sole government of China. It is all written in our treaty. What we want most of all is a peaceful China. Of course, there will be inevitable disorders following the war, but eventually there will be a working arrangement between the Yenan Communists and Chiang Kai-shek. For one thing, both sides must come to realize that one of the first things to be done is to make China a nation. It is ridiculous to speak of a Chinese nation under present conditions. It is a country of many tongues and many peoples divided into little valleys who do not know the language or customs of their neighbors in the next valley. Until it gets transportation and communications, China can never be a nation. Then, too, there will be tremendous pressure from abroad for a peaceful China—not only from Moscow but from New York and London. China is worn out from eight years of war and needs foreign investments and foreign products to rebuild itself. Your bankers and manufacturers and salesmen are looking for markets for your industrial products. They will not invest in a warring China and cannot sell to one. So there will be peace."

But peace, it would seem, at a price. China's Communists had done a great deal in fifteen years toward unifying large areas of the hinterland and it was their aim eventually to relieve the country from its dependence on foreigners, which inevitably had meant for China a loss of political independence. The coming years would bring the test as to whether China could become one nation. It needed American and British skill and machinery to build up industry, irrigation projects, and communications, but always in the past the presence of foreigners and foreign money had meant a divided China, and foreign bases and troops on Chinese soil.

We drank another toast to the Big Three. "And you can believe me," said my Soviet friend, "when I tell you that the three points I have outlined are the limit of what Moscow wants—immediately—in the Far East. We will get out of Manchuria and out of Korea."

172

All of which was very interesting to recall in the light of subsequent developments in Manchuria.

It is my opinion, which some may find naive, that my Red colleague was talking the straight Kremlin line and that, despite the later stripping of Japanese-built factories in Manchuria by the Red Army, Moscow did not have any large territorial or other ambitions in the Orient for the predictable future. The Russians see the world strategic problem today as a question of Who is pushing Whom? They look at a map in Moscow and note that American troops are in Korea—only 200 miles from Russia's Siberian border but 7,000 miles from Washington—that Japan has become an American military stronghold, and that other American troops are in Berlin and Austria, 4,000 miles from Washington and only a few hundred from Russia. Consequently, they take steps to defend themselves against the military forces of a country whose inhabitants are in overwhelming majority enemies of their form of government. If the Soviets had very strong forces in Bermuda and in Newfoundland, and in Mexico, the Washington government would be criminally remiss if it did not take similar defensive steps.

A point of view similar to that of my Soviet friend in Shanghai had been given us a few days before by Pat Hurley, then our Ambassador to Chungking. He had quoted Stalin himself as authority. That was still some weeks before Hurley resigned in a huff against subordinates whom he accused of being pro-Russian to the extent that they deliberately betrayed Washington's announced policies. I will not say that I think Hurley's performance on the occasion of his resignation was brilliant, but I do believe that he is a good American and that the diplomatic missions he performed during the war were helpful to our country. It is the fashion among the be-spotted State Department careerists to sneer at Hurley as an Oklahoma hick, but for my money he is worth a hundred of them.

At our meeting in Chungking, Hurley described his first encounter with Stalin. The Russian rose to shake hands and then the two men sat down in the Kremlin and looked each other over coolly. Stalin broke the ice.

"They tell me you're a tough guy who won't take 'no' for an answer."

"You're damn right I'm a tough guy," the American answered. Stalin roared with laughter. Then the talk turned to China, where Hurley was headed, on an assignment given him by President Roose-

173

velt. "Are you going to help the Chinese Communists?" Hurley asked.

"No," Stalin answered. "In the first place, they are Chinese—not Communists. I think it is very difficult for a Chinese to be a Communist. In the second place, which do you think is more convenient for Russia—a China in civil war, or a peaceful country on our borders? I have promised to recognize only Chiang Kai-shek's government as the government of China and that is what I intend to do."

"And," said Hurley, in telling of the meeting, "I have heard Uncle Joe and Molotov promise a lot of things and neither of them has gone back on any promise. They do what they say they'll do."

Hurley went on to relate the hitherto unpublished story of the partial failure of his mission to Chungking. It is a far better defense of his actions than the one he offered at the hearings in Washington after his resignation. "Mr. Roosevelt gave me a directive," he said, "and the first point of that directive was: 'Support the National Government of China and keep China in the war!' It didn't say, 'Keep China in the war if you feel like it.' It didn't say, 'Keep China from collapsing if you admire the color of Mr. Shek's eyes.' Nor did it say that Chiang Kai-shek's government was Fascist and that, according to John Carter Vincent and George Acheson, the Yenan Communist government was truly the representative government of China and therefore must be supported. It said, 'Assist the Nationalist government and keep China in the war.'

"You may remember that at that time China's morale was very low; we ourselves had taken a lot of lickings, and there was talk of the Chinese making a bargain with the Japs. So my first job was to encourage the Nationalist government—which Russia and Britain also supported—to forestall any peace movement in Chungking and give them a boost generally." In that, Hurley was successful.

"The second point in my directive," Hurley went on, "was to try to arrange an agreement between Chungking and the Chinese government at Yenan so that instead of fighting each other they would fight Japan." Well, Hurley did his best and his work was sabotaged not by the Communists but by some of the Nationalist clique in Chungking, and especially by one man whom Hurley had befriended. When Hurley reached the Chinese capital, he found that T. V. Soong, the generalissimo's brother-in-law, was in bad favor and even, according to newspaper reports of the time, in danger of being liquidated. Hurley intervened with the generalissimo to get Soong out of the doghouse, partly for humanitarian reasons and partly because the American found that he could not make himself understood with the then Chinese foreign minister, whereas Soong, a Harvard graduate, could readily talk Hurley's Oklahoma-cussword language. Through Hurley's efforts, to a large extent, Soong was returned to good graces and became foreign minister.

Following the second part of his directive, the American Ambassador flew up to Yenan to negotiate with the Communists. He got along famously, and at his invitation Chu-teh, the No. 2 Chinese Red, overcame his suspicions and his fear of flying and accompanied Hurley back to Chungking by plane. With them, Hurley took an historic document which he himself had composed. It quoted the Magna Carta, the Bill of Rights, Lincoln's Gettysburg Address, and a few other immortal charters of freedom, and it provided for an agreement whereby the Communists would share in the government of China. More important, it bore the signature of Mao The-tung, the Red leader. I saw the signature, written in both Chinese and English.

Hurley confidently expected the generalissimo would sign it quickly, but "Mr. Shek"—as Hurley called him—began to stall. Investigating behind the scenes, Hurley found that the opposition came from none other than the man who owed him his job, if not his life, T. V. Soong. He went to call on the foreign minister, and Soong explained, "We can't let these Communists come here. Why, they may stage a coup overnight and we'll wake up in the morning and find that we're either dead or prisoners."

Hurley roared back. "Stage a coup! They're willing to come here to your stronghold, where you could wipe them all out at once, yet you talk about them seizing the government. It's more likely that you'd seize them." Then he gave the foreign minister a thorough but undiplomatic bawling out. "The trouble with you, Soong, and all your gang, is that you are too rich and comfortable, and too afraid. All you can think about is your money and your safety. Wake up to the problems of your country!" Soong, however, remained adamant, and under his influence the generalissimo refused to sign any comprehensive agreement with the Reds until months later, after General Marshall went out to China, and after signing it they refused to live up to it. This was a violation of Chiang Kai-shek's agreement with Roosevelt in Cairo, but our side had violated that agreement too by permitting British ships to return to Hong Kong which would never have been allowed if F.D.R. had been alive.

175

While we were talking these things over with our Soviet pals in Shanghai, most of our gang from the B-17 had disappeared here and there into the city. I found only Jim McGlincy in the lobby of the Metropole when I returned, and he explained, "A couple of them went off with White Russian girls to dance. Some are seeing which way the street cars run. Others were invited to the homes of Chinese or Russians; and some guys and girls who looked to me like Nazis took a few others off."

Jim's eyesight was good. They were Nazis. A group of them came to call at the Metropole next morning, very self-assured, as they requested me to communicate with their friends. My anti-Nazi friend, Baron Harro von Zeppelin, gave prophetic warning about them. "Since Germany surrendered, they have been laying plans on how to deceive the Americans, and buying their way into good favor with the Chinese. Their propaganda line is to congratulate America on its success on obtaining strategic positions from which to combat the 'Communist menace.' They are pretty sure they can outsmart you." As indeed they did. By bribing the Chinese, most of them were still out of prison camps much later. One of those who failed to stay out was Dr. Klaus Mehnert, a former professor at the University of Hawaii and an ex-Nazi geopolitical expert. Mehnert came to call and left his card with a note: "It was my pleasure back in 1941 to present you with the first copy of my XX Magazine. [The name was Twentieth Century, but we called it the 'Double Cross.'] I now present you with the last." Mehnert belonged to the intelligentsia and worked in the background, whereas the German businessmen—all loudly proclaiming themselves non-Nazi—put themselves out to entertain our generals and admirals when they entered Shanghai.

That morning in Shanghai, we were invited to a friend's house for breakfast, and the hostess proudly produced a can of American tinned milk—"cost thirty-five thousand Chinese dollars." "How in the world did you get it?" "Oh, it's American Army supplies, came down through the lines from Chungking."

They told me that a thriving business had been carried on across the Chinese and Japanese lines, and a good deal of American equipment and supplies had passed from the Chungking side to Shanghai. The two armies were supposedly at death grips, but actually it was possible to travel freely between the areas which each occupied. I asked about one friend, the wife of a Chinese banker, and was told that she and her two sons had gone recently to Chungking. "You just

176

get on a train to Shanghai and ride to Hankow. Then you pay so much squeeze to the Japs for a pass to get by their sentries. When you reach the Chinese lines you pay some more squeeze. It takes quite a while, but it's a safe enough journey. Goods come down in the same way, including American Army stuff."

There were several released Americans from the internment camps at breakfast, and they said they had been crowded and uncomfortable for three years, but their lot had been by no means as bad as what we had told them of conditions in Manila and elsewhere. A good many of the Americans, British, and French were planning to stay in Shanghai and pick up their businesses.

One cotton man said, "In the past few days, my old Chinese contacts have been swarming to see me. They have been doing business under the Japs, but Shanghai has been a half-dead city without its American and foreign trade. Now they want all the cotton we can sell. The only trouble is going to be finding a way to pay with the currency running wild as it is. As soon as there is financial stabilization, we'll be doing more trade with China than ever before. You just can't keep this city down. It always bounces back, wars or no wars." A few months later I heard that the cotton man's company had orders for U. S. $20,000,000 in Shanghai. The exchange had been officially stabilized at 2,000 to 1, but that did not enter the contracts. Payment was to be made in U. S. dollar bills which GIs had spent and which had been rounded up in the black market by Chinese businessmen.

But such deals grew rarer and rarer. Our visit to Shanghai was made at a period of celebration, of a brief turning back to old times. As the months passed and the marines poured into Shanghai and the other Chinese ports, and the businessmen followed them in to resume trading at the same old stand, they found that times had definitely changed. The Chinese were no longer subservient to the white man. They wanted their country back and they made that fact very obvious; by pushing marines on the streets and stoning sailors, by charging outrageous prices, by passing laws tending to eliminate American and British middlemen and drive them out of the country. The Japs had taught the Chinese a lesson, and the Chinese began to apply it.

Still, Washington kept the marines in China and clung to its old policy of backing the corrupt Chiang Kai-shek government. UNRRA supplies were diverted into the black market by the Kuomintang

177

officials, and kept from reaching Communist-held areas. T. V. Soong, whose God is money and the power that money gives, got richer and richer every day. Unlike his old friend Franklin Roosevelt, he did not think of dam projects or flood-control works in terms of benefits to the people. Every such project made money for T. V. Soong and his henchmen.

General Marshall, in his special role of peace negotiator in China, became quickly disillusioned as the Kuomintang broke its word time after time. He made a trip to Washington to try to convince the President and the State Department that we would have to stop our all-out armed aid to Chiang Kai-shek and to recognize the fact, palatable or otherwise, that the Communists did represent a dynamic force in China. But the marines stayed on and Chiang, his armies equipped by the United States of America, made plans to wage war on the Communists, who, less well equipped and armed, were equally willing to fight. As long as Chiang had American support, bloodshed was inevitable. If it were withdrawn, then there might be a chance of settlement in China. Or it might be that for the next decade China could know no peace, but would have to fight civil war just as the United States had struggled internally for four long years before it could find the path to unity.

In one thing, though, the Chinese were united. Yenan might follow the Moscow line and Chiang Kai-shek be a tool of Washington policy, but Nationalist and Communist alike wanted the foreigners to get out, wanted to take their country back after a century of white domination of China's trade and finances, and armed occupation of its key cities.

Yes, times had changed in China. The morning after our arrival in Shanghai I met a French newspaperman whom I had known for eight years. Back in the days of extraterritoriality and foreign courts, he had been involved in a hunting accident. Taking aim at a pheasant flushed from a rice field outside of Shanghai, he had shot and killed the four-year-old daughter of a peasant as she suddenly stood up in front of his gun barrel. The farmer had demanded Ch. $3 to pay for the loss of the girl's life; the Frenchman offered Ch. $2. The court settled the dispute by awarding damages of Ch. $2.50, the equivalent in those days of U. S. $0.75.

In the spring of 1946, a Swedish businessman came to see me in Honolulu with a letter of introduction from the Frenchman. "I am going back to my country," said the Swede. "It is no longer possible

178

to live in Shanghai. Why, a Chinese delivery boy spat in my wife's face in the kitchen of our home. She complained to the police, and instead of arresting the boy they took my wife to the police station and held her all night in a dirty cell. A Chinese judge tried her in the morning and I had to pay a fine of seven hundred and fifty U. S. dollars to obtain her release. The white man is finished in China."

It was a pretty shaky gang that gathered at the Metropole Hotel in Shanghai twenty-four hours after our unsanctioned arrival. We paid our bill of $1,300,000 Chinese dollars, and then the boys said goodbye to the girls who had gathered, White Russian, Chinese, Eurasian, American, English, Portuguese—some smiling and some tearful. Out at the airfield, I went up in the cockpit and asked the pilot, "How was that blonde White Russian, Mark?" "Blonde, nuts!" he said. "I met an Indian princess. I am going to fly over her house to say goodbye."

Colonel Norman Ross of our party, who is a veteran pilot and a sensible man, and consequently had been scared stiff by our antics the day before, came up front to warn Mark, "No more monkey business. Take off into the wind, climb to one thousand feet and don't bank at more than fifteen degrees. You can fly once over the city to let the photographers get another picture, but no buzzing. That's an order!"

"Yes, sir," said Mark.

We took off sedately, circled the city, and then spotted the princess' house out in Frenchtown. Samari herself was on the rooftop, waving a big red silk scarf. Mark nosed the Fortress over in a sharp dive and swept over the roof at close to 300 miles an hour. I hope the princess' scarf was big enough for a parachute, because it looked as though the prop wash blew her off.

Chapter Sixteen

But They Won't Get Hong Kong

THE SHANGHAI WE HAD VISITED WAS ABOUT TO
become a Chinese city again. But 900 miles south and west down
the coast was another city, an even finer port than Shanghai and of
equal importance to the country's economy, which was *not* becoming
Chinese. The city was Hong Kong, which the British had stolen from
China a century before by bloodshed and by threat and by the liberal use of opium, and which post-war Britain did not propose to
give up at any price.

We went to Hong Kong after Japan's surrender, stopping at the
British colony while en route in mid-September, 1945, on a flying
trip through southeastern Asia to see how the countries in that former stronghold of European imperialism were faring after nearly
four years of Japanese occupation.

They weren't faring well. Two colonies were in revolt—French
Indo-China and the Netherlands East Indies—and the repercussions
were being felt not only in Paris and Rotterdam, but in Bombay and
Calcutta and throughout China, where millions watched with interest the struggle of brown-skinned men against white. There was no
revolt as yet in the other three countries that make up southeastern
Asia—Malaya, Burma, and Siam. But the Japs had left behind them
in all the vast and rich region a legacy—however fictitious—of freedom.

Only Siam, of the five countries, had been independent before the
war. In the dying days of their rule the Japanese had granted "freedom" to the others and the significant thing, the unforgettable thing,
was that while nowhere in the area had the native peoples fought

in any large numbers against occupation by their fellow Asiatics, the Japanese, they were now fighting with fanatical bravery in Java and in Indo-China to preserve their Jap-sponsored independence and to resist the return of white dominance. They had lived quietly, without resistance, under the Japs. Now they preferred death to restoration of European colonial power.

The Crown Colony of Hong Kong—part of the Empire which Churchill did not become prime minister to dismember—was our first stop en route to the embattled regions. Hong Kong has always meant wars for me, and not for the reason that I was married there in 1938. I had been there when the Japs stepped slyly along its border to capture the South China metropolis of Canton in 1938, and again in late November, 1941, a few weeks before this supposed stronghold of Empire was overwhelmed by the southward surge of Japan. Then it had been practically undefended—a few thousand Canadian and Indian troops, a destroyer or two that soon turned tail and ran for Singapore. Now the picture was different.

In the beautiful harbor dominated by the steep hillsides of the Peak, on which the British Taipans had made their homes, were scores of British ships, ships that might, had they been available in December, 1941, have enabled the Canadian and Indian defenders of the colony to hold out for more than the sixteen days they resisted Japanese air and amphibious attacks. I say "might" because it is also a reasonable possibility that they would have been caught in the harbor as our ships were caught at Pearl Harbor, and equally possible that they might have sallied out without adequate air defense and been slaughtered as were the "Prince of Wales" and "Repulse" off Singapore.

The Taipans—managers of British firms and banks, exporters, importers, newspapermen, big merchants—were gathering again with their ladies in the lobby of the Peninsular Hotel across the harbor in Kowloon, and on British Navy rations they were beginning to pick up some of the weight they lost during nearly four years of internment in Stanley Prison and other camps. The hotel was intact and running full blast, in contrast to those in Hong Kong itself where coolies were busy knocking apart blast walls, removing sandbags, and replacing plate-glass windows. As if from nowhere, but actually out of caves and hiding places in the carefully segregated Chinese quarter, came large quantities of American and British goods to go on sale at fabulous prices. Knowing the tastes of sailors but over-

181

estimating their pocketbooks, the Chinese were asking U. S. $30 and $40 for pre-war imported liquors. There were abundant stocks of American cigarettes in the trays of the street-corner vendors. Newspapers were publishing again.

The Taipans, and their No. 2s, 3s, and so on down the line of foreign commercial hierarchy, had not yet recovered their confidence sufficiently to resume their browbeating of the Chinese. Those giant gray ships in the harbor were very reassuring, but the Colonials could not forget overnight the nightmare of four years when the enslaved Asiatics had suddenly become their masters; and if they needed a reminder they had only to lift up their eyes unto the hills, to the massive monument erected on the Peak by their temporary conquerors to the glory of "Greater East Asia." These were bones and skulls and broken rifles mixed with the concrete of the monument's base, not only of Japanese but of Canadians and Indians and a handful of Englishmen who had fought very bravely indeed, in defense of this distant outpost of Empire.

Yet the British were determined to make one more try to hang on here, 12,000 miles from London. Over cups of tea in the Peninsular lounge, a British banker asked, with pathetic need of affirmation, "It is true, isn't it, Lee, old man, that Mr. Churchill said that Britain will never give up Hong Kong?" Yes, it was true, even though the more outspoken Chinese newspapers were insisting that in return the Republic of China should take over the port of Liverpool and surrounding territory as a Chinese colony. "Insolent beggars!" said the banker. "We'll put them back in their places."

That was going to take a lot of doing. In Hong Kong itself the Chinese were turning out readily enough to assist the erstwhile prisoners to get business running again, but outside the colony, along the Kowloon borders, we encountered a different breed of Chinese. The troops holding the outposts were Chinese Communists, of the old Eighth Route Army and they looked like first-class soldiers. Through an interpreter, a Red captain told us another chapter in the amazing story of a China within a China and an army within an army.

These Communists had been driven out of the provinces south of Shanghai by Chiang Kai-shek back in the early 1930s. While a majority of their comrades had made the epic "long march" to the west and north and finally set up headquarters in Yenan, this group had worked south to the vicinity of Hong Kong. They had separated to find jobs, but they had never lost their identity or their contacts with one another and with headquarters 3,000 miles away—this in a country that is almost without communications. Recently they had been working with British and American Intelligence teams dropped into their area, and they had received arms and equipment. Depending on the reader's viewpoint, their actions may be regarded in either a favorable or an unfavorable light. Their continued existence was a testimonial to the strength of Communist discipline and beliefs. On the other hand, they admitted they had not been very active against the Japanese.

By this time, all the Japanese troops in Hong Kong, mostly marines, had been disarmed by the British. Some 2,000 of them in Kowloon were prisoners of the R.A.F. and they were having a pretty rough time. We saw British Tommies seated in carts, their pale backs stripped to absorb the sunshine, while Japanese pulled them through the streets at double time to an accompaniment of billingsgate, and an occasional blow. This was in sharp contrast with the American attitude in Japan, where MacArthur himself had set the keynote: Japan was to pay terribly for the war, criminals and murderers of prisoners were to be punished, but there was to be no petty brutality against individuals. MacArthur expected that some day the Japanese people could be taught to take their place in the world as a decent nation, and he didn't think the way to teach them was by a slap in the face. The British had a different view of the subject.

With an R.A.F. officer as our protesting escort, we were taken to see the Japanese admiral who had been in command at Hong Kong and was now confined with several hundred marines in their former barracks behind Kowloon. The flight officer gave us detailed instructions, "Don't salute them! Don't smile at them! Act tough!" We told him that in Japan our troops were required to return salutes, and he replied angrily, "Don't do it heah!"

The admiral's aide offered to escort us into his quarters, but the Englishman insisted that the old man come out personally to lead us into his living room. Our interview started quite well, with the admiral answering all our questions. He told us his fleet had consisted of one mine layer, and his air force of one scouting plane. He had only occasional communications with Tokyo, but had been prepared to defend Hong Kong to the end until the surrender orders came. We were talking along, not making buddies with the old boy but not, on the other hand, calling him a dirty Jap bastard in every other sentence. The R.A.F. man got more and more agitated. He had kept his hat on in the house, obviously to show his prisoners what was what, and suddenly he pulled a pistol out of a holster and cocked it noisily. We looked at him in amazement then and saw that he was shaking with emotion, but whether anger or fear it was difficult to determine. In either case he succeeded in breaking up the interview.

We found the British back at the Peninsular agitated, too, but over a more concrete thing. Some of them wanted to tear down the big Jap-built monument dedicated to the New Order in East Asia. It got under their skins to see the huge tower standing there against the sky, high up on the Peak. There had been very rigid rules of social order on the Peak. The Chinese, the masses, lived at its foot and were not permitted to approach the big houses of the Taipans, the governors, the generals, on the top half of the hillside. "Upper-class" Chinese, bankers, doctors, merchants who were rich enough, were allowed to build homes halfway up the Peak. And now here, at its very crest, was this insulting monument that stood above even the most lofty homes of the British. It was unthinkable! But there was a problem involved in its destruction. "After all," a businessman said, "there actually are the bones of British Empire soldiers in the concrete, and we do not wish to move them." Others argued that the monument should be done away with forthwith.

One of the party scandalized the British by suggesting that an "eternal flame" monument be built in place of the hated Jap structure, and that the new memorial should be constructed in the shape of an opium pipe, with the everlasting light consisting of a glowing heap of opium.

This, of course, will never be done, but the suggestion had considerable merit, for Hong Kong itself was built on opium—was a trophy of the opium trade. Opium and European imperialism had always gone hand in hand in southeastern Asia, in fact, in all Asia outside of Japan and the Philippines.

Opium had been the chief weapon of the British, Dutch, and French colonists. They had resorted to it because, only a handful numerically, they had feared the millions upon millions of Orientals whom they were determined to subject to economic enslavement. Opium would keep the millions docile and stupefied. Both England and Holland introduced the traffic and it became so lucrative that government monopolies were set up in India, Burma, Malaya, the

184

Netherlands East Indies, and in the Portuguese colonies. There are still opium factories in Batavia and Singapore.

China saw her people becoming enslaved and she tried to resist the white man's poison. The Opium War was fought in 1840 to free the Chinese from their servitude to the drug, but England won the war and, as a prize, took Hong Kong—that bright pearl in the glorious British Empire. The defeat of 1840 was the beginning of the end of Old China, being followed by the slow collapse of the Manchu dynasty and the increasing encroachments of foreign powers, not excluding the United States.

In 1934, as part of his New Life movement, Chiang Kai-shek was spurred into launching a drive against opium and attempted to cut off supplies to the estimated 10,000,000 addicts in his country, where the growth of the poppy had become a vast industry and a source of income for the warlords. Chiang was making considerable headway when the Japanese invaded China in 1937 and, taking a page from the book of Europe's imperialists, used drugs for their own ally.

In the years before Pearl Harbor, the Japanese concentrated on manufacture of heroin, an opium derivative, and exported it to the East Indies, Malaya, and other places to compete with government-monopoly opium. The Japs were even more aggressive in pushing the sale of opium than the white imperialists had been. Replanting the poppy fields of North China and Inner Mongolia, they established narcotic factories whose product was peddled throughout occupied China and slipped through the lines into Chinese-held areas. I had been in numerous gambling-opium establishments in Jap-controlled portions of Shanghai before the war, where you walked around between bets on fantan or bird-cage dice and looked at the human wrecks who, openly to the public gaze, lay in dazed dreams on wooden pallets—young and old alike, men, women, and even children.

From 1941 until the end of the war, the picture became even blacker. In the four-square-mile Japanese concession area of Tientsin there were 200 heroin factories operated by 1,500 Japanese experts and employing 10,000 Chinese. There were more than 1,000 hotels, shops, and stores where the Japanese openly sold drugs, using their destructive powers to weaken the will of the Chinese, and the bait of huge fortunes to win traitors to their side. That had been the British-Dutch-French-Portuguese pattern, and the Japanese simply put it into mass production. Strictly for export, however, since the

185

Japanese were too smart to allow drugs to be used in Japan itself.

The results were horrifying. In China alone it was estimated that the number of addicts had jumped from the minimum of 10,000,000 in 1934 to some 30,000,000 people by 1945.

With the end of the war, something was finally done about this tremendous menace. The Netherlands government promised it would completely suppress opium smoking in the N.E.I. "after the liberation of the islands from Japanese occupation." Inasmuch as there were admittedly some 100,000 Jap soldiers unaccounted for in the N.E.I. hinterland, in addition to 250,000 whose whereabouts was known, and since the Dutch and British were using Jap troops to shoot down the liberty-seeking Javanese, this was a somewhat nebulous promise.

Malaya took more concrete measures, the British military government in Singapore announcing a month after the reoccupation of that city that opium smoking in Malaya and all British protected territories would be abolished "immediately." This was not a move calculated to please the tycoons and Taipans who, because of the huge returns to the government from the opium monopoly (the raw opium was bought in India or Persia and processed at the British government factory outside Singapore for sale in government shops), never had to pay income taxes.

These British and Dutch government monopolies in a business of degradation and death had prevented effective enforcement of League of Nations efforts to control the use of opium by limiting the planting of poppies throughout the world. Because the British and Dutch asserted that they could not give an accurate annual estimate of the needs of their monopolies, it was impossible for the League to fix quotas for poppy-growing countries.

At war's end, the Chinese also resumed their war on opium. Huge quantities were burned in Peking and other cities, and the Chinese seized and destroyed stocks of heroin which the Jap army had distributed through retail outlets. In Japan, MacArthur banned the growth of the opium poppy and the manufacture of opium products except for medicinal and scientific purposes. Similar measures were ordered in the American-occupied section of Korea.

American narcotic agents sent to the Orient after the surrender discovered that the Jap army had paid a price for its lucrative opium and heroin business. Thousands of Japanese officers and enlisted men became slaves to the drugs in spite of an Imperial booklet which

186

informed them: "The use of narcotics is unworthy of a superior race like the Japanese. Only inferior races that are decadent, like the Chinese, Europeans, and East Indians, are addicted to the use of narcotics. That is why they are destined to become our servants and eventually to disappear."

But Hong Kong, which was built on narcotics, seemed destined to a few more years of life as the most distant bastion of Britain's Empire, for the British were determined to cling to it with all their might and the Chinese were too law-abiding to take back by main force what belonged to them. Just why the British wanted so desperately to retain Hong Kong was difficult to understand. It had proved defenseless pre-atom bomb, and in the atomic age it is just a giant death trap.

Chapter Seventeen

Siam—Enemy or Friend?

THE ONLY INDEPENDENT COUNTRY IN SOUTHEAST-ern Asia has two names. One is Siam, which means Siam, and the other is Thai, which means free.

Siam had remained relatively free because the British and French decided over a half-century ago that it would be to their mutual interests to maintain a neutral buffer state between their respective colonies and spheres of interest in southeastern Asia. The British chipped and chiseled large slices off of Siam to add to Malaya and to Burma, and the French did the same thing to increase the size of Indo-China which borders Siam on the east. Britain, for example, got four rich states in return for surrendering extraterritoriality.

Then the Europeans kept hands off as Siam underwent a revolution in the early '30's which limited the power of the monarchy. In the years that followed Siam turned more and more to Japan and, opening its doors to Japanese invasion in 1941, soon joined up as a full-fledged Axis war partner. So, when we landed at the Bangkok airport from Hong Kong in late September, 1945, we were landing in what was supposedly an enemy country—but you'd never know it from the way the people acted.

The English-speaking air-force officers met us with friendly camaraderie, apparently not the least bit abashed by the fact that they had been allies of the Japanese until a few days previously. They were competent-appearing and smartly dressed and they were, oh, so glad to see us. Their planes were antiquated by modern standards but in first-class condition. In their officers' club with its modern furniture, they served us Siamese-made mekhong whiskey, and except that the food they supplied was duck eggs and rice, the atmos-

188

phere was far more European than Oriental. Our first impression of Siam as a militaristic little land of plenty, which didn't intend to apologize—very much—to anybody, grew stronger every hour. In the long run, though, they were forced to apologize. Britain never forgives or forgets.

Siam, the cleanest and most fertile and most spotless country of southeastern Asia, was on the spot. The Siamese had been bad boys for ten years. Shortly after the Japanese occupied their country in 1942, the Siamese declared war on us. Britain declared war right back, but Washington ignored the whole thing and, immediately the shooting had stopped, there was a concerted effort by our State Department to play up a supposedly widespread underground anti-Japanese movement.

This was a good story, but from all we could discover in Siam the movement was small and had no great popular support, although it is true that the American-trained Siamese parachutists who dropped into the country provided us with valuable Intelligence information and assisted the escape of downed Allied fliers.

Washington quickly recognized what was called a "new, liberal" government of Siam, although the fact was that most of its members had served the Japanese throughout the war with no outward signs of protest. Here and there in Siam cautious men came up to us to whisper that the government was "the same old gang," the original group of revolutionaries who took away a large portion of the king's powers in 1932 and established a form of representative government.

However, Washington accepted at face value the contention of the Siamese "liberals" that their country had been led astray by a single man, former premier Luang Pibul Songgram and that it had been Pibul alone who had thrown Siam into the arms of Japan. It was hard to keep a straight face as you heard this obvious absurdity repeated time after time. However, the State Department may have had perfectly understandable motives. Siam had been a good customer of ours before the war, and Bangkok is a logical stop on a world airline touching at Calcutta and Manila. Also, Washington may have hoped by supporting Siam to prod the British, French, and Dutch into carrying out, sooner than intended, their promises of increased freedom for their Asiatic colonies.

Washington should have known better. Britain took the position that Siam was in fact an enemy and forced her into a separate peace giving Britain some lush territorial plums, including the formerly Siamese sections of Malaya which had been restored to Siam by the Japanese during the war. Even the French, the imperialist weak sisters of the Orient who contributed nothing to defeating Japan, began to bully the Siamese by force of arms in the hope of regaining the regions that Siam had taken from Indo-China by the same means in 1941.

At first, on our arrival in Bangkok, the British appeared to be following the Washington Line. Major General Geoffrey Evans, in command of British troops engaged in disarming the Japanese and, on the side, in helping to suppress demonstrations by Siam's Chinese minority, told us he was "treating Siam as a friendly country." But later Britain had a change of heart, a typically British change of heart.

The British forced the Siamese to tear up the 700-mile railway across the Kra isthmus which the Japanese had built with prisoner labor. They also forced the Siamese to sign a pledge that no such railway would ever be reconstructed. Now, looked at from any but the British point of view, the railroad would seem to be a benefit to the peoples of the world. If it could be paralleled by a canal, it would cut the steamship distance from Europe to the Orient by some 2,000 miles. But the railway and the canal (which Japan had long urged should be built) by-pass the great British port of Singapore, and Singapore, like Hong Kong, is one place the British don't propose to give up.

Destruction of the railroad and the prevention by Britain of construction of a Kra canal will, of course, force the people of Europe and of Asia to pay more for the products interchanged between those two sections of the world. But the British don't care about things like that.

When we reached Bangkok, we found the new Siamese government engaged in attempting to cement its newly reestablished good relations with Washington and, at the time, with London. We were driven from the airport into the capital and to the Ratanokosinder Hotel, a lofty, spacious building in tone with the other German-tropical-style edifices that lined the wide-paved main street. Then we were given a course in Siamese methods of winning friends, a program that took the immediate post-war form of supplying the needs and demands, professional and otherwise, of visiting newspapermen. This was done through the medium of an ambitious and well-organized Bureau of Information, whose alert, well-dressed, bright young men all spoke at least a smattering of British-English. At the drop of a bead of sweat on a visitor's brow, they whipped up some mekhong or some iced beer. We were told by British correspondents who reached Bangkok just ahead of us that the Information Bureau had a standard three-day friendship schedule:

1st night—Chinese dinner.

2nd day and night—Interview with the prime minister and the regent, and then dinner with the prime minister.

3rd night—Sojourn at a nearby beach resort for the night with girl companions, music, food, and liquid refreshment all supplied and paid for by the government.

Our party left after the second night, so we missed what was apparently the most interesting part of the schedule. We did get the Chinese dinner—in the midst of a pitched street battle—and a Siamese lunch of highly spiced curries, shrimp, fish, and perfect fruits. The curfew prevented our attendance at the prime minister's party, but we interviewed him and the regent. All of our hosts were fast talkers and they had plenty to explain—if not to apologize for.

Siam got into the bad books of the democracies back in the 1930s when Luang Pibul Songgram emerged from the revolution as the country's strong man. He beat the drums for a chauvinistic program, and Siam's people fell in line without any noticeable reluctance. A rubber-stamp assembly provided funds for a Japanese-trained army and a built-in-Japan miniature navy. To whip up nationalistic spirit the country resumed its ancient name of Thailand. The Siamese became the bullies of southeast Asia, its small-fry Nazis. With Japanese backing, they defeated the French of Indo-China in 1941 and took away from them some portions of Cambodia that had formerly been Siamese territory.

When the Japanese attacked at Pearl Harbor and landed simultaneously on the shores of Siam, Premier Luang Pibul Songgram ordered his forces to cease fire after eight hours of indifferent resistance and in a few days all of Siam was in Japan's control. Luang then declared war on the democracies and Siamese troops served side by side with Japanese as occupation forces in captured Burma and Malaya, or relieved Jap soldiers for front-line duty. In return for these favors, Japan recognized Thailand as a full ally and gave the country a lavish present of four Malay states and two Shan (Burmese) states—formerly Thai territory.

191

In the eyes of Washington, however, all these facts were out-weighed by the gallant performance of the Siamese underground. Washington had not even administered a rebuke or a slap on the wrist. The bright young men of the Siamese Department of Information were quick to emphasize Washington's attitude when they greeted us in Bangkok. With the B.Y.M. of the D.O.I. was a member of the ubiquitous O.S.S., Navy Lieutenant Alexander MacDonald of Honolulu. Mac told us that the D.G. had arranged a Chinese dinner. You fell quickly into the habit of using initials for everything in Siam. The Siamese called the prime minister the P.M., and the director general the D.G. of the D.O.I. which is the Department of Information. Yes, W.C. meant the same thing in Bangkok as it does everywhere else in the world. The W.C.s weren't working too well, because one of the power plants was still shut down as a result of a B-29 raid—a practice mission for the later assaults on Japan—and water had to be hauled up to the third-floor rooms in buckets.

We met the D.G. in a Chinese restaurant on the fifth floor of a fine, new building in Yarawat Road in Chinatown, where we drove through darkened and deserted streets that occasionally echoed the sounds of shooting. As dinner went on, the shooting increased and so did the embarrassment of our hosts. They explained that some Chinese "Communists" were firing on the Siamese police. From the balcony, we saw an occasional rifle flash and once in a while a machine gun stuttered briefly and nervously, and then was still. Between the seventeen courses, all of them excellent, we took an occasional look at the fighting.

Actually, it was no great shakes as a battle, and the Chinese had no chance to win with Bangkok under occupation by thousands of British troops. Only a few people were killed, one of them an Australian prisoner of war from Singapore who had survived three years of work on the railroad built at Jap bayonet point through the jungle—the railroad that killed 40,000 Asiatics and 25,000 white men through starvation, disease, and beatings—the railroad the British have now ordered torn up instead of leaving it as a useful monument to those dead.

The shooting in Bangkok was a flare-up in a long feud between Siamese and Chinese. A minority of 2,000,000 in a nation of 15,000,000, the Chinese had been victims of Thai racism. In 1940 and 1941, newspaper dispatches compared the persecution of the Chinese with Nazi terror in Europe. Now with the war over, the

192

Chinese, contrary to Washington's view, took the stand that Siam was a defeated enemy nation. They refused to fly the flag of a vanquished enemy country, and insisted on showing China's colors in victory celebrations. So the Bangkok police, who were old hands at that sort of thing, turned machine guns on them.

In their stand, the Bangkok Chinese were significantly not supported by Chiang Kai-shek, although his government had made many protests against persecution of its nationals in previous years. Chiang's attitude toward Siam was outwardly that of Washington, but there was a difference. Even though some of its citizens suffered in Siam, China wanted that country on its side in the future as a fellow Asiatic nation.

One morning in Bangkok we were awakened by a parade of singing soldiers passing the hotel, soldiers followed by several hundred men in civilian clothes—but not ragged or dirty—who stepped along smartly to the martial cadence of a national song. They paused in front of the D.G.'s building to participate in the ceremonious raising of the flag, and in the evening the colors were hauled down in another ceremony, while loudspeakers blared out another song and all over the capital people stood at attention. The marchers were "underground" troops, some of them carrying American carbines. Their immediate excuse for parading was to prepare for a "liberation" parade a few days hence, but you could see that they enjoyed the music, the songs poured from many throats, the marching in unison. Even the kids jumped to attention as the colors passed and saluted smartly. The youngsters had learned the V signal and "O.K." and they shouted it whenever they spotted our American uniforms. They never begged for chewing gum.

We found the prime minister in a home that spelled hundreds of thousands of dollars, U. S. money, in any part of the world. Indeed, the homes of the politicians reminded me of the lavish palaces of victorious Mexican generals, and it seemed that having been a Siamese revolutionist in 1932 had been a very profitable business for everyone—except the princes of the royal family who lost the incomes which had formerly drained the country of much of its wealth. These reforms were favored by the then absolute monarch, King Prajadnipok, but it is doubtful if he foresaw the future affluence of those who took over the government.

The new prime minister was S.M. Seni Pramoj (since replaced by Luang Pradit), who had been Siamese minister to Washington.

He was flown to Bangkok after Japan's surrender and was immediately appointed P.M. by the regent, Pridi Banomyong. Seni Pramoj received us on the second floor of his residence and immediately insisted on serving whiskey although it was early in the morning. Forty-two years old and looking considerably younger with his thick, slicked-back, black hair, Pramoj was a lawyer with extensive experience in evading questions.

He told us the Chinese minority problem had been a source of concern and trouble both to Siam and China. Under Siamese law, Chinese born in Siam were Siamese citizens, while China regarded them as Chinese. "That is the main difficulty," Pramoj said. "There is no discrimination here against the Chinese. They can own property and even can vote."

Siam was not alone in having a Chinese minority problem, a condition which is common to all southeastern Asia. There are some 400,000 overseas Chinese in Burma, 600,000 in French Indo-China, 1,800,000 in Malaya where they outnumber the Malayans, a million and a half in the N.E.I., and 150,000 in the Philippines.

Hard-working, smart traders and businessmen, having plenty of initiative and a fine organization, the Chinese were not only laborers but bankers, retailers, money lenders, importers of European, American, and Japanese manufactured goods. They bought real estate, and in many places controlled rice distribution. Others worked as artisans. Earning fortunes by their ingenuity and devotion to business, they won the enmity of the native populations in whose countries they lived—as people apart. For they remained strictly Chinese, and when countries like Siam tried to make them take out citizenship, the Chinese home government cracked down.

The overseas Chinese have long been an important factor in China's economy. Sending their wealth home, they financed Sun Yat-sen's revolution. They supplied one-third of Chiang Kai-shek's war chest. In 1936, they remitted $115,000,000 (U. S.) to China, contributing one-half as much of China's foreign exchange as was supplied by the 400,000,000 Chinese at home. Chinese investments in the N.E.I. exceeded those of Britain and America in the pre-war years.

Chiang Kai-shek has denied that China wants to replace Japan as the organizing power of Asia. He said in November, 1942, "There has been some talk of China emerging as the leader of Asia, as if China wished the mantle of an unworthy Japan to fall on her shoulders. Having been the victim of exploitation, China has infinite sympathy for the submerged nations of Asia, and toward them China feels she has only responsibilities—not rights. China has no desire to replace Western imperialism with an Oriental imperialism or isolationism of its own."

The generalissimo probably meant what he said, but would it be "imperialism" if China at some future date were to demand the return of Hong Kong, of French Indo-China, and of other countries that were Chinese before the Europeans took them at bayonet point? And there is plenty of justification for Siam's pre-war charges that the widespread business control exercised by alien Chinese amounted to economic imperialism.

Sidi Pramoj assured us that Siam's one desire now was to place itself in a good light in the eyes of the United Nations. They were even willing to hand back to French Indo-China the territory seized in the 1940 border war, provided that "an international tribunal decides that it is rightfully a part of Indo-China." Although Siam believed that the seized land, and a lot more, was justly Siamese, Pramoj promised that Siam would not "in the interests of international harmony" seek to press any further claims. All this was, of course, evidence of a guilty conscience. To atone for its unadmitted sins, Siam would not even ask for that which it believed its own.

The most interesting statements by Sidi Pramoj and all the other Bangkok politicians concerned Luang Pibul Songgram. They insisted volubly that he alone was the villain of the piece; he alone had surrendered to Japan and declared war on the United Nations. The case was open and shut, black and white. Yet, for months, nothing was done about Pibul, who continued to live in his country home thirty-five miles from Bangkok. Pramoj explained to me, "There is an old Siamese proverb: 'Step over a fallen log but never step on a fallen man.'" Finally Pibul was arrested and then released without trial. One theory we heard in Bangkok was that he had too much incriminating information about his fellow revolutionaries, and the last thing in the world they wanted was for him to tell his story to a war-crimes commission. As long as Washington maintains its attitude, he and his colleagues are safe from trial and exposure.

Now, it is not hard to understand why Siam sided with Japan. For many years they had been given nothing but dirty deals by the British and French. They had been up against the soul-searing barricade of white superiority. In Japan's war on the white man, they saw a chance for the yellow races to reach a place of equality with the European bullies who had dominated them. They knew—and Britain's terribly harsh peace terms have proved them right—that unless Japan won they would be worse off than ever. I am glad that Washington has not been swayed by Britain's vindictiveness.

But if Washington thinks that its friendship will pay off in cash, the State Department may have another think coming. In his interview, Sidi Pramoj was quite frank about Siam's future economic plans. "We will shop around and buy in the best market, no matter what country it is, or what its politics. We hope to resume our trade with the United States, but—we must purchase where goods are cheapest." Before the war, it had been Japan which sold cheap silk and consumer goods to Siam, plus guns and warships, in return for rice and metals. This was a natural exchange between natural markets.

When we were in Siam, youthful King Anantha Mahiden (later shot to death on his return to Bangkok) was in Switzerland at school. We called on the regent in his airy stucco palace down by the waterfront. Regent Bayem Banomyong served warm beer in the pink-walled reception room with its Occidental porcelain bric-à-brac and its Oriental treasures. Banomyong was more outspoken than the prime minister, but like Sidi Pramoj he insisted that Siam should not be punished as a defeated nation. "The declaration of war was unconstitutional. I was then one of three regents and my name appears on the document—but it was a forgery." Maybe so. Also, Banomyong showed the same disposition as Pramoj to avoid "stepping on a fallen man." He thought it likely that Pibul had plotted in advance to turn Siam over to the Japs, but then, one couldn't be sure.

The regent was known in Bangkok as head of the resistance movement which was claimed to include a force of 10,000 "Free Thais" who built secret airdromes, hid American aviators from the Japs, and furnished target information by radio to Allied bombers. The story was that the underground forces had been ready to rise against the Japs, but had been told by the Americans and British to sit tight.

"How many guerrillas were there?" I asked the regent.

Banomyong smiled, "Well, we estimated ten thousand at the end of the war. However, the number is growing every day and there will probably be twenty-five thousand guerrillas in the parade next Tuesday."

Sure, the Siamese loved a parade and now that the war was over everybody in Siam was rushing to jump on the democratic band-wagon. With the shooting ended, everybody was a "guerilla."

Most of what I have written about Siam has been critical, but there is one thing I remember with pleasure. We saw one American there of the type that makes enemies for our country all over the world, one of the kind who could sabotage the most far-sighted foreign policy—if we had a foreign policy. He stood up in a truck driving through the streets of Bangkok and with loud shouts, threw cigarettes onto the pavement and gutter, expecting the people to scramble wildly for them. They didn't. Not even the ricksha boys. They just looked with contempt at the apparition, ignored the ciga-rettes, and kept on about their business. Just from that, I think there is hope for Siam—even if it is proved that the politicians are crooked.

Chapter Eighteen

French Colonials Are Sad Sacks

IT HAS LONG BEEN THE CUSTOM OF MANY FRENCH residents of French Indo-China to indulge in a little opium smoking in lieu of pre-dinner cocktails or post-prandial highballs. The French said opium "is very enjoyable and does you far less harm than alcohol." They added that if one reclined on a comfortable couch, preferably with a companion of the opposite sex and smoked a few pipefuls of the drug, the most pleasant dreams were experienced.

Now, flying down from Siam in October, 1945, we found the French living the most ghastly kind of nightmare—without benefit of opium.

The British were coming, hurrah, hurrah, but they were coming too late and with too few forces, for in the interval between the surrender of Japan and their arrival a full-fledged revolution had broken out in Indo-China and the French could do absolutely nothing at all to control the unruly natives whom they had governed with an iron hand for more than three-quarters of a century.

We landed at the Saigon airport in a fierce rainstorm, just missing the tall towers of Radio Saigon, and on the short watersoaked runway one of the tires of the B–17 blew out. This precipitated a hot argument between passengers and pilot, with the latter claiming that the mishap was not his fault. The verbal dueling was halted just short of fisticuffs by the arrival of an R.A.F. officer who jeeped over through the wet twilight to where we were standing, dripping, under the wing.

"Stop fighting among yourselves, chappies," he suggested. "There's plenty of that going on here already."

"What do you mean?" There had been only meager reports out of Indo-China since the surrender.

"The natives are revolting. They have the city surrounded and hold positions between the airfield and the center of town. I suggest you stay here tonight and meanwhile we'll get off a message to Calcutta asking for a new wheel and tire for your aircraft."

We still weren't convinced. What about the restaurants, the hotels, the famed night life modeled on the Parisian pattern? Weren't the French celebrating the victory over Japan, the regaining of this rich and fertile corner of Asia?

"You've been given a bad steer," said the R.A.F. man. "There's only one decent hotel and it's overflowing with French. One restaurant is open. You chaps don't understand that there's a war going on down here and it will be very dangerous until we get in enough troops to handle things."

Nevertheless, we insisted on going into Saigon and after we had stood in open trucks in the rain for an hour the British rounded up some Gurkha guards for us and sent us into the city. The quick, tropic twilight faded as we drove along country roads across the flat rice-lands, and it was late in the evening when we reached the main street of the Paris of the Orient and drove up to the Majestic Hotel, just recently vacated by the Imperial Japanese Army. The Japs had taken with them most of the plumbing fixtures, the beds, and even the mosquito nets, so we didn't get much sleep there during our stay. We walked out the first evening to the Rue Catinat, a narrow paved street that extends for a mile from the cathedral to the yellow and winding, swift-flowing Mekong River—the main artery of this port seventy miles inland from the South China Sea. French men and women in white clothes wandered up and down the Rue Catinat, whose sidewalk cafes and trees did remind you of a French provincial town. But the names on the stores were not so much French as Chinese, Indian, Japanese, and Siamese.

In the next few days in Saigon we were to get to know the French quite well, with that intimacy that comes quickly under the stress of shared danger. We disliked them thoroughly, even more than the British in Hong Kong or Singapore or the Dutch we were to meet in Java. Imperialism is a bad business at best, but when the conquering power is so strong that the oppressed people cannot hope to fight back then there is an outward appearance of orderliness and the scene is not messy. But when the superior beings are weak and ineffectual, when even their arrogance is stripped from them, then it is like a botched-up surgical operation with blood spurting on everyone and sticking to everything. As a general rule the people who go out from their homelands to live in foreign colonies or countries are second- and third-raters, mediocre businessmen who could not make a place for themselves at home and harassed missionaries who get an extra $250 yearly for each additional child and consequently raise large families. These people, American, British, French, Dutch, Portuguese, deliberately turn their backs on their homelands for most of their lives, taking the easy way out, avoiding the struggle against first-class competition and being rewarded with a life of relative luxury, many servants, and the illusion of being important. I think the Americans in the Orient stood up best of all under the impact of the Japanese wave that swept away that ease and luxury overnight. The British maintained some of their dignity, even in prison camps. But the French in Indo-China were something else. They not only were traitors to the cause of their homeland and of her allies, but cowards as well. They were really sad sacks.

We went into the Papillon restaurant the first night in Saigon and quickly ran into the nervous uncertainty and naked fear of the French men and women. Our idea that they might be celebrating proved ridiculous. All they could do was pray that the lights would stay on a little longer and that the rebellious Annamites would not attack the Rue Catinat. We had just crowded into a booth when two men walked over to shake hands. Major François Verger, a veteran of the French underground, was already known to us from England and France. With him was Lt. Colonel A. Peter Dewey, a slim European-educated American from Washington, D. C., who had served with the Polish and French resistance movements after representing a Chicago newspaper in pre-war Europe. Both Verger and Dewey had parachuted into Indo-China. To Verger, we brought the news that his American wife, War Correspondent Lee Carson, was about to get a divorce. We had no bad news for Dewey. But as he sat and talked to us over watered anisettes, the American had only sixty-four hours to live.

They told us what was happening. "The Annamites are revolting. They are willing to die rather than be colonists of France again. British Gurkha troops are opposing the Annamites and the Japs, who were supposed to be disarmed, are helping the British. It's a stinking mess."

200

The picture in Indo-China was this: Some 23,000,000 of Indo-China's 28,000,000 native inhabitants are Annamites and nearly all of them wanted to end France's eighty-year rule over their homeland, a territory as big as France itself and rich in coal and rice and other agricultural products. They had risen in arms once before in 1929, but the French machine-gunned and bombed them into submission. Now, the Japs had apparently given them their big chance for freedom from a regime whose colonial record was shameful. For instance, after eighty years in the colony, the French had permitted only five per cent of the people to learn to read and write.

Trouble came into Indo-China in 1940 when the Japs shot and bullied their way into the north, ostensibly for the purpose of closing off one of China's last supply routes through the Indo-Chinese port of Haiphong, from which a railroad heads into Chinese Hunnan. A year later, Vichy opened the door to Saigon and the south for the Japs, ignoring the obvious fact that they wanted Saigon as a springboard for their attacks on Singapore and the Dutch East Indies, and for their occupation of Siam. Economic agreements were reached between Tokyo and Vichy for the exchange of Indo-China's rice and metals for Japanese manufactured products. Instead of the 5,000 tons of rice they were getting, the French supplied Tokyo 1,000,000 tons annually to feed the Japanese troops who were shortly to besiege our starving forces in Bataan.

The Vichyites, headed by colonial governor Admiral Jean de Coux threw in their lot wholeheartedly with Japan and its Axis partners. That their own homeland was in Nazi chains meant nothing to these French Colonials. Their first concern was the preservation of their own interests and for three years—all during Pearl Harbor, Tarawa, Saipan, even the liberation of France—the Japanese occupation forces and the colonial French lived in perfect harmony, collaborating enthusiastically and doing business to their mutual profit.

With the collapse of Vichy, Admiral de Coux took over complete control in Indo-China with the support of the French Fascist, Pétainists, businessmen, and government officials, and the Banque de l'Indo-Chine clique—plus, of course, the Japs. Some Frenchmen and Annamites wanted to resist the Japs and made a brief stab at organizing an underground. They were ruthlessly suppressed by de Coux. Some were exiled to the penal colony of Poulo Condore, where conditions were so bad that they even horrified the Japs. Two Tokyo newspapermen who visited the island described finding 1,500 political prisoners who "were subjected by the French to all conceivable atrocities . . . who stood mute and expressionless like dumb animals."

A few French escaped to Allied territory, but not many of them could make the long trek to India or China through the Japanese lines. Not trusting the French Colonials, the United States made no serious effort to get arms to the few resistance leaders.

Major Verger told me, "There was no underground worthy of the name. A very few of the French assisted American aviators to escape after they were shot down, escorting them to the coast where they were picked up by submarines. There was one French captain who had a secret radio set and supplied important Intelligence information for our planes. Outside of that, I regret to say that my fellow countrymen did nothing to resist the Japanese or assist our forces. There was an army revolt in 1941 against admitting the Japanese to the colony without a struggle, but it was suppressed and the survivors either fled to China, were imprisoned, or abandoned their activities."

The French-Japanese honeymoon ended on March 9, 1945, when the Japanese suddenly surrounded the homes of de Coux and of the French officers and quickly disarmed the 6,000 French troops in southern Indo-China. Simultaneously the French in the north surrendered, and the French men and women were interned.

Then the Japs played their trump card. Knowing that Tokyo would surrender shortly and that the end for them was not far off, they permitted the Annamites to form their own government to replace the French regime. A coalition government of Communists and Nationalists was set up with branches in Hanoi and Saigon, and was promised complete independence by the Japanese. When Tokyo surrendered, the Japanese gave the Annamites some arms and told them to carry on with their government and defend their independence. Meantime, all during the war, the United States and the provisional government of France had been sparring about the future of Indo-China. Roosevelt fought the churlish deGaulle and the stubborn Churchill for a new status for all Asiatic colonies. For Indo-China he wanted an international trusteeship to pave the way for total freedom. But as soon as he was dead, Truman and Byrnes forgot his desires and concentrated on the "get tough with Russia" game to the oblivion of such trifling matters as freedom for a hundred million Asiatic colonials. During their wartime discussions, the French indicated their willingness to grant freedom "within the Indo-Chinese federation and French union, plus recognition of democratic liberties for all and education in native and French culture." But de-Gaulle and other officials made it clear that France renounced none of her Far Eastern possessions.

The situation was further complicated in the north by Chinese claims to the Tonkin area, which blocks Yunnan province's only convenient doorway to the outside world. Some 400,000 lived there and most of them looked to Chungking for guidance. With the end of the war, Chinese troops moved down from Yunnan into Tonkin and by Allied agreement occupied all of Indo-China north of the 16th parallel. But when the French tried to move their own armed forces into the area in March, 1946, again by Chinese-French agreement, Chinese forces around the port of Haiphong fired on their landing craft and warships. After finally getting ashore, the French found that the Chinese had not ousted the Annamite officials but had strengthened their position.

When we reached Saigon in October, 1945, the Annamites were still occupying the government buildings from which they had officially functioned since August 17th, when the Japanese installed them in complete power. They called their government the Viet Nam Republic, substituting that pre-colonial name for Indo-China, a French importation.

"Now," said Colonel Dewey on our first night in Saigon, "the British troops are driving them out. The Annamites are determined people and it is taking a lot of shooting."

The British commander, General D. D. Gracey, a self-proclaimed Tory and believer in Empire, was willing to use whatever means were necessary to restore white supremacy and try to rebuild the shattered self-confidence of the French. In negotiations with the Viet Nam prior to the landing of British troops, the British assured the Annamites that Gracey's mission was to disarm the Japanese and to restore order. The Annamites were foolish enough to believe that story. Instead of carrying out the promise, Gracey returned the Japanese troops to their posts, allowed them to keep their arms, and used them to attack the Annamites who were likewise using Japanese arms when they had any at all beyond sticks, clubs, and spears. Thus, as was to be the case in the Dutch East Indies, the British used their former enemies, the Japanese, to shoot down other Asiatics. If the Japanese were planning a comeback in later years in their "Asia for

203

Asiatics" campaign, they could not have asked for better propaganda ammunition.

Gracey's defense was: "What do you want? Do you think we will surrender European supremacy to the first group of outlaws that point guns at us?" In other words, the words not only of Gracey, but of his superior officers and the London Labor government—defend the Imperial system and the hell with these outlaws who believe in the Four Freedoms.

The French who saw us at first in Saigon cheered enthusiastically for the arrival of "les soldats Américains." They said openly, "Now we can put these Annamite beggars back in their places." They were crestfallen when we told them we weren't troops, but correspondents, and that no American forces were coming to the colony.

Actually, the American "forces" consisted of Colonel Dewey and his mission, plus a group of eight Air Transport Command personnel headed by Major Frank Rhoades. Dewey jumped from a transport plane into Saigon right after V–J Day and quickly got the 136 American war prisoners out of their camps and headed home. Then, instead of leaving, he got mixed up in a game that was too fast for him. "I am remaining to protect American property," he explained. What property? He had hung out the American flag from the offices of Standard Oil, Texaco, and Singer Sewing Machine. Also, he had intervened dramatically a few days before when Annamites had prepared to storm the Continental Hotel and threatened to kill the French people sheltered there. Dewey had bluffed the Annamites into believing the hotel was American property, exhibiting a "bill of sale" made over to him by the Corsican manager, and had waved the American flag to turn back the would-be attackers. Tragically enough, it was the lack of an American flag on his jeep that caused his death.

The British were more concerned in talking to us about the A.T.C. mission than about Dewey's. The A.T.C. men were under orders to set up a base on a line from Shanghai to Singapore, a "temporary" line to operate for a limited time. The British found that hard to swallow. "I understand," General Gracey told us, "that the A.T.C. is establishing a line to carry letters. Who the letters are from or what necessity there is for carrying them, I do not know." It was the suspicion of the British and the French that far from being temporary the American base was to be used by future American globe-girdling airlines. Since then, the Civil Aeronautics Bureau in Washington has licensed American routes to Indo-China and Siam.

If our arrival was a disappointment to the French, it was even more so to the Annamites. Like all of the people of Asia they looked to Americans in the first weeks after the surrender as true liberators and believers in democracy for everybody, everywhere. They hoped the United States would guarantee their freedom. They knew the French would not give an inch more than they had to, despite the "liberal" promises of deGaulle and his henchmen. If there had been any doubt in the minds of the Annamites about the French, it disappeared when the colonial overlords were released from internment after the Japanese surrender.

Feeling their oats once more, the French resumed their old habit of kicking around—literally—the despised natives. This was a grave mistake, because the French were not strong enough to get away with it pending the arrival of reinforcements, of guns, tanks, rifles, and hand grenades. Then the Annamites turned back on them and suddenly the French realized that they were dealing with people who were willing to give their lives to demonstrate to the world their desire for freedom. The Annamites were still fighting when the vanguard of British troops came in, and it was at this stage of the struggle that we reached Indo-China.

The Japanese just stood by and chuckled while the Annamites turned their arms on the French, kidnaped and killed many of the most hated of their tormentors, and drove the terrified Colonials out of their suburban homes and into a narrow section of Saigon paralleling the Rue Catinat. Inside the city the Annamites quit their jobs. Most of them faded away into the countryside, hiding in villages which the British troops attacked and burned in reprisal for attacks on their supply lines. The city, stripped of ninety per cent of its populace, was paralyzed. We found the water supply off, the lights working only fitfully. To the disgust of the French, who for years had been accustomed to regard their servants as pieces of furniture, the servants disappeared. There were no rickshas in the streets, no public transportation of any kind.

Along the Rue Catinat and the small "safe" area surrounding it, the French gathered in little worried knots. They were ashamed of their war record, their cooperation with the Japs, their inability to do anything now about the Annamite uprising. The men huddled in the cafes, unwilling even to take rifles and go out and protect their city. They shouted for more help—Japs, Gurkhas, Americans, it didn't matter—and they plotted how they would avenge themselves on the Annamites when their turn came.

Starting at seven in the morning, the French came out to parade up and down the Rue Catinat, stopping at the sidewalk cafes for an aperitif of anisette, ice, and water. At eleven they went into the few restaurants still open, but soon to close, and ate heartily for two hours and then disappeared for a siesta. About four in the afternoon, people started to emerge again and an hour before dusk everyone had gathered either in the candle-lit lobby of the Continental Hotel or on the sidewalk outside. We learned a new line there. All around the world, in Sicily, Italy, France, Germany, Egypt, the Philippines, Japan, young kids had approached us with outstretched hands and pronounced the local equivalent of *"cigarette pour papa."* In Saigon, Frenchmen stopped us on the street and, too ashamed to ask for themselves, begged, "A cigarette for my wife."

It was pitiful to watch the French when the sound of shooting was heard. One night a platoon of Japanese ran up on the double to take sentry positions outside the hotel, and there was a panicked rush for inside. Another night Annamites set fire to the market place four blocks from the Continental. The French, silent and terrified, refused to go near the fire—even though the supply of food was growing scantier every day—but the Chinese stall owners made frantic and futile efforts to drench the flame with small splashes of water from leaking buckets. Most of the time there weren't any lights and in the confusion of that pushing mass around the hotel, more than one Frenchwoman wound up in the room of an English officer or a correspondent. Despite this amateur competition, the bright-looking half-caste girls roaming the Rue Catinat did a big business.

During one outbreak of shooting, the owner of the Continental called us into his office for an aperitif with him and some friends.

"Why," they demanded in an aggrieved tone, "do not you protect us from those devil Annamites?"

We baited them, "This is not the quarrel of Americans. For all we know, justice is on the side of the rebels. We hear that the French have been inexcusably cruel to them. In fact, we would just as soon shoot French as Annamites." This last remark was accompanied by an ostentatious fingering of carbine triggers.

"Ah, monsieurs," the hotel owner gushed, "it is quite right that you are. All of us in this room are not French. You are surprised, no? The fact is that we do not come from Metropolitan France. We are Corsicans. This local political squabble is not of our making, but the fault of the French who have treated the Annamites inconsiderately."

Meantime, Frenchman and Corsican alike continued to plan for vengeance. They got it after the French troops under irascible General Jacques LeClerq finally arrived to take over behind Gurkha and Japanese guns. Witnesses later described the long lines of Annamite prisoners, manacled or trussed up, being marched down the Rue Catinat to the filthy jail, where they were fed miserably, given drumhead trials lasting a few minutes and then sentenced to many years at hard labor on Poulo Condore Island—or even condemned to die for distributing leaflets asking independence. In this and other ways, the French finally got retribution for the humiliation that we watched them undergo.

At night, Annamites would slip into the city, set fire to the power plant and other buildings, and shoot off their rifles. The harassed Gracey was unable to stop them with his small force, whose forays into the countryside and across the river to the Chinese quarter proved fruitless. He blamed the Japs for his troubles, accusing them of instigating the Annamites to fight, and at the same time he called on the Japs to assist him in putting down the fighting. In desperation, the British commander visited the home of the aged and ailing Japanese field marshal, Count Terauchi, and warned him that unless the Japs behaved themselves they "would not be sent back home to Japan." Gracey pointed out that the Allied plan was to repatriate the Japs in Nipponese shipping. Very few bottoms were available, Gracey said, and he threatened that unless Terauchi saw to it that his troops were good boys, no ships would come to Indo-China for them. This provided another big laugh for the Japs, who didn't care very much either way whether they stayed or went—after all, it was France that wanted the colony back.

Meantime, the fighting was getting sharper every night and more and more factories and homes were being burned by the Annamites. On the third night of our stay, Captain Joe Coolidge, a distant relative of the late Calvin and Colonel Dewey's No. 2 in the O.S.S., was shot through the throat and arm while escorting a group of French women and children through an Annamite barricade.

We got word of it through Colonel Dewey, who sent for us to come to his room at the Continental. Perhaps it was a premonition that made Dewey talk at length about something that was on his mind. He had been doing a great deal of running around in the midst of the fighting, and had found the Annamites friendly when they discovered him to be American. "It's the French they're after. Not us, nor even the British. They won't shoot at the Japanese at all." Dewey's difficulty was to identify himself as an American. "I had an American flag on my jeep," he said, "but General Gracey forbade me to fly it. When I go up to one of the barricades, there is always a chance that the Annamites will kill me before I can identify myself."

Several of us stormed up to see Gracey and protest against his refusal to allow the American flag to be flown from automobiles. "I cannot permit it," he said. "That is a privilege of general officers only." If you chose to be strict about it—and Gracey did, for obvious reasons of European Imperial prestige—the British general was correct in his position, according to military regulations. He went on to say that he had no objections to flags being painted on jeeps and cars, which was a meaningless concession in view of the total absence of paint in Saigon. Likewise, he agreed to flags being tied to the side of vehicles, but that was no assistance whatever since the important thing was to be recognized well before you drove up to a barricade, and a flag on the side was not visible from a distance.

The following day Colonel Dewey invited two of our party, Bill Downs and Jim McGlincy, to lunch at the O.S.S. house on the northern edge of Saigon. They drove out with Major Verger and with Captain Frank White, a member of the nine-man O.S.S. mission, and sat in the patio to have a drink and wait for Dewey to return from the airport.

Five minutes later there was heavy firing up the road, and an American officer came running toward the O.S.S. villa which was also, in effect, American Army headquarters in Saigon. The officer halted every few yards to crouch and fire his .45 back down the road at some invisible pursuers.

Hurriedly, Captain White issued carbines to the correspondents and to the other four men in the house, and they got behind the garden wall and fired at a crowd of Annamites who suddenly came into sight pursuing the American. The Annamites took cover—there were about a hundred of them—and the officer staggered into the yard behind the protective wall. He was Major Herbert Bluechel. His head, neck, shoulders, and most of his body was covered with blood and he appeared to be seriously wounded.

208

"They got the colonel," he gasped hysterically. "They killed the colonel."

The blood on Bluechel was Dewey's blood. The two Americans had been passing a barricade in their jeep. Dewey gestured to the Annamites ahead to remove the crisscrossed trees forming the road block, but they suddenly opened fire with a machine gun. The colonel's head was blown off. Bluechel, unharmed, jumped out of the jeep and sprinted frantically up the road.

"What a pity!" Bluechel exclaimed. "The Annamites liked Dewey and he liked them and he believed they should be free. If they had only recognized us as Americans, they would never have shot."

Meanwhile, the Annamites began pushing toward the house. The Americans ran inside and took positions at the windows. Like Dewey, they did not want to kill Annamites, but they were being fired upon and there was no choice except to shoot back. Yelling and shouting, the Annamites advanced down a drainage ditch parallel to the road, pausing from time to time to fire their guns. They were bad marksmen and although their bullets bounced off the house, none of the Americans was hit.

Spacing their shots, the Americans picked off the attacking men. Three fell as they tried to run across an open field. Several others were wounded. Bill Downs shot down at least one man, and he says that the sight of the little brown figure falling will haunt him for years. But blood was being shed, hysteria had taken command, and there was no chance to stop and argue things out.

Briefly, the Annamites retired, and then returned with a machine gun. They fired one burst into the front of the house and then ceased fire. In this interlude a jeep with three more O.S.S. men drove squarely down the road without drawing a single shot, and turned into the yard. Meantime, six Japanese sentries who were on duty guarding the villa had taken a casual part in the fighting, firing once or twice but mostly just crouching out of the way.

After more than two hours of skirmishing, the Annamites began to withdraw, and McGlincy and Downs volunteered to walk across the fields and try to reach the airport in search of reinforcements. They took their sidearms for defense, a bottle of "Old Crow" for courage, and on the theory that nobody will shoot at a singing man they walked along caroling at the top of their voices, "For he's a jolly good fellow." They made it to the airfield without trouble and dispatched a message for help. Then the two correspondents, with Major

Rhoades of the A.T.C., drove back in a jeep through the Annamite positions, where a group were picking up wounded under a Red Cross flag. The Americans waved their arms and shouted, "Chee-Wee, Chee-wee," which means American in the Annamite tongue.

Back at the house, the Americans decided to go out after Dewey's body. Major Verger took the precaution of changing his French army shirt for an American jacket. He tied a white handkerchief to his carbine and waved as the jeep gingerly approached the Annamite positions. "Where is the commandant?" McGlincy demanded of the sentries.

An excited young man—in civilian shirt and shorts like the other fighters for freedom—stepped forward and delivered a fiery speech on liberty and the rights of man, intermingled with violent protests against the Americans, who loved liberty, killing Annamites who sought it. Another young Annamite, about sixteen or seventeen, assisted in translating the leader's discourse.

Downs explained, "We would like to get Colonel Dewey's body."

There were lengthy negotiations, and finally the commander agreed to return Dewey's body if the Americans would bring back the bodies of the Annamite casualties. These terms were accepted. The Americans drove back to the scene of the battle, picked up three bodies, and piled them on the hood of the jeep.

When they returned to the barricade, the Annamite leader became even more violently excited. "Three for one is not fair exchange," he protested through the interpreter.

"Where is Colonel Dewey's body?" Downs asked.

"It is not here," the young man said. "I cannot go through with this agreement when you ask three for one." The Americans insisted that they had kept their part of the bargain.

The negotiations were broken up suddenly by the sound of firing. A group of Gurkhas were coming down the road, shooting off their rifles and driving before them a terrified group of native refugees, mostly women and children. The Annamites at the barricade glared at the Americans, as if they suspected that the negotiations had been a trap to hold them until the Gurkhas arrived. Then they faded away into the woods and behind nearby houses.

Dewey's body was never recovered. For months afterward the French used the missing American's body—the body of a man who believed they should be free—as a bargaining point against the natives. They refused to enter discussions until the body was produced and the Viet Nam government even offered a reward for the corpse.

Reports of Dewey's death in his flagless jeep—there had been a flag but it was wrapped around a pole and thus unidentifiable—quickly reached Lord Louis Mountbatten in Singapore as our stories went out. He sent an urgent message to General Gracey to fly down to Singapore and report on the incident, and the general asked for a lift in our B–25, which had returned after making a trip to Calcutta to pick up equipment for our crippled B–17. As we drove to the airport, we passed through a deathly quiet mile of no-man's land, with torn trees and the bodies of animals on the road—souvenirs of the Gurkhas drive the day before. Native villages along the road were aflame, and here and there Frenchmen crouched behind the stone walls of fine villas. Every few hundred yards there was a Japanese soldier with a rifle and a bayonet—unconcernedly guarding our route. Our own carbines and pistols were cocked as we peered over the sides of the truck.

Throughout the night there had been the sound of drums and shouting from the perimeter around the city and sporadically the noise of shots smashing into buildings. Circling over the city in the B–17 we counted a half dozen large fires, several of them quite close to the besieged Rue Catinat. These fires were symbolic funeral pyres of many natives, for the French came back in and with American arms and with the help of the British engaged in bloodletting and slaughter. But eventually they would be the signal fires of freedom.

Chapter Nineteen

The King's Cousin, the Coal
Miner, and the Sultan

THE GREAT WALL OF CHINA WAS A SMART IDEA—IN
its time.

So was the Singapore Naval Base. It cost $50,000,000 to build and
millions more to furnish and man. Its eighteen-inch guns could toss
huge shells for twenty miles to sea—in certain directions. It was considered impregnable until 1942 when the Japs came from the other
direction, crashed through the back door in a terribly brief period of
days, and hauled down the Union Jack which had flown over the
island for more than a hundred years.

This loss was as much of a shock to Britain as the collapse of
France's Maginot Line. Singapore was the eastern anchor of Empire,
and Malaya one of the richest jewels in the imperial diadem. The
Singapore base had an interesting background. In the early days of
this century, British imperialism in Asia began to fret a great deal
about Czarist Russian expansion toward the Pacific and toward India, and Britain decided to play off Japan against the Russian Bear.
In 1902, London signed a five-year alliance with Japan, the first treaty
of modern times between states of the Western and Eastern worlds,
and an especially important document because Japan was recognized
in the treaty as an equal.

Thus backed, Japan went to war with Russia and, thanks in no
small part to the Portsmouth Treaty, came out the winner with a
stranglehold on Korea and the Kwantung Peninsula. In the World
War, Japan's navy performed important chores in escorting Aus-

tralian and New Zealand fighting troops to the European front, but when the Anglo-Japanese treaty came up for renewal in 1922, Britain did not renew it. This action, forced in the main by American and Canadian fears of the growing Japanese strength, was taken at the time of the Washington Naval Conference.

At that meeting, a dirty trick was played on the Japs. The British agreed that they would not fortify Hong Kong, which the Japanese regarded as a threat to them, and in return the Japs promised not to fortify the mandated islands of the Pacific which had been their prizes for participation in World War I. After everything was signed, sealed, and delivered, the House of Commons threw a bombshell at Japan by announcing that a great naval base would be built at Singapore—outside of the agreed-upon, non-fortified area. The United States had known all along that this was to be done and indeed had agreed to it. Before long, the United States fleet moved to the Pacific, while Britain's stayed in European waters. Japan saw this as American underwriting of European imperialism in Asia, and as the first definite lining up of White forces against Yellow. Very shortly, Tokyo said to hell with naval treaties.

So the naval base was built, paid for in part by profits of the government opium monopoly. Its guns commanded the straits through which ships proceeded from Europe to Asia and return. Each year 30,000 ships put into Singapore to load and unload cargoes. Malaya supplied three-fourths of the tin and three-fifths of the rubber used in the United States each year. The British like to tell a "romantic" story about how the rubber industry started. A gallant chappie named Sir Henry Wickham had smuggled rubber seeds from Brazil to Kew Gardens in 1876 and two years later seedlings were sent to Singapore. From this patriotic theft had grown a huge and profitable industry.

The tin business was less romantic but no less profitable. British cartelists controlled not only the production but the smelting. Thus tin ore which Americans bought in Malaya had to be shipped to England for smelting. The British, like the United States, sold to all comers, including Japan, which even had pre-war concessions to mine iron ore. That the Japs were making the iron into missiles to kill Chinese did not bother the British, as was explained by one of the Singapore papers: "Japan needs increasing quantities of iron, perhaps for purposes of which Malaya does not approve, but it would be futile trying to starve her of them by irritating restrictions. On the contrary we should be grateful to her mining companies for seeing the possibilities of Malaya's resources. . . ."

That gratitude disappeared in the dreadful days of February, 1942, when Singapore was going down in smoke and flame. Some of the signs of those days were still visible as we flew down from Saigon, crossing the Straits of Johore which separate Singapore Island from the State of Johore, which is the most southerly part of Malaya and of the Asiatic mainland. Wrecks of partially sunk Japanese ships stood up above the mile-wide waters and the great naval base—which Britain had pronounced in 1941 to be capable of sheltering and repairing the warships of all "Britain's allies and prospective allies"—still showed scars of the damage done by B–29s.

There were tall and solid buildings in Singapore, and the homes of the Taipans quite fittingly decorated the green hillsides, but somehow the city had the look of the overgrown fishing village which it is. It reminded you of Tonga Tabu or Suva, Fiji.

The R.A.F. officer who jeeped over to our plane was surprised to see us. "Where are your papers, old boy?" he asked Colonel McCrary, the head of our party. Of course, McCrary didn't have any papers. But he spotted Lord Louis Mountbatten's big de luxe plane parked alongside of ours and he said, "The supreme commander invited us down." Which he had—in a way. What saved us was that General Gracey, the commander in Saigon, had flown down with us to report to Mountbatten on the death of Colonel Dewey. So the R.A.F. men dug up a couple of trucks and we drove into the town and to Raffles Hotel.

Raffles Hotel was itself a monument to Empire. It bore the name of Sir Stamford Raffles who had raised Britain's flag and kept it flying in this distant outpost halfway around the world from London and only sixty miles north of the equator. The building was romantic and storied, a setting often used in adventure novels and movies of the Orient. In the rambling structure, planters once sat in their white suits and discussed the price of rubber over stengahs or gin pahits, or celebrated with champagne the latest Tory victory back home. Now it was overcrowded with recently rescued civilians from the internment camps; thin people—but not so thin as those in Manila—with the inevitable look of confinement that takes a long time to wear off. It was evident from the angled eyes of some of the smaller children, and from their complexions, that the once so sharply drawn line between the men of Britain and Asiatic women had not survived the

214

war. Proximity had been the bed-maiden of miscegenation. In the old days, those coffee-colored, lively kids and their plainly Oriental mothers would not have felt at home in Raffles; and indeed it was serving them now only as a temporary shelter until they could be moved out and the pukka sahibs came back to resume rubber planting, harvesting, and tin mining.

A good many of the real big guns of the rubber business had succeeded in being exchanged by the Japs and had returned to England by diplomatic ship to sit out the war. But a few had been interned, and we talked to them in Raffles over lemonades served by British Tommies from a NAAFI refreshment bar. A gaunt-faced man with gray hair and a guardsman's mustache said, "Funny thing, but these Jap blighters did not destroy the rubber trees. We estimate ninety per cent of production can be resumed within a year. We hear, though, that this business of synthetic rubber has come along fast during the war. Do you think it will ever take the place of natural rubber?" Not, we ventured, for some years to come; and this prediction was fulfilled a few months later when the United States began buying large quantities of crude from the again-producing rubber plantations of Malaya.

We turned the discussion to the uprising in French Indo-China. Would there be revolution here in Malaya?

"Oh, no," the planters said. "These people have no political consciousness." Naturally not, when their education had been limited to training them to plant rubber trees and work as clerks in government offices or for British exporting and importing firms. Politically Malaya was the most backward part of southeastern Asia, and its population of Malayans, Chinese, Indians, Burmese, and Siamese had never united to seek their independence or even a measure of self-government. It was this political disorganization that caused the Japs to rely chiefly on their own military government during the occupation, rather than establish influential puppet regimes as they had in the surrounding countries. The Malayans had not fought against Japanese seizure of their country, but neither did they turn around and fight the British when they returned to take over and disarm the Emperor's troops.

"We know how to handle the colored man here," the planters went on, "but the French and Americans don't. The French are too tough and the Americans too soft. There can be no equality with an Asiatic. Give him a whiff of equality and he wants the whole bottle. You'll find in China that as soon as the White Man is no longer master, the Chinese will make it impossible for you to live in his country. The Oriental understands only force!"

"And how about the Philippines?" we asked. "Oh," the planters shrugged, "that's different." America's program in the Philippines had certainly been different from England's in Malaya. In return for the sugar and gold we took out of the Philippines and for the bases we established there, we had at least given the Filipinos schools and public health and had tried to prepare them for self-government. Britain had given Malayans a subsistence standard of living in return for the great Singapore Naval Base, whose "impregnability" proved to be a myth when Japan attacked.

All during the war there had been rumors of something sour in the surrender of 60,000 Australian and other Empire troops at Singapore in February, 1941, while Bataan and Corregidor were still holding out with smaller forces. There had been tales of mutiny and near-mutiny among the Australian forces which were larger than the Jap invading armies. It was rumored that the Aussies had thrown down their guns rather than be killed fighting for rubber plantations "owned by those old school tie barstards in London." We inquired among the released prisoners. They admitted that morale had been low once the Japanese had landed on the Malayan coast and worked their way swiftly down through the jungles and into positions at the back door of Singapore, where the fixed guns of the naval base could not be swung around to fire on them. "But there was no mutiny, nor anything like it," they said. "The R.A.F. blokes put up a good show in their old planes as long as they lasted. The Navy got itself sunk by Jap planes. But once the Japanese began crossing the Straits of Johore and landing on Singapore Island the game was up and everybody knew it. The whole thing was useless; no help was in sight, and the psychology was to try to escape from a death trap and live to fight another day. When some of the top commanders left, it didn't do morale any good. Everybody who could, grabbed a boat and beat it for Sumatra or Java. The rest of us surrendered rather than wait to get killed."

A good many of the Australians were to wish later that they had been killed instead of surrendering. Thousands and thousands of them died in captivity, slaving on the jungle railroad which took a higher toll of Allied lives than any other single prisoners' work project carried out under the guns of Japanese sentries. Now the surviving Australians were sitting in Raffles, sipping lemonade, and getting ready, at long last, to go home.

From Raffles we went up to Government House where we had the rare opportunity of seeing the old Britain and the new together in the same room in this, once again, great bastion (except for the A-Bomb) of farflung Empire. The age-old Britain was personified by Lord Louis Mountbatten, cousin of His Majesty the King, and the new by plain Mr. Jack Lawton, ex-miner and now British Secretary of State for War. Our first impression was this: The aristocrat and the miner in Britain may fight over the wages of men in the coal pits; they may disagree violently and even bloodily over such matters as unemployment insurance and old-age pensions and the amount of taxes to be paid by the wealthy. But when it comes to the Empire, you will find them standing shoulder to shoulder, waving Union Jack for Union Jack.

Our party, and the English and Australian correspondents in Singapore, were invited at sixty-thirty in the evening to Government House, where we stood for a quarter-hour on the thick red carpets and drank iceless whiskey drowned in water and waited for the bigwigs to appear. Government House is a noble structure, a fitting dwelling place for the proconsuls of imperialism. It stands on a high hill overlooking the sprawling city, and it is palatial in its spaciousness, its vast grounds, high-ceilinged rooms, and long, wide halls. British paratroop sentries did a formal present arms in heel-clicking cadence as our jeeps drove up.

Mountbatten seemed to bound up the stairs to greet us as "unexpected visitors." He was obviously surprised to find us there. Dicky —as his chums Noel Coward and Edward, Duke of Windsor, call him—is very tall and very handsome, as everyone knows from his pictures, and no small amount of fun has been poked at him because of his manly beauty. Also, during the time when his command was at the end of the line of war priorities and he had no troops, planes, or ships to enable him to do more than harass the Japs, it became fashionable to refer to him by the odious nickname of "Lord-Noncombatten." Actually, to use one of Lord Dicky's favorite words, Mountbatten was in the best tradition of the dashing English fighting man —the kind of leader you would like to serve with, or under, in a slugging match at sea; or to have lead your bomber formation on an especially tough mission, or command your ground troops in an assault that required plenty of nerve and intelligence and coolness.

217

The wartime mission of Mountbatten's Southeast Asia Command (SEAC) had been the reconquest of the European colonial areas of Southeast Asia, namely Burma, Malaya, and Singapore, French Indo-China and the Netherlands East Indies. They had already retaken one British sphere—Burma—and were to have attacked and recaptured Malaya in September, 1945, an operation which was turned into a peaceful occupation by the Japanese surrender. SEAC was mostly a British show, which means that the men who died that imperialism might live were mostly Indian, native South African, and Chinese troops, together with some British and American fliers and infantrymen. That SEAC was British was no accident. England, more than any other power, had lost face as a result of Japan's early conquests and England wanted the major share in getting back the lost colonies. The British wanted to fight not in Okinawa, or in Japan proper or in China, but in areas where the natives could see them and be once again impressed by the strength of the white man with his colored-skinned troops who died for him.

And because any weakness in the system of European colonialism would be a reflection on England's position also, the British wanted to get back not only their own colonies but those of France and Holland as well. This was why the British poured troops into the N.E.I. and French Indo-China after the surrender and promptly turned their guns—and those of the Japanese—on the liberty-seeking natives. Britain "had to" do this for two reasons: first of all, she frankly admitted needing the goods and trade of southeastern Asia, which meant prolonging the colonial system even at the price of holdup and mass murder, and secondly she expected that France and Holland would return the favor by joining the western European bloc against Russia.

Meanwhile, the United States was, to all public appearances, keeping hands off in recognition of the fact that most Americans abhorred what the British, French, and Dutch were doing. That great statesman, James F. Byrnes, attempting to quell American indignation, told the British to remove "Made in U.S.A." labels from the arms with which they were murdering Indonesians. Then it would be all right, said Mr. Byrnes, for the British to use them.

And Lord Louis Mountbatten (formerly Battenberg), that fine and handsome gentleman, was the man who was using them now. He was no gallant soldier now, but a man in the dirty business of imperialism—a business that required neither courage, brains, nor

218

sangfroid. It was his duty, carrying out the edicts of the British Labor government, to order British (and Japanese) troops to kill the native peoples who wanted their freedom. At the time of our meeting with him in Singapore, our immediate concern as reporters and Americans with Mountbatten's business was that our fellow American, Lt. Col. Dewey had lost his life when he became involved in this killing. The handsome Lord Louis anticipated our questions.

"I understand," he said, "that someone of you wishes to question me about the American flag on Colonel Dewey's jeep. I understand your position is that Colonel Dewey would not have been killed if he had been permitted to fly the American flag. Now, my commander in Indo-China, General Gracey, tells me that he advised all foreign nationals in Saigon to paint their country's flag on both sides of their cars and to fly a flag across the radiator, so that there could be no chance of mistaken identity.

"I am also told," he went on, "that Colonel Dewey did quite a bit of running about during the shooting. That can be quite dangerous. Also that he would not accept an escort of Gurkhas that was offered to him and that, against advice, he selected a house outside the perimeter held by our troops."

Jim McGlincy pointed out that the last two statements were correct. "But, sir," he added emphatically, "the part about the flags is bunk. Dewey was forbidden to fly the flag from his jeep. As for the painting, there was no red, white, and blue paint in Indo-China, so General Gracey's order was an absurdity."

"So sorry," murmured the graceful Englishman.

I asked Lord Louis if Dewey had been on his staff. "No," he came back quickly, "he was on General Donovan's staff. You know, the O.S.S. . . ." He held up his left arm in front of his face, like a mysterious figure shrouding his feature with a dark cloak, placed his right forefinger over his lips and whispered, "Shhhhssss. Cloak and dagger."

Mountbatten announced that he had a treat for us. Mr. Jack Lawton, minister of the new Labor government, was staying with him at Government House and would come up shortly to meet us. Lord Louis gave Lawton a tremendous buildup and every few minutes he would interrupt our questioning to say, "The secretary should be here shortly." He did it so dramatically that we expected Lawton to appear on a pillar of fire. When Lawton did finally walk up the wide stairway and stand beside Mountbatten, there was no fanfare of

219

trumpets or roulade of drums. He was there suddenly, a white-haired man in tropical battle dress without ornament or decoration.

A greater contrast in men and personalities is hard to imagine. Mountbatten, tall, dignified, and unobtrusively but inescapably the English gentleman in his white admiral's shorts and shirt. And Lawton, a short, aggressive man with pugnacious chin and a sideways, thin slit of a mouth, belligerently and inescapably working at being the underdog—the poor but honest laboring man risen to power. But Lawton, as Secretary of State for War, shared the responsibility for the fact that British troops were shooting down unarmed natives in Indo-China (and a day later were to start doing the same thing in the Dutch East Indies) and that Great Britain was using Japanese troops to fight against these same natives. Neither Lawton nor Mountbatten offered any excuse for this overnight alliance between the British forces of so-called democracy and the Japanese whom they had denounced the day before as brutal barbarians. Neither of them put into words the obvious answer, from the British point of view, that the "nigger" must be once again subjected to the Royal Dutch Shell and the French business empire, and if you had to use Jap troops to do it, that was all right, too. In fact there was a precedent for it right here in Singapore, for Jap forces had aided the British in quelling a mutiny during World War I.

As Lawton chatted nervously, Mountbatten began to fidget more and more, swinging his arms and pounding one fist with the other. All during the interview he had exhibited signs of the typical English gentleman's self-consciousness, acting as if he were balanced on pogo sticks, but now the symptoms became more pronounced.

"What the hell is the matter with him?" I whispered to an English colleague.

"He's embarrassed by this ruddy bloke," was the answer. It should be stressed that my colleague works for a paper which was definitely not pro-Labor in the British elections of 1945.

Finally, Mountbatten dashed off down the stairs, muttering something about "must take my shower." An Australian woman correspondent started to dash off after him and then, considering his destination, stopped with a profane "Bugger!"

"I came here to see Supremo," she announced loudly. "And now he hares off to the shower. Bugger!" The Australian girl called Mountbatten "Supremo." They all did in Singapore, even in the newspapers. We called him "Sir."

220

While Mountbatten enjoyed the refreshing coolness of a shower pumped through the pipes from Singapore's undamaged water works, we questioned the war minister. Did he have any plans for studying the independence movements in French Indo-China and in Java? Were there any plans to grant Malaya a measure of self-government? Did the British Labor government, which sought increased freedom for the Englishman at home, have any plans to aid the peoples of Asia in obtaining some small share of independence? No, said Mr. Lawton, there were no such plans.

An Indian correspondent, turbaned and in white gown, asked, "Does the Secretary think the British troops will object to being asked to shoot down or fight against people seeking their independence?"

Lawton answered in a broad accent, "I've been negotiating for twenty years and ye'll not catch me with such questions as that." Eventually, however, he did state that Britain's policy in southeastern Asia was "to carry out its obligations to the United Nations," but he did not know what those obligations were.

Then he put his finger on the reason why the British Labor government, like Churchill, is not eager to preside at the "dismemberment of the British Empire." "Yes," said Lawton, in answer to a question, "I am confident that we can handle the problem of reconversion and reemployment. We'll not let the same things happen that did after the last war—a boom for twelve months and then unemployment and hunger that was felt worst in the depressed areas. I am a working man and I lived in those depressed areas, and I know myself what they are. I walked into a shop here this afternoon and they have no goods at all except those in the window. I'm sure we'll be busy for a long time supplying their demands." So here was why Britain needed Empire, needed markets—the factory worker in Birmingham and the man at the cotton loom in Lancashire would have employment filling the shop windows in Singapore. If the storekeeper in Malaya didn't purchase British goods, the English laborer wouldn't have enough pounds, shillings, and pence in his weekly envelope to insure full bellies for little Tom, Dick and 'Arry.

What Lawton was saying made sense to any Englishman. The British had no stupid delusions about Four Freedoms for Asiatics. They were fighting to reconquer markets. In their wartime "background" propaganda circulated to commentators and editorialists interested in southeastern Asia, the London government passed over the "moral issues" of war in a few sentences and went on to say, "The fact remains that we have got an additional motive because a great deal of our own children's bread and butter depends on the Far East. That is to say, we as a commercial nation need a rising standard of living in the Far East if our own is to be so much as maintained." Pointing out the countless products Britain needed from southeastern Asia—rubber, petroleum, tea, sugar, rice, lead, teak, quinine—the circular stated, "Britain will have to export about fifty per cent more than in pre-war years to balance its initial accounts and maintain its standard of living."

Why, you ask, couldn't Britain grant the Malayans some political independence and still sell them British goods? The answer is that unless they were forced to Buy British the people of Malaya would purchase the same items cheaper, and sometimes better, from Bombay or Shanghai or Tokyo or San Francisco, and would dispose of their own products elsewhere at better prices. Then the British would be out in the cold, they would have less to eat and wear, and that they couldn't afford.

That's the trouble with imperialism. Once you force a people to become dependent on you, you become dependent on them and when they want to break the relationship, when they want their freedom, you can't afford to give it to them. You have to maintain your relationship by killing, if necessary, and that is what Mountbatten, Lawton, and the rest were doing when we saw them in the fine big government palace in Singapore.

Before long, Mountbatten came bounding back up the stairs. He had changed to green jungle dress with four rows of decorations across the chest of his jacket. With him was another of Britain's great and dashing war heroes, Lt. General Miles Browning, paratrooper, commando and husband of novelist Daphne du Maurier.

The Australian woman correspondent shouted, "There's Supremo!" She burst through the circle and over to the top of the stairs, where she linked her arm in Louis', turned him about, and headed him back down. They had descended a few steps when they met Lady Mountbatten coming up, a squarish blonde woman in semi-uniform with two decorations. The Australian dropped Lord Louis like a hot cake and leeched onto his wife, talking with machine-gun rapidity. Mountbatten joined our group and chatted affably for a while—all strictly off the record. Then, with an airy, "Goodbye, chaps. I do hope you'll be comfortable," he half-loped out of the room. His wife followed at a more sedate pace.

We piled into a big Packard sedan to drive back to Raffles for dinner. The Australian woman was jubilant. "Well, pets," she announced, "I got me story! Asked them about their love life and they said they were much too busy. I got a lot of intimate, boudoir angles for the woman's page. Let's get drunk to celebrate me scoop."

The English correspondents did not even cable a line of Jack Lawton's interview. He had said the same things before in India and Hong Kong. But one did send a service message to his imperialist editor in London: "Lawton's press conference miserable failure his references to forty years in coal pits puzzling to Americans seeking information about Britain's southeast Asia policy." That was not exactly fair to Mr. Jack Lawton, who had been given his instructions in London and would have caught hell if he had exceeded them.

Meanwhile, troops of Jack Lawton's war ministry under Lord Louis' command were shooting down the men of Asia but there was no shooting here in Malaya. Britain's colonial record here had been shockingly bad, but Japan had not been much more successful. It is true that during the occupation Singapore had been the headquarters for the Indian patriot Subhas Chandra Bose's independence army, and a good many Malayans, Burmese, Siamese, and Indo-Chinese had joined that anti-white organization together with thousands of overseas Indians. Bose's troops did cross the border of India side by side with the Japanese, but his dreams were destined to failure and he was not to live to see India at last freed from the claws of the British Lion.

Now, to all outward appearances, the Chinese and Malayans were not unhappy at having the British back in Singapore. There was not a single case of a Chinese or Malayan shooting a British soldier; the people turned out en masse to cheer the arrival of the imperial troops. Possibly because the presence of so many Chinese in Malaya complicated the situation, the average Japanese soldier had treated the Malayans with the same stupidity that had defeated Tokyo's long-range plans for winning the friendship of China. Instead of proclaiming themselves liberators of Chinese and Malayans alike—both fellow Asiatics—the Japanese had tried to drive a wedge between the two races by favoring the Malayans and mistreating the Chinese. Their scheme backfired. (The fact that the Chinese outnumbered the

223

Malayans in the latter's own country was no more an accident than was the British leadership of SEAC. The British had brought the Chinese there to help them keep the Malayans in line and the Chinese, shortsighted and avaricious, had obligingly done this chore.)

One afternoon in Raffles I talked to an Australian ex-prisoner of war over lemon squashes. How had it been for three and a half years as a prisoner of the Japs?

"Bloody awful," the Aussie said.

"Worst thing," he went on, "was that you were subject to the whims of the man running the camp you happened to be in. Some of them were perfect barstards. They would feed you or not, according to their whim of the moment. There was even one barstard made us work at double time. They got him now and are going to try him as a war criminal."

Street scene, Singapore, later the same day:

Two hundred Jap prisoners, most of them in shorts and sneakers and nothing else, were tearing down a blast wall—a large barricade of earth enclosed by wooden boards which were held upright by poles cut from tree trunks. Indian guards lolled under the shade of trees. An English captain was seated in a wicker chair under a store awning, smoking and looking bored.

"How are they taking it?" we asked.

"Big," the Englishman answered. "Watch this."

He called over a Jap major and snapped out an order. The Jap stood stiffly at attention, saluted rigidly, and then turned away, apparently very happy. He shouted an order to the other prisoners. Immediately, all of them doubled the speed of their work. Those carrying earth-filled baskets on poles across their shoulders ran from the blast wall to a hole 200 yards away, dumped the baskets, and then ran back at double time. Sweat poured from their brown backs.

"See," said the British captain, "that officer is pleased as punch and so are the men. All they want is an order to obey."

"How long do you work them?" I asked.

The Englishman yawned and looked at his watch. "Let's see. It's two now and I'm supposed to work them to four, and if I'm not satisfied I can work them four hours more and then four hours after that and so on, just so long as I get them back to their barracks in time to go out for their next job in the morning. All depends on how I feel."

He pointed to a big-bellied Jap major. "See that blighter? He's no good, the worst man of all. Even the Japs hate him. I'm not going to give him any food this evening. Hasn't worked enough to suit me today."

He lit a cigarette. "As for the rest, I think I'll let them off at four. Have a date tonight"—big wink—"new batch of nurses just got in today."

This story is reported not to arouse any sympathy for the Japs, but rather to attempt to throw some light on the difference between their mentality and ours. There can be no sympathy for the men who starved and beat 56,000 men to death on the notorious jungle railway. The point is that with the shoe now on the other foot, the Japanese were accepting their lot without the slightest complaint against the whims of their conquerors. *They* could not understand, or pretended not to understand, our indignation over the way they treated our prisoners. To their way of thinking, it is the right of the victor to do what he likes with the defeated.

The Japanese had no feeling of guilt, not even the Butchers of Bataan or the assassin-guards in the prison camps. General Massaharu Homma, who went to his death before a firing squad for the Bataan death march, was amazed at the anger aroused in the United States by that parade of "grim, gaunt, ghostly" Americans and Filipinos. "I didn't think it was such a tough march," Homma said.

Now, as the defeated, these Japs in Singapore were doing what they were told and were ready to accept without complaint whatever fate held in store for them. It is the nature of the Jap that he feels most at peace with himself when obeying orders, whether from his father, his sergeant, his general, his Emperor; from MacArthur, or an English captain in Singapore. Regardless of the origin of the orders, he carries them out as quickly and efficiently as possible.

There were a few faded pictures of Tojo still clinging to walls in Singapore, and across the Straits of Johore we found the mate to the Japanese warlord's Samurai swords—one of which had nearly been liberated by photographer George Burns on the day Tojo shot himself. It was a beautiful sword, encased in brocaded silk over its polished leather holder, and its current owner was the Sultan of Johore, legendary ruler of 7,000,000 Mohammedans living in the State of Johore.

"I'll take this damn thing to England on my next trip," the Sultan said, "and give it to the king. What the hell good is it to me?"

The sword was just one of the many presents that the Japanese showered on Johore in an effort to make friends with him and win him to their "Asia for the Asiatics" program. There was no way for us to tell what the Sultan's inner feelings had been about the matter. If he really did hate the white man and subscribed to Japan's propaganda, he had been too intelligent to make any public statements to that effect. Thus his record was clear. He did receive Tojo and other Jap leaders in his home, but he had no choice about that. He and his Viennese-born wife were virtual prisoners during the whole Japanese occupation in one of their smaller "palaces"—actually it was just an airy, expensively furnished villa overlooking the straits and Singapore Island beyond.

I had expected a tall, thin, severe man with a turban around his austere head, but when the Sultan walked out into the garden to meet us at nine in the morning, a half hour early for the appointment arranged by British correspondent Dickson Brown, he turned out to be vigorous and alert, for all his seventy-odd years, and far from austere. His hair was white and he smiled in friendly fashion from behind his horn-rimmed spectacles. His khaki shorts were amply filled, which seemed to testify that at least he had eaten well under Japanese occupation, but despite the bulge above his belt he looked as if he could still play a fast game of polo. His fifth wife, some thirty years younger, was an attractive brunette. Five years of each other's company, without the diversions of world travel and the luxuries they formerly enjoyed on the Sultan's multimillion-dollar income, might easily have caused them to become a trifle bored with one another's company. The contrary seemed to have been the case, and they appeared genuinely attached to each other.

As religious leader of a people forbidden to indulge in alcohol or to covet an infidel woman, the Sultan enjoyed special privileges which he exercised in more ways than by his marriage to a succession of foreigners. Now, when we called on him, he clapped his hands and a servant brought excellent dry champagne, already iced. His Royal Highness sipped a glass of sauterne slowly, which was a decided change of pace from the old days when he tore through the streets of Singapore in his powerful cars, driving terrified pedestrians to the alleyways for safety. The British had finally ordered a curfew for him, forcing him to return across the Causeway to his own state

226

before dark. The Sultan had resented that order bitterly, but from the way he talked he had found the British restrictions far more bearable than "house arrest" at the hands of the Japs.

His speech had no trace of Oxford; it sounded more Australian plus Pacific-island pidgin. But perhaps he was talking down to a Yank.

"These damn Japs used to come here and spit and throw their cigarettes on the carpet," he said. Then, remembering his hospitality, he asked his wife to pass cigarettes, apparently convinced that we would use ashtrays instead of the rug. She produced, with apologies, a heavy silver case containing four Jap cigarettes and one mildewed Lucky Strike. "I've been saving it for years for the first American to come here," she explained. Fortunately, we had some fresher ones.

"Yes," His Royal Highness went on, "that Tojo came here and sat right where you are sitting, and do you know what he told me? He said that now Malaya had been captured the Japanese were going into Burma, then into India, meet the Germans at the Suez Canal, and then cross the Atlantic to attack the United States and end the war in Washington!"

Smiling at his memories, Johore added, "I told the interpreter to say, 'How the hell you going to conquer the world when nobody can speak that infernal language of yours?'" Tojo had answered: Everybody in the world would be required to speak one of the three Axis languages—Japanese, German, or Italian.

At the time of Tokyo's surrender, Johore received another visit from the Japanese. This time it was General Itagaki, the commander in Malaya. "Why the god-damn hell did you stop fighting?" His Royal Highness asked.

"The American atomic bomb," the general said, "killed thirty thousand people in an area three miles wide."

Johore "played dumb like hell." Then, "I asked the interpreter to tell him he must think I'm crazy to believe anything like that." Saying goodbye, Itagaki warned, "If this war is like the last one, we'll be back in Malaya in ten years. It may take us a little longer—twenty years perhaps—but we'll be back." Then the Japanese general got back into his car and drove across the Causeway to Singapore to wait for the British to come and capture him.

Not long after our interview the Sultan and his Lady departed for London, en route to New York, but before leaving to resume their pre-war playing the Sultan was betrayed by a typical dirty British trick. Sir Harold MacMichael, Colonial Office expert and a ranking Tory, sped to Malaya and persuaded (or "coerced" as it was charged in Commons) the nine sultans to sign away all their sovereign powers as a prelude to a Malayan Union in which England would take over sovereign rights of each of the nine native states and the Straits Settlements, leaving the sultans only their religious leadership.

Citizens of Malaya would have the right to vote for representatives in this government, but the last word would be exercised by a British governor so that, in the final effect, British control would be strengthened. On top of that, Singapore was made a separate Crown Colony, divorced from Malaya.

And, in reality, the Malayans would have little voice in their own "representative" government. There are some 2,000,000 Malayans in the whole area, compared to 2,000,000 Chinese and 750,000 Indians—the latter better educated and better off economically than the natives and certainly fully able to outmaneuver them in any struggle for control of the government.

Chapter Twenty

Uncle Sam and Our Little Brown Javanese Brothers

I GOT INTO AN ARGUMENT WITH A DUTCHMAN IN A honkytonk in Batavia our first night in the Javanese capital. He was a personable guy of twenty-eight or so, blond and clean-looking in his white shorts and shirt and very well fed for a man who had spent nearly four years in Japanese prison camps. And he was very disagreeable. He disagreed with nearly everything we said.

"You certainly speak good English," I commented.

"I should. I graduated from Yale, class of thirty-five, and I lived in America for eight years altogether."

"It didn't make you like us very much, did it?"

"No," he said, agreeing for a change.

The Dutchman's companion, a thin and saturnine man in his middle thirties, ordered four gins from the barmaid. She was a blowzy White Russian whose whiteness had faded under years of living just over the edge of the equator and who now looked washed out and lifeless. When she lifted her arms to pour the drinks from a dirty-looking bottle, you saw sweat stains on her cheap cotton dress. The fourth gin was for a Chinese-Hawaiian boy who had come into Batavia that afternoon on the first American Victory ship to reach Java with a load of post-surrender relief supplies. We had seen the ship—the "Canton Victory"—as we flew over the harbor at twilight to land at the Batavia airfield, and farther out in the bay there had been a British task force bringing the first of Lord Louis Mountbatten's troops on the supposed mission of disarming the Japanese in the

Netherlands East Indies and reclaiming the country for the Imperial Dutch government of Her Majesty Queen Wilhelmina. The mission was to prove a flop on both counts. The Javanese wanted no part of the Imperial government of Queen Wilhelmina. They wanted their freedom. We had seen their slogans and signs as we rode from the airport over fine highways to the clean red-roofed town set in the middle of the rice fields. Street cars and buildings were plastered with them: "Up Republic Indonesia!" "Better go to hell than to be colonial." "Life, liberty, and the pursuit of happiness is the right of all nations." "The Monroe Doctrine—America for the Americans and Indonesia for the Indonesians."

The signs in English were unintelligible to most of the Javanese. They had been painted and posted as an appeal to the American forces who the Indonesians had expected would come into the country after Japan's surrender. Poor innocent little people. They thought Truman and Byrnes and the Tories, the French and Dutch would really keep Roosevelt's promise of freedom for all the oppressed nations of the world. They thought the United States would help them gain their liberty and independence.

I asked the Dutchman in the honkytonk, "What are you going to do about the demands of these people for their freedom?"

"To hell with the dirty little brown bastards," he snapped.

The Chinese-Hawaiian, whose skin was brown and who still bore the physical and mental marks of a long career as an amateur lightweight, had been getting more and more annoyed. He didn't follow all of the conversation but he disliked the Dutchman's attitude. Now he cocked back his fist. "Can I let him have it, Clockilee?" he asked, using the name by which I am sometimes called in the Hawaiian Islands. I made a sign, "Not yet." Behind us, the long narrow room that was the Black Cat Cabaret was getting more and more noisy. Some of our pilots had taken over the ancient piano, squeaky violin, and rattletrap drums from the girl orchestra. A couple of reporters had cornered a willing-looking Javanese girl in a scarlet dress and were pouring fiery gin drinks into her. At one side of the bar two English merchant sailors stood in a little pool of silence, drinking steadily and wordlessly. I turned to the blond Dutchman again.

"You people weren't strong enough to hold your colonies. The way you folded up back in 1942 when the Japs came down taught the Javanese that your toy warships and your Wright brothers airforce couldn't protect them, and you had kept them subdued for a long

230

time on the pretense that your military power would keep them safe from invasion. You couldn't have gotten the islands back in a million years if the United States hadn't defeated Japan. And now you mean to say you intend to come back here and try to play that master-race game again?"

"You altruistic Americans are just nuts about giving everybody 'freedom,'" he said with a sneer. "You're just dying to export your phony democracy."

The Chinese-Hawaiian kid pulled my arm. "Now, Clockilee?" he implored.

"Not yet," I said. And to the Dutchman, "Sure, we're a long way from being perfect. But we've kept our promises to the Philippines. We are suckers enough to believe in freedom and democracy for everybody who wants those things."

The Dutchman laughed nastily. He was feeling his drinks. "I'm going to give you a little lesson," he said. "How in hell can you export democracy when you don't have it at home, when your country is controlled by trusts, cartels, syndicates, and combines. And just why do you think you are here tonight, twelve thousand miles from home? You're here because your cartelists and imperialists have involved your country inextricably in Asia. Most Americans are too stupid to realize that simple fact. America has been intervening in Asia since long before Perry opened Japan. Your ships were in the opium trade. You had marines and soldiers in China for decades to protect the oil, cotton, tobacco combines, the airplane industry—the people who did business with Japan. You built a great navy to protect those interests. Where did the Navy come from? The Navy League, backed by the steel industry and Wall Street, forced it to be built as an instrument of imperialism. You didn't give a damn how many Chinese were killed by the Japanese. You kept hands off until your own interests were threatened and those of the British. Your imperialists counted on the British to be the watchdogs against the Yellow Races. England failed, but she'll be back in business again with the support of Wall Street and the State Department, while you stupid American liberals holler about 'perfidious Albion.' But you're wasting time here. Bolshevism is the threat to civilization. You will find that Hitler was right about the Bolsheviks."

"How was that last?" I asked.

He slugged back another straight shot of gin.

"Hitler was right," he repeated. "And you can baby these little

231

brown bastards if you want to, give them their freedom to fall into Russia's arms. Or back up the Dutch, those miserable weaklings. We should have killed all the swine in Rotterdam. We . . ."

"So that's it," I interrupted sharply. "You're not a Dutchman at all. You're a damn Kraut!"

"Sure I'm a Nazi," he said, drawing himself straight with considerable difficulty. "You wondered why I looked healthy after being locked up for four years. Well, I was locked up all right, but not in any prison camp. I was on that submarine out in the harbor. Since the end of the war in Europe, we have been attacking American ships in the Pacific."

The Chinese-Hawaiian kid looked at me. I nodded, "Now!"

I don't think the Kraut knew what hit him. In a few seconds he was lying in the gutter outside the Black Cat. The other German stumbled out, followed by a chorus of boos from the members of our party who had seen the hostilities but had not overheard the preceding argument. The violence of course, didn't answer any arguments. But at least it ended them. It also precipitated an indoor football game whose object was to entice the Englishmen to play so that they could be mussed up a bit, but they wisely stayed on the sidelines and we ended up by boffing each other around a little and the next morning half our gang had black eyes or split lips.

That was about the last quiet night in the Netherlands East Indies.

The British came ashore next day with a few Dutch troops and some Indians, and their American-made Sherman tanks backed up by American-made P–47s. Everything had been very quiet up to then. Expecting that American forces would land and bring the answer to their prayers the Javanese had not caused any disorders. With a minimum of good judgment and honest intentions on the part of the Dutch and their British strong-arm partners, there would have been no revolution in Java. The Dutch had proclaimed their intention of granting the demands of the Indonesians but when the showdown came they quickly demonstrated that they had no thought of making good. Instead, they deliberately began to provoke "incidents" with the Javanese. Trigger-happy Dutch and Amboinese sentries fired their guns indiscriminately in Batavia and Javanese were wounded and killed. Other groups of gangster Dutch soldiers broke into and searched the homes of suspected revolutionaries and dragged them away to an unknown fate. As they watched the Dutch go about these chores in trucks marked "USA" which had come in on the "Canton Victory," the Javanese quickly realized that their hope in the United States had been misplaced.

Despite all the provocations, the Javanese kept order. The head of the "Indonesian Republic," Dr. Soekarno, ordered an eight-o'clock curfew and told the Javanese to get off the streets at that hour to avoid clashes. He and his people kept their tempers as long as possible. Then, to the utter amazement of the Dutch who had wanted only to punish their subjects a little bit, a full-fledged revolution got underway. The Javanese began to fight back. The British military commander, who had come to Java under orders to disarm the Japanese, did nothing of the kind. He promptly backed up the Dutch and ordered the Japanese army to attack and capture the city of Bandoeng from the nationalists. Fighting was on in earnest and the British went to it with a vengeance.

With their artillery, and their American tanks and planes, they wiped out whole villages in retaliation for the killing of British soldiers. They bombed and shelled Soerabaya and other cities. Armed mostly with spears and clubs, sticks and stones, plus some weapons they had taken from the Japs, the Javanese stood up to the white man's guns and bombs. In only one way could the fighting have been stopped, and that was to yield to the demands of the nationalists. But naturally neither the British nor the Dutch could agree to anything like that so the Dutch temporized and stalled and tried to double-talk the Indonesian leaders and the British went about what is an old familiar business to them, the killing of people who want to be free. The fighting decided nothing. In a few months the British saw that the whole island could not be conquered without pouring in large armies to fight across the rich rice country and into the mountain cities of the interior. So they established perimeters around the principal seaports while the Javanese held the interior, with a no-man's land between the opposing lines.

An additional complicating factor in the struggle was the fact that some 30,000 Dutch men, women, and children who had been prisoners of the Japanese in internment camps were now in territory held by militant native armies and were in effect hostages. Subsequently the Dutch were to blame Mountbatten for the plight of the prisoners. They pointed out that Lord Louis had instructed the Dutch to remain in their camps after the surrender, whereas—except for those orders—they could have made their way to the seacoast and safety in the interval between the capitulation of Japan and the outbreak of armed hostilities.

Little news came of the hostages from the interior camps, but some of the Dutch were reported to have been killed by Indonesians in retaliation for the British bombing and slaughter of civilians in Soerabaya and elsewhere. Queen Wilhelmina's government could no doubt have obtained the release of these prisoners and their safe conduct back to the ports by agreeing to the Javanese demands, but that would have meant surrender of the country to the people whose country it was, and you don't give up such a rich prize easily, even though you no longer have the strength or means to defend it. If the 30,000 hostages were all killed, said the Dutch in effect, why, that wasn't too big a price to pay for hanging on here, somehow, for a little longer.

The center of the resistance movement, the fight for freedom, was Dr. Soekarno. Both Soekarno and the Indonesian Republic of which he was president were to some extent creatures of Japan and as such were living proof that willy-nilly the Japanese had given life and meaning to their slogan of "Asia for the Asiatics." The pattern was different from the one the Japs had followed in Indo-China where they had used French puppets to handle the natives and where "Asia for the Asiatics" had not been translated into practical terms until a short time before the surrender, when the Viet Nam government was formed under Japanese sponsorship. In the early days of the Japanese occupation of Java, Dr. Soekarno had worked with the invaders openly and enthusiastically, believing that they really intended to make the Javanese free and, even if that were only partially so, welcoming any change from Dutch rule. Then had come disillusionment as the Japanese, repeating the same mistakes they made in most of their conquered countries, betrayed the trust of the Javanese. The Japanese exported several million Javanese for forced labor in various parts of the "Co-Prosperity Sphere." They drafted another million for slave labor in Java and many of these starved to death. Japan betrayed her own ends, but even so her over-all record of brutality is not nearly as black as, for example, that of the British in India where after three hundred years of benevolent British rule millions of people die each year of hunger.

The record, however, was enough to disgust Dr. Soekarno. He had gone into partial retirement from which he emerged again when the Japanese, at the time of Tokyo's surrender, turned the country over to the Indonesian Republic once more and supplied the Javanese with arms.

These arms were used to equip the T.R.I., the government army, which in turn was backed up by other militant organizations including the People's Army, whose weapons were usually spears; the Pomoeda, or youth organization which was trained by the Japs; and numerous local guerrilla bands. There were also some 100,000 Japanese soldiers in the interior of Java, still armed, well fed, and perfectly content to sit there. The Dutch government in Holland reported six months after Japan's surrender that "all kinds of Japanese deserters and Japanese influences are still playing a most objectionable part in Javanese society, their actions contribute to a situation in which neither persons nor property are safe." Those Japanese still in the hills will be heard from again some day. They are no doubt pointing out to the Javanese that they never could have hoped for their freedom except for Japan's war on the white man, and they are certainly telling their fellow Asiatics that one day Japan will rise again and lead the united nations of Asia to victory over the white world. All reports say they are having a hell of a good time.

This situation would never have developed if the British had gone into Java promptly, with strong forces and with honest intentions of disarming the Japanese. Or better still, if American forces had been dispatched from the Philippines, where plenty were available, for this job. But Washington and London, which saw eye to eye on creation of the British SEAC as an instrument not only for defeating Japan but for restoring European colonial rule, didn't want Americans to go in there. Britain didn't give a tinker's dam about disarming the Japs. They preferred (with the tacit consent of Washington which supplied many of the arms and weapons) to use the Japanese to kill Indonesians.

As the eyes of his people were opened to the real intentions of the British and Dutch and to the lack of interest of the United States and the United Nations, Soekarno broke off his negotiations with the Netherlands Government. He had entered them with great reluctance, after telling us that he would never deal with the Dutch because they had proved unworthy of being trusted.

We found Soekarno in his home in Batavia in the first days of the revolution. Driving in from the headquarters of the Kempetai, the Japanese military gendarmerie, where we had been fed cold Dutch beer and tall tales about the "ungratefulness" of the Jap-trained Javanese who were now attacking Japanese troops and seizing their arms, we came to a house which was guarded by a miscellaneous collection of sentries. Some of the Indonesians wore sarongs and others freshly laundered shorts and shirts. They were handsome, lithe, compact men who admitted us with smiles when we identified ourselves as Americans. We walked across a long, level lawn to the verandah of a buff-colored residence and Soekarno rose from a swing and came to meet us. He is tall with a strong face and fine eyes, and a Mohammedan skull cap covered his black hair.

The Dutch had educated him as an engineer. He was one of the few who enjoyed such benefits, for the Javanese—as Soekarno told me—have the lowest literacy rate in the world. The Dutch were to regret giving Soekarno book learning. As one of them said, "We never should have done it." After graduation in his profession he had become an agitator for independence, and long before the war he was arrested for inciting the Javanese to riot against the Dutch. Since the Japanese surrender, his regime had become the de facto government of Java, moving in to take over when it became obvious that the first group of Dutch to return with Mountbatten's mission did not have the organization to run the country.

Talking to us, Dr. Soekarno felt no need to apologize for his collaboration with the Japanese, although he did regret the results. "Dutch rule had become so intolerable by 1942 that any change was for the better and so it was that the Japanese were welcomed. Before that, Java had suffered three hundred years of foreign domination. Now we intend to be free!" Soekarno is a convincing talker, a magnetic man with the undisguisable stamp of a leader and crusader.

We asked if he would arbitrate his demands with Dr. Charles van der Plas, the representative of the Netherlands government.

"No," he answered, "the promises of the Dutch cannot be trusted."

He told us that his government would agree to a plan of independence like that of the Philippines, but only if the United States or the United Nations supervised the transition. "Not the Dutch, because the Dutch cannot be believed."

A little later Soekarno changed his mind and did enter negotiations with the Dutch but it was quickly apparent that they were leading nowhere. The Dutch are past masters at stalling, as they had proved in their talks with the oil-hungry Japanese before Pearl Harbor. Soekarno demanded that his republic be recognized as a sovereign state to include all the Dutch colonies of the N.E.I. He was supported in his demand by all the Javanese, conservatives as well as Communists, Sultan, Prince, and rice-field worker as well as the middle class.

But the Dutch, deaf to the stifled cries of the 30,000 hostages, were unwilling to go that far. Thinking, as always, in terms of their $2,000,000,000 investment in Java, they turned down Soekarno's demand as "incompatible with the responsibilities of the Kingdom with respect to Indonesia, and to its international responsibility." They offered instead a copy of the Viet Nam Free State in Indo-China, making Java a free state in the Federal Commonwealth of Indonesia which the outer islands could join or refuse to join as they desired. Other members of the Dutch Commonwealth would be the Netherlands, Surinam, and Curaçao. The Indonesians, said the Dutch, must recognize Dutch sovereignty and "such fundamental rights as proper administration and sound finances."

The Indonesians said Nuts! Soekarno withdrew his representatives from the discussions and himself retired to the inland city of Jogjakarta, the capital of the republic and the stronghold of the independence movement. Nine months after Japan's surrender, Soekarno's Republic controlled, outside of the British- and Dutch-held seaports, ninety per cent of the wonderfully fertile island of Java with its 48,000,000 people, of whom 47,000,000 are Indonesians, 600,000 Chinese, 200,000 Europeans (mostly Dutch), and the remainder Asiatics from neighboring countries. (Plus, of course, the 100,000 Japanese that Lord Louis Mountbatten's SEAC was to have disarmed and shipped home.) The most densely populated area on the whole earth, Java has twice as many people as inhabit all the other East Indies islands combined.

In contrast to the unhappy seaboard cities, where inflation raged, where there was no trade, no business, no work, where foreign troops held uneasy perimeters under the boiling equatorial sun, the interior of Java was cheerful and busy. Rice and other crops were being grown, schools were opened. The people rejoiced in their newly won though not yet consolidated Meredka—Freedom. Yet the Dutch were convinced that they had to upset the situation and restore the *status quo ante* so that the wealth of the plantations and mines, the oil wells, the rubber trees might pour once more into the banks of distant Amsterdam. They even told themselves that they had a moral obligation to do all this.

"In this respect," one of Soekarno's aides said, "the Dutch are very much like the British. They convince themselves that what is good for them is right for everybody. Thus morals and self-interest become intertwined."

It was incomprehensible to the Dutch, as it was to the French in Indo-China, that they had created such a terrifying store of hatred toward themselves in the years when they had imagined that they were performing as benevolent and enlightened bearers of the White Man's alleged burden. Yet revolution was not new to Java. Soekarno's assistant said, "The world press is just discovering, as I note by the presence of your party of correspondents, the existence of the native nationalisms of southeastern Asia. In fact, the anti-Dutch movement here dates back to the last century in the Indies. For seventy-five years we have been plugging away, trying to gain some measure of freedom. There were armed uprisings in Java in the 1930s and one group even captured a Dutch cruiser and put to sea with it. The Dutch ruthlessly suppressed these uprisings and the patriots were sent to horrible exile in the prison camps of New Guinea. Our vice-president, Mohammed Hatta, was an exile. If you have seen one of those camps, you will feel no false pity for the Dutch now in prison camps in the interior of Java. The Japanese gave us our chance and now we are taking it."

Dutch propaganda, like that of all other imperialist nations, had striven to impress the world with the picture of a benevolent super-race sharing its super-culture with backward people. The truth was that the natives of southeastern Asia were "backward" only in that they did not possess machines or the weapons of mass destruction, the battleships, tanks, airplanes. Great and highly civilized empires flourished in these regions even before Europe floundered into its Dark Ages. Some of the monuments are still there, like the magnificent and mysterious ruins of Angkor Wat in Indo-China. The Javanese are fine artists and, left alone, artists of living as well, laughing, hard-working, happy, clean people. Like other empires elsewhere, their early ones had fallen because tyranny and oppression had crept in, those same destructive forces that are now surely writing the doom of the White Man as the overlord of the Orient.

In their struggle since October of 1945, the Javanese received sympathetic support from only two quarters—Australia and Moscow. Australian labor unions actively backed up the Javanese. They refused to load ships carrying supplies to the anti-native armies. Their spokesmen tried to interest world conferences in the plight of the Indonesians and the Annamites of French Indo-China. This was against the London-Washington line, but Australia did it anyway. By geography, if not by racial background or skin pigmentation, Australia is a very near neighbor of southeastern Asia. Its trade unionists, many of its leaders, are liberal and far-sighted men. They see that British (and American) imperialists are building up their country as a bulwark against the Yellow Man and as a base for an ultimate bloody showdown between the White and Yellow races in which Japan's war was only a curtain raiser. Economically, the British are strengthening Australia to counterbalance the great industrialization of India, which is more and more passing into Indian hands.

The British see no alternative to a White-Yellow struggle. They cannot conceive that possibly, by treating the yellow man with decency, you could avoid a test of arms. But Australia believes otherwise and places its hopes and faith in the United Nations. So it is that the spokesmen of Australia—who are more and more becoming the spokesmen for the British Empire—have the courage to stand up to London and Washington and to their own, native Australian imperialists. In doing this the Australians are "betraying" the British, who thought that by the flattery of important posts the Australians could be won to the side of Empire. But the Australians do not want their land converted into an arsenal for military or economic war. They are for the UN first and Empire last.

The Australians try to speak up for the people of Java and Indo-China, but their voices are drowned by London and Washington. That leaves only Russia as a possible friend of the people of southeastern Asia. In Java, life has long been on a communal basis although not politically communistic. Each man contributed so many days of work yearly to village irrigation projects and similar communal endeavors. In pre-war years the Javanese did not take to the Russian brand of communism. Signs were posted in many interior villages warning that anyone joining the Red party would be expelled from the village.

In those years and at the time of the Japanese surrender, the Javanese placed their trust and hopes in Washington. Now they have been ignored, neglected, and betrayed and they are turning to Moscow which may similarly ignore, neglect, and betray them. But they don't know that for sure yet.

239

Chapter Twenty-One

"The Philippines Are Free.   Or Are They?"

O NE AFTERNOON LATE IN 1944, HAM FISHER, THE famous cartoonist and creator of Joe Palooka, was walking down a New York street with a Filipino official. Ham, who himself isn't quite as tall as Palooka, was annoyed by the fact that he and his companion were being constantly separated in the New York street crowds. This was due in part to the Filipino's small stature which made him inconspicuous among the comparatively gigantic Americans. Passing an Adler shoe store, Ham had a sudden inspiration. Inside, he whispered to a salesman who brought out a pair of shoes and tried them on the feet of the Filipino.

"Walk around," said Ham. "Take a look at yourself in the mirror."

"I don't see anything deeferent," the little official answered.

"You're about two inches taller," Ham pointed out. "Those shoes have built-up heels."

"It looks the same to me," said the official unhappily.

Ham got another idea. "I remembered when I was a kid just growing up and waiting for the day when I would be able to go to the bathroom and stand up like my Pop." He told the official, "Go into the men's room."

A few minutes later there was a triumphant shout from behind the partition. "Eureka," cried the official, "Eureka! Ham, you should see! I am a big man now!"

Several months afterward the official returned to Manila with our reconquering forces, and in a short time a letter reached the late

240

Mr. Adler. It was an urgent plea from the official, ordering many pairs of shoes like his for his friends and relatives.

And so it was that the Philippines faced the future as an independent nation on July 4, 1946, from a new and more lofty vantage point.

In forty-eight years of American occupancy they had come a long way—from bare feet to high heels and from Spanish colonialism to American-sponsored freedom—if you can call it freedom when a stronger power demands military bases on your soil and, in effect, continues to rule your economy.

In the story of our generally benevolent program in the islands, and in the saga of Bataan we have sometimes lost sight of the fact that our early record was as bad as that of any power motivated by imperialism. For twelve years after we purchased the Philippines from defeated Spain in 1899 and embarked, protestingly and uncertainly, on expansion far beyond our continental borders, American soldiers battled Filipinos. The Filipinos wanted independence; we wanted the gold in their mountains and the green gold of their sugar fields. There was a black chapter of water cures, of native villages going up in flames set by our troops, of rule imposed by armed force.

We were doing just what Holland was doing in the Netherlands Indies, Britain in China and Malaya, France in French Indo-China. Then our imperialists found a new outlet. Ready to land in the United States were the immigrant labor masses brought from Europe—millions of human beings ripe for exploitation in the steel, coal, cotton, tobacco industries. So, while the British, French, Dutch made slaves of the brown and yellow men far from their shores, America's imperialists did it at home to the new immigrants.

This took the pressure off the Philippines and because of it, and because, fortunately, most Americans are not imperialistic, we began to live up to President McKinley's policy: "The Philippines are not ours to exploit, but to develop, to civilize, to educate, to train in the science of self-government."

We gave the Filipinos schools and a public-health system and helped them to a decent standard of living. To their minds, these acts more than compensated for the fact that our imperialists were taking far more out of the islands each year in the form of gold and sugar and hemp than our government was putting back in. In 1914 we made them a definite promise of eventual independence, and subsequently we took other steps to prove we intended to live up to that promise. These policies were to pay dividends from December 7, 1941, through the surrender of Japan in Tokyo Bay in September, 1945.

The Filipinos were loyal to us because we had two decades in which to change our first, mistaken policies. Given time, the Japanese might have changed their ways, too, and eventually won over the Filipinos. We did not give them that time.

I have a special interest in the Philippines, having been there when the war started and when it ended; and because I saw how bravely the Filipinos died for us I have a special love for them. I say "died for us," because they knew that to avenge our own honor and to defeat Japan we would necessarily one day have to recapture the lost islands and redeem our pledge of freedom for the Philippines. They did not, in the last analysis, have to fight, but they did because they loved us and believed in us.

Now, some of them are beginning to regret it.

To me the most impressive part of the story of the Philippines underground movement is not the armed exploits of the guerrillas. It is the loyalty of 17,000,000 common people who shared a secret that was known at least in part to all of them and yet was still kept secret from the Japanese who held their land captive.

The mountaineers of Baguio, the wild and warlike Moros of Mindanao, the liquid-tongued Visayans of the central islands—nearly everyone of them was either connected with the underground or aware of the existence of an organization which under the very eyes of the enemy turned the Philippines into a vast intelligence network.

After the shock of Bataan's fall, the loss of Manila, the total defeat and surrender of American forces, the Filipinos began spontaneously and almost at once their hidden war against the invaders. Soon they established contact with MacArthur through patched-up radio sets, and under the direction of Filipino and American leaders sent in by submarine, the vague resistance movement took on organization and purpose.

Whether one admires MacArthur or not, it cannot be denied that he was the heart and soul of that movement, not only as an individual but because he typified America to the Filipinos and they still had faith in America even after watching the skeletons of Bataan parade like ragged ghosts under the bayonets of an Asiatic conqueror.

242

Colonel Dyess, who survived the death march and escaped to lead a guerrilla band, said before his death, "For my men, there were two idols—MacArthur and God, in that order." Which is hard to understand unless you have seen the tears in the eyes of Filipinos at the sight of MacArthur's tall figure, the intense emotion with which they greet him.

"I shall return!" was the keynote of the underground campaign. The slogan appeared on pencils, matchboxes, chewing-gum wrappers. Kids painted it on walls or traced it in the dusty roads. Like a religious cry the words rang through the islands. Schoolchildren repeated them, even while mouthing difficult Japanese words they were forced to learn in place of American history and literature.

The wireless network spread and grew, until there were more than seventy radio and weather stations on the island of Luzon alone, some of them within a stone's throw of Jap headquarters. Thousands of people knew of those radios—tens of thousands—but nobody talked.

When José Laurel, president of the puppet Philippines Republic, went to Japan and signed a secret treaty, MacArthur wanted to know about it. Laurel kept the treaty in an unlocked briefcase. Two days after his return to Manila, MacArthur had the complete text. The guerrillas even furnished daily lists of the guests in the Manila Hotel. They supplied reports on the movement of every Jap platoon, every commander, anywhere in the Philippines.

While millions of Filipinos assisted in gathering and transmitting this information, thousands of others took up arms and fought the Japs.

This brilliant record of loyalty was only partially offset by the defections of some high-ranking Filipino politicians. A number of them lost heart and hope and actively collaborated with the conquerors of their country. Current conquerors, that is. Others joined up with the Japs because they wanted personal glory and wealth. Still others pretended to join but at heart were still loyal to the United States and to their own exiled government. They worked with the guerrillas to outwit the Japs.

Ex-President Sergio Osmena, the quiet, scholarly leader who became chief executive in exile after the death of Manuel Quezon, had a personal problem in his own family. Two of his sons were accused of working with the Japs.

But two other sons died as heroes. Dr. Emilio Osmena, a graduate of Vienna and of Johns Hopkins, took to the mountains with the guerrillas and was captured by the Japs. Refusing to sign a pledge of loyalty, he was executed. Teddy, twenty-seven, a pre-war socialite, was a guerrilla who died under the guns of rival guerrillas—specifically at the hands of a group commanded by an American piano player who had taken to the hills to fight the Japs.

Most of the collaborationists came from the ranks of the highborn, the fascist-minded, the rich landowners, the fanatical antiwhites. The real guerrilla leaders were men like Marking, a Manila truck driver, who lost his temper when his face was slapped by a Jap sentry and who in revenge organized one of the biggest and most effective underground fighting forces.

Of course, not every Filipino was a hero, although after our reoccupancy of the Islands it was difficult to find one who did not claim to have been a guerrilla leader. I remember a lad called Carlos, at whose home on the outskirts we stayed during the battle of Manila. Our first night at his house, Carlos had our eyes popping as he told of his deeds with the guerrillas. "I was a sergeant," he said, "and I killed sixteen of those damn Japs. They are buried in the back yard. I have one more Jap prisoner hidden away, and we are going to skin him alive. You are all invited to watch."

As the nights went on and Carlos repeated his story for newcomers, some of the details became confused. Eventually, he had promoted himself to a full colonel of guerrillas and the number of damn Japs buried in his back yard had decreased to six. When we pressed him for the date of the skinning of the prisoner, he confessed the Jap "had escaped." Finally, he told me one night the true story of his "guerrilla activities."

He had belonged to the "slick chick" gang of boys and girls whose hangout was the A-1 barber shop in Manila. They played pool, shot craps, and danced for the first two years of the war and by early 1944 Carlos had acquired a small fortune of 70,000 pesos—which would have been $35,000 pre-war but now was about $500. With this money in the pocket of his flashy sport jacket, he made a trip to the Pines Hotel in Baguio, posing as a "rich sport from Manila." His "secret" assignment, secret from everyone except himself, was to get into the quarters of General Yamashita, the Japanese commander in the Philippines who was living in the hotel.

"I cased the joint," Carlos told me, "and discovered that the Japanese girl who took care of Yamashita's room also doubled as bartender. So I went into the bar and threw five hundred pesos on the mahogany and told her, 'I'm a bigtime sport from Manila. Put twelve bottles of beer on the bar. Six for you and six for me.'" Young Miss Butterfly-san, overwhelmed at this display, drank her share of the Jap-made beer and quickly became enamored of the big city slicker. Very soon, Carlos was her lover—"By gosh, she was a firgin,"—and had access to Yamashita's room when the girl went in to clean up in the mornings while the general was out riding horseback.

In the room he caught glimpses of Japanese battle maps showing the disposition of troops in the Philippines, but when he returned to Manila—leaving behind a weeping poor Butterfly—he couldn't get any real guerrillas to listen to the information he wanted to pass on. Knowing him as a member of the "slick chicks" they refused to take him seriously.

But, despite the failure of such all-important missions as the self-assigned one of Carlos, the Filipinos did a master job of espionage. All in all, they were faithful and loyal to us. Thousands upon thousands of them died in the underground struggle, in the battle of Bataan, and in the later reconquest of the Islands. Their cities and towns were ravaged, their country torn and laid waste.

All this—the struggle, the bloodshed, the deaths—were forgotten in the joy of their liberation, forgotten except in that they held a promise for the future. It was the promise that white Americans, at least, could and would deal on terms of equality and friendship and respect with brown Asiatics. Without saying anything about it, the Filipinos felt they had earned the right to equality and to respect which, after all, can be little things. Sometimes they are negative things—like not slapping a face, like not posting a sign on a white man's club saying, "No Dogs or Asiatics allowed."

So what did we do to fulfill that promise, to repay their loyalty? We did absolutely nothing worthwhile!

We sent $3,000,000 of UNRRA supplies to feed 18,000,000 people.

Then for a year and a half Congress sat on its fat backsides, and padlocked the treasury doors, refusing stupidly and stubbornly to vote the funds that would have saved countless Filipinos from near-starvation. Bills introduced in Congress promised them limited preferential treatment of their exports of sugar, copra, coconut oil, and other products. In return, we insisted on monopolistic rights for "established" trading firms—which meant American and Spanish firms. We also insisted that Americans be given the special privileges of acquiring land, owning businesses and industry, and, of course, made no gesture toward offering the Filipinos reciprocal rights in our country. And all the time Congress would *not* vote $400,000,000 for reconstruction, would *not* authorize the money that the Philippines needed to build new roofs over their heads and to fill their empty stomachs.

Certainly, we agreed to go through the forms of independence on July 4, 1946, and eventually did so, but at the same time we demanded naval and air bases. And what nation can be independent with foreign troops on its soil?

In short, our program amounted to imperialism however you spell it, nor could that fact be obscured by the cloaking of our motives in pious righteousness.

When I went into Manila with our liberating troops in February, 1945, crawled with them through the burning streets, the air drenched with the stench of corpses, there was—despite all the death—a feeling of new life, of resurrection. The living did not stop to mourn their dead—burned alive by the Japanese, shot down with their hands behind their backs, bayoneted, gutted, chopped up, raped. Instead, they worked and fought to help finish the job of liberation. They were indescribably happy, even while their city went up in smoke and flames around their heads.

Eight months later, when I flew up to Manila from the Dutch East Indies by way of Singapore, the American Army and Navy had turned the ruined city into a giant honkytonk, an obscenely corrupt monument to a capital that had died in fire and horror. The buildings that were still standing, and the shacks that had been erected from fragments of wood and tin were plastered with signs: "Whiskey $3.00. Gin $2.00. Rum $1.50 per drink." Arrows pointed to nipa huts off the highways: "Kit-Kat Night Club." "Rendezvous." "Passion Pit." With his chewing gum, cigarettes, and chocolate bars the GI had corrupted into prostitution far more girls than had ever been condemned by the Japs, at bayonet point, to this way of life.

When a Yank went into a Filipino town, the native came running to meet him with open arms, trying to express in his grammatically correct but strangely inflected English something of the happiness in his heart, something, too, of the sadness for those who had died to make this day possible. He offered his last chicken, his last bowl of rice to the liberator. He quickly found out that the GI was interested, seven cases out of ten, only in getting drunk and getting laid.

246

I blame the GIs and not the Filipinos for what has taken place, because the Filipinos are essentially a sober, orderly people, though, certainly, not all Filipinos were ideal citizens. There had been prostitution, gambling, crimes of passion, and occasional gang holdups in the Islands before the war. There had been a Ganap organization dedicated to fighting the United States. But, as the pre-liberation booklets informed our GIs, "The Filipino is an individual of great personal dignity with a natural respect for law and order." And, "With the girl of good family, the 'Hi, Babe' approach is *not* appreciated." The GI did not read those booklets very well.

If he had been forced to do so, if he had been indoctrinated in his mission, indeed, if the United States itself had been imbued with a sense of mission, a purpose, things would have been different. But having none of these things at home, how could we expect to have them for export? I should explain that by GI I do not mean every GI, nor only GIs. The guilty include people of all ranks, officer and private, soldier, sailor, and civilian, newspaperman and Red Cross worker. It has been said with nauseating repetition that the GI did not know what he was fighting for. It is still true.

In blaming the GI for conditions in the Philippines post-occupation, I am not ignoring the fact that these conditions could not have come about without the Filipinos who did, after all, sell whiskey to Americans, did operate black markets, and did become prostitutes. But the point is that despite our long stewardship and the training for self-dependence, the great majority of Filipinos were emotionally still dependent on us. My friend General Romulo writes that there were four Filipinos for every American in the Battle of Bataan. True enough, but there would have been no Bataan without those Americans to inspire and lead the Filipinos, to teach them by their own self-sacrifice that there are things worth dying for; men like Wainwright and Johnny Pugh, Wermuth, Bridget, Pierce, and hundreds more.

In Bataan and in the long years of their resistance, the Filipinos grew up emotionally but they still retained enough of their spiritual dependence on us to look to us for an example when the Islands were retaken. If our occupation troops had gone in and distributed history books, held seminars on street corners, led discussion groups to explain the war and the victory, given language lessons, provided an educational program, the Filipinos would have supported these efforts wholeheartedly. But our troops did nothing like that. So when

247

a hundred thousand drunken soldiers wanted whiskey, the Filipinos sold it to them. If they wanted women, the girls offered themselves. It was not a case of a liberated populace or a conquered one, like those in many parts of Europe, sniveling and chiseling and defrauding the Americans. It was a grateful people supplying to their supposed friends what the friends demanded.

Instead of assisting the Filipinos to restore their ruined economy, the deluge of soldier and sailor pay was poured over the Islands and nearly drowned their currency in a tidal wave of inflation.

On top of that, the American Army—not as a matter of policy but through many of its personnel—introduced Jim Crowism to the Islands. We started to draw the color line, and that was too much for the Filipinos. Then, in addition, they saw that U. S. arms were being used in the N.E.I., Indo-China, and elsewhere to shoot down their fellow Asiatics whose own hopes for independence had been based on America's record in the Philippines. These people had counted on us to intervene and we did—against them, by supplying guns and planes to the armies of imperialist Europe.

The whole picture added up to a national shame and disgrace. Our post-occupation actions have gone far toward wiping out a half-century of friendship. They have, unless we can promptly reform, sowed the seeds for a future "Asia for the Asiatics" movement that will make the recent Japanese-sponsored war look like child's play. We had a foot in the door of the so-called "yellow menace" problem. Now we have slammed the door on our own toes.

It has been said that Congress' hesitancy to aid the Philippines was due to our dissatisfaction over their treatment of alleged collaborationists. President Roosevelt had warned, "Those who collaborate with the enemy must be removed from authority and influence over the political and economic life of the country." President Truman made it even stronger in a later statement.

But neither Roosevelt nor Truman, nor any other American leader in recent history, has lived in an enemy-occupied country, so we cannot predict with any certainty that there would be no American Pétain or Laval or Quisling. We do not know if millions of our population, driven by desperation and hunger, would work for scant rations supplied by the occupying enemy and available from no other sources.

Peoples whose country has been conquered and occupied have a different view of collaboration than those who have never under-

248

gone such experiences—and the United States is about the last nation remaining in that category. The Filipinos who worked for us, the conquerors, after '98, the Japanese who are on our side now, are collaborators, but no stigma is attached to collaborating with the winners. So it was that President Osmena, who himself escaped with MacArthur and thus did not live under the occupation, had the courage to defy Truman and Roosevelt and to state that as far as the Filipinos were concerned, "We must not close our eyes to the realities of the occupation. . . . Not all public officials could take to the hills to carry on the struggle. Some had to remain at their posts to maintain a semblance of government for the protection of the population and the comfort of the people. . . . We must look into their motives . . . and judge . . . whether those holding office were prompted by a desire to protect the people, actuated by fear of enemy reprisals or by disloyalty."

The Filipinos went on to defeat Osmena in the elections for the first presidency of the Republic and to choose instead (former Brigadier General) Manuel Roxas.

While still a general officer in the United States Army, Roxas had served in the Japanese-sponsored government of the Philippines and helped to write the constitution for that "republic." Nevertheless, standing before the court of public opinion, Roxas was elected by his fellow countrymen to the highest office at their disposal. This was due in no small measure to General MacArthur's announcement that even while he was cooperating with the Japs, Roxas had been a key man in aiding the guerrilla organizations. Perhaps he was sincere when he worked with the Japs, perhaps he was being honest when he worked against them while in their pay. Perhaps his motives were "to protect the people." In any case, it is certainly true that at the time Manila was recaptured, Roxas was the great popular hero.

But if we had not succeeded in retaking the Philippines within a reasonable number of years, if we had been repulsed and driven off Leyte, it is my belief that Roxas and other Filipino political leaders— and the great masses of the country—would have abandoned their guerrilla work and actively supported the Japanese. I think that if Manuel Quezon and General Romulo and Osmena and others had not been taken to safety with MacArthur they would, like Roxas, have "collaborated" with the Japanese for the good of their people and that if we had not returned after a few years they would have become sincerely convinced that their destiny lay in unity with Japan and not with us. These statements imply nothing of faintheartedness or treachery. The American Tories eventually gave in to the Revolution when they were convinced that it was best for them; the South laid down its arms and rejoined the Union and these acts were recognition of the "realities" of the situations.

In any case, in view of the undisputed record of Filipino loyalty, it was ridiculous for Congress to delay the appropriation of funds because of alleged Filipino collaboration during the occupation.

This continued delay inevitably resulted in a wave of anti-American reaction. A few educated Filipinos blamed MacArthur for "deserting" the Islands. One of them said, "If General MacArthur had consented to remain here instead of going to Japan, if he had become Ambassador to our Republic or High Commissioner prior to its establishment, I am sure that his influence in Washington would have been sufficient to save us from starvation and economic chaos. He would have demanded the necessary funds and gotten them. But the job wasn't big enough for him. Once the Philippines were off the front pages he began campaigning for the leadership of the attack on Japan, and won his fight. He forgot us completely in his devotion to what he considered the more important job of ruling the Son of Heaven and seventy million Japs. And so we are starving."

Thirty-three-year-old Brig. Gen. Macario Peralta, Jr., guerrilla leader who held out on Panay Island for three years and who later became deputy chief of staff of the Philippine Army, implied much the same thing in May, 1946, on his return from an unsuccessful trip to Washington in search of aid for his country. He was turned down flatly in his effort to have Philippine soldiers included in the GI bill of rights, and he was angry about conditions in general.

"Instead of sending millions of tons of rice to feed the 'poor' Japanese," he said, "the Philippine soldier believes the money could be better expended to feed, clothe, and educate the guys who fought. The hell with the Japs!" But, meanwhile, American rice was going to MacArthur in Japan for distribution among the ex-enemies of the Filipinos.

When Roxas took over the presidency on May 28, 1946, he was thus confronted with the problem of governing an economically prostrated country which had been deserted by the great and powerful nation on whose side it had battled for more than three years. He was also confronted by an armed minority, most of them peasants who had actively fought the Japs, who insisted that Roxas was in fact a collaborator and was a fascist. Roxas, of course, denied such charges. "Despite the allegations of fascism against me," he said with no great show of modesty, "I am sure that I am the greatest champion of democracy that this country has."

Nevertheless his opponents branded him a friend of the rich and powerful Catholic landowners and the Catholic church which controlled most of the country's agricultural lands. They pointed to the fact that those in his favor included such men as Andres Soriano, a colonel in the United States Army. Soriano became a Filipino citizen shortly before Pearl Harbor under circumstances which aroused wide comment in the Manila press. Rich, internationally powerful, owning businesses in the United States, Singapore, Batavia, and the Philippines, a Catholic of Spanish descent, Soriano had been decorated by General Franco. The Filipino peasants regarded men like Soriano as enemies of their aspirations.

Behind the peasant unrest was an increasingly vocal demand that Roxas take action to break up the huge estates and distribute them more equally among the people of the nation. In pre-war years Roxas had publicly backed Quezon's proposals in this direction, but in his inaugural address he threatened strong measures against "demagogues [who] using economic injustice as a rallying cry . . . have destroyed the precious fabric of public faith in democratic procedure."

By "demagogues" the president meant the leaders of the Hukbalahaps and the other peasant organizations. Because the Filipinos are essentially fair-minded people and willing to give anyone a chance—just as they gave us a chance to demonstrate our good intentions toward them after our early bad record in the Islands—these opponents of Roxas announced a few days after his inauguration that they would surrender the arms they had acquired as guerrillas. These were the organizations that had backed Osmena—the friend of the United States—in the elections.

I think their decision—perhaps only temporary—to cast their lot with Roxas was in no small part due to their disillusionment and disappointment at the failure of the United States to live up to its obligations.

Chapter Twenty-Two

What Goes On in Asia

THE WORLD ABOUT WHICH THE PRECEDING PAGES were written no longer exists except by the sufferance of the United States. We could put an end to it tomorrow with the atomic bomb. We have the planes to carry the bombs, and airplane bases within easy range of all the Pacific-Asiatic countries. We could end colonialism with the bomb, or we could blow up the people who are fighting for freedom from the imperial system. In the following three chapters, there are some sidelights on the atomic world, post-Bikini.

Meantime, a brief look backward at the old world that is comforting to contemplate—for all its confusion, its suffering and injustices. As this is written, some of the things that have been forecast, predicted, or implied in the foregoing pages have come true, and others have not. This is the way things look, for the present and the future:

SOUTHEAST ASIA

The Dutch-Javanese stalemate, political and military, still exists. A few English and Dutch troops die each day and quite a few Javanese.

In Indo-China, France has recognized the native Viet Nam Republic as the government of the northern and eastern half of the colony, subject of course to French sovereignty. The colony has come into the UN limelight as a result of attacks across the Siamese border by French troops seeking to win back by force the disputed areas of Cambodia which Siam took by force in 1941 and which had been taken from Siam by French force a half-century earlier.

Siam is on her best behavior, and hoping to win UN membership.

The British, after the exposure of their dirty trick on the sultans of the Malay States, are still busy trying to think up another one that will get by. (To their everlasting credit, it was a handful of Englishmen who exposed the duplicity of the Foreign Office.)

Outside of southeastern Asia, Britain has at long last been forced to recognize that the Sun of Empire is setting fast. The Labor government has promised to withdraw British troops from Egypt and in due course to grant India its independence. Southeast Asia is almost the last stronghold, and even there the thin white line of imperialism is near the cracking point. But the imperialists, with their superior weapons and their disregard for human lives, are a hardy breed and do not surrender easily. In the late hostilities we fought against Japan's "fanatical determination to rule the world." But Europe's imperialists (and those of America) are imbued with a no less fanatical belief in the divine mission of the Anglo-Saxon-Gallic-Dutch races to rule the colored peoples of the world.

There have been secret discussions between British, French, and Dutchmen of the possibility of pooling air, naval, and military forces to strike more effectively at native revolts. Even such an alliance, however, could delay for only a few years a final, successful rising of the Asiatic people against absentee ownership and tyranny. The native nationalisms are a profound and deeply rooted force in Asia and they must be satisfied and they will be—unless. Unless the imperialists use the atom bomb to quell them.

Some people of anti-imperialist beliefs say such use of the atom bomb would "only delay the inevitable for a few years."

That is to underestimate the fearful power of the bomb. In teeming Java, for instance, millions upon millions could be killed by a few bombs and the whole land area of the island be rendered agriculturally useless and uninhabitable by the employment of weapons now in existence. But such an unproductive, uninhabited wilderness would be valueless to the Dutch and consequently it is to be hoped and believed that in the next few years the Dutch and the other imperialists will abandon their unjustified and eventually hopeless struggle to continue the enslavement of distant peoples. It is hoped that the UN will make such things impossible.

This may be a forlorn hope when you consider the entrenched power of the imperialists in London and Wall Street and Washington and Rotterdam, their tight-knit brotherhood all over the world. But the choice is now clear . . . justice and peace for all; or more bloodshed and then a final war of annihilation.

All this should have been clear to the lined-up democracies in the United Nations meetings. What was happening in southeastern Asia, especially in the Netherlands Indies and Indo-China, was an open and shut case. Here were situations which not only could "lead to war" but which constituted war, shooting and killing. But London assured Washington and Paris and Amsterdam that the British and Dutch and French forces, with their American-made arms, could keep the situation under control. That meant Byrnes and Bevin could devote their full time to heckling the Russians over Iran— where there was no war and where nobody was getting killed. So the poor little Indonesians and Annamites went on dying, and only Russia and Australia raised voices on their behalf. But nevertheless we must continue to hope that the UN will get around someday to seeing that justice is done in this remote corner of the world.

Meanwhile, the people of southeastern Asia are turning more and more to the idea of a union among themselves. The first step, proposed and supported by Filipino leaders, would be a Malayan Union to take in the people of the Philippines, the N.E.I., and Malaya in a loose-knit federation, a sort of local United Nations which would later include all of southeastern Asia and which would safeguard the welfare and importance of this region—sandwiched as it is between two of the most ancient and populous countries on earth, and two of the most unaggressive—India and China.

It seems inevitable that someday there will be a federation of all the Asiatic states, great and small. If in the years that it takes such a union to grow, the world continues to be divided into two great power blocs—USA versus USSR—then the Asiatics would have to choose between them, to take sides. At present the natives know they cannot expect any UN aid from America, the "splendid interventionist" on behalf of imperialism. But there is still time for us to change, still time to make the UN work for everybody.

The next few years will tell whether Asia will become united against the white man. Meanwhile, we should remember again the warning of General Romulo: "It must never be forgotten that Japan nearly accomplished her purpose in the Far East. Until this war the white man was considered a god in the Orient and often an unjust and fearsome divinity. Japan broke that fetish and revealed him as a man who could suffer humiliation and defeat. That was an Asiatic victory that will not be forgotten by races who have suffered and resented imperialism." And who, long after Japan's defeat, are still suffering and resenting.

PHILIPPINES

Congress finally voted half the funds required for the economic and physical reconstitution of our late ally.

But the Filipinos whose countrymen died because they loved liberty, are paying a high price for their choice of Manuel Roxas as president, a choice which was due in large extent to General MacArthur's support of Roxas and was also influenced by Congress' delay in giving the government of President Osmena the money it needed to start setting the country in order.

The truce between Roxas and the peasants was short-lived. Backed by the 90,000 American troops in the Philippines, Roxas directed his American-armed and -trained constabulary forces to open civil war against the small farmers living on the fertile plains north of Manila. Instead of initiating land reforms that would break up the huge holdings of the Catholic church and of his Spanish-Filipino friends, Roxas turned loose tanks, armored cars, bazookas, and machine guns against the men and women who sought to put an end to the tenant-farmer system and to win for their children a place in the new world for which so many Filipinos died.

President Osmena had been broad-minded enough to recognize that there are several kinds of collaborationists: those who work with the enemy to save their people from suffering, and those who are power-crazed and who desire wealth and position and favors for themselves. Roxas claimed to have worked with the Japanese to spare his fellow Filipinos, but his record as president of the first Philippines republic shed doubt on his motives. The record of his first months in office was one of purges of all opposition in the legislature and in government service, of a ban on radio criticism of his regime, of a rapid centering of control in the hands of one man—Roxas. The president named feudal landowners to his cabinet, appointed known Franco-sympathizers to high places, appeared in public with collaborationists awaiting trial for betraying their country.

The Battle of Bataan might never have been fought. . . .

The first food riots, the first anti-American incidents have occurred but they have been minor. MacArthur and Hirohito go serenely along governing this well-disciplined nation which is economically prostrate, its industry flattened, its navy and merchant shipping at the bottom of the ocean, its vast and rich colonial empire gone.

MacArthur's latest estimate is that it will take three years to "democratize" and "liberalize" Japan to a point where it will be safe to turn over the government to the Japanese and withdraw all but a handful of our troops, who would remain to suppress any attempts to revive the country militarily.

MacArthur may be right, but personally I distrust the Zaibatsu and their overseas friends. The greatest contributory factor to Japan's growth was the boost given by international cartelists and bog concerns, notably in America. The core of the Zaibatsu is intact, so is much of the international organization that backed Japan's rise to power. Japan has seen other nations come back from defeat and knows that it normally takes about twenty-five years from war to war. The Japanese have before them the lessons of two Germanys—the imperial and the Nazi—and the secrets of how Germany came back after 1918. There's a lot of bounce left in the Japs.

I distrust certain of MacArthur's generals who are still arguing that we should make Japan a bulwark against Russia and insisting that the Japs would fight as hard on our side as they did against us.

These hot-headed American militarists, betraying MacArthur's dream of establishing in Japan a system that will show the world the way to peace, are the worst type of war-mongers. Given their way, they would have us in war tomorrow, for their passion for blood-letting was not slaked in the recent slaughter.

George Acheson, the American Ambassador, has gone so far as to state that the aims of Japan and America "are now identical" which can only be interpreted as another case of Moscow-baiting.

And what of Hirohito? An official of his household announced on the first anniversary of the surrender that the Emperor's position was "stronger than ever." Which would be, perhaps, all right if Hirohito were actually a peace-loving man. But I am still unconvinced about that.

257

As my Russian newspaper friend in Shanghai prophesied, the Red Army did finally pull out of Manchuria, although they took nine months to do it—instead of the three to which they were pledged—and when they departed they took with them a good deal of the Jap machinery from Mukden and other industrial centers. From Chiang Kai-shek's point of view it might have been better if the Red forces had remained a little longer. But with American backing and the hysterical support of the American press, Chiang and the UN insisted that the Russians leave post-haste. So the Russians pulled out, leaving a vacuum in Manchuria. Chiang's armies were not prepared to move in; they lacked the shipping and transport to reach Manchuria. Consequently, the Chinese Reds swarmed in and Chiang's forces had to fight to dislodge them.

My Soviet colleague had denied, too, that anybody could buy Russia. But it is now apparent that there was a deal and a sellout. China was sold out at Yalta in return for Russia's entry in the war against Japan, and it was China who had to pay the price in the form of Soviet occupation of Port Arthur, the "internationalization" of Dairen, and Soviet management of the Northern Manchuria railroads.

By taking Port Arthur, Russia turned the clock back twenty-five years. Then, she renounced her concessions and special privileges and denounced imperialism. Now, she resumes these practices after all other nations have verbally abandoned them in China with the exception of Hong Kong, where the British hold on stubbornly. I say "verbally," because the United States has done no such thing.

There are two governments in post-war China. One is notoriously corrupt. Its officials live on graft and extortion and misuse of tax monies for their own purposes. The peasants in its areas are starving, kept in terrible poverty. The government has no visible public backing and the people have no representation whatever, for it is a government imposed from the top by force of arms. That is the government of Generalissimo Chiang Kai-shek and his American-educated wife, the beautiful Mei-ling Soong.

The other government claims to be a government of and for the people. In the eleven years of its existence it has brought education and enlightenment to many regions of the remote hinterlands of China. It has accomplished miracles in ridding the peasants of the crushing burden of taxes. It has cracked the landlord system and distributed lands to the needy. Its soldiers fight for a cause, not for money. Given time, the leaders of this government may become as corrupt as those of Nationalist China because corruption and power historically go hand in hand in China—and elsewhere. They may betray the people, although so far they have not done so.

But this second government has been tagged with the name "Communist," and because the leaders of the United States are deathly afraid of that name, the United States backed with armed force the government of Chiang Kai-shek, which not even our own leaders deny is corrupt and crooked and non-representative.

In backing the Nationalist government of China, we were playing a dangerous game, the old game of armed imperialism. In the year after Japan's surrender every important Chinese seaport with the exception of Hong Kong was patrolled by U. S. battleships and airplanes and marines. Once having intervened in China, we were caught in a trap. The Chinese people did not want American marines on their soil. They killed a few marines. And so the marines found justification for shooting down Chinese on Chinese soil, for doing exactly what the British and Dutch and French were doing in southeastern Asia. Once the marines had been killed, we could not withdraw from China because that would mean "loss of face." So we were dragged in deeper and deeper, and eventually it might become a question of sending whole armies to China to avenge the death of the marines who should not have been there in the first place; and after that the next step would be to find justification for dropping the atom bomb on the people of China. Killing with marine machine guns or with atom bombs is just a matter of degree, after all.

Behind the marines and the battleships and the airplanes, the traders swarmed in, the oil men, the machinery salesmen, the automobile peddlers, doing business under the protective guns of Americans in uniform. They were finding it difficult to do business. China's currency was shot to pieces. The old, soft life for the foreigner had largely disappeared in Shanghai and the Chinese weren't quite so quick to jump to the white man's call of "coolie" or "boy."

In contrast to our own armed intervention, Soviet Russia lived up—as far as could be determined—to its own promise to refrain from active participation in China's civil struggle. It is true that the Red Army turned over Japanese arms to the Chinese Communists, or abandoned them in places where they would fall into Communist

259

hands. But the Reds, unlike ourselves, did not send Soviet fighter pilots or warships to take sides in China's war.

Even without outside assistance on a major scale, Chinese Communists kept on fighting and Communists and Nationalists continued to kill each other. But, as a people, the Chinese too had learned from Japan's war that the white man is not a deity—except in that he now possesses the atom bomb.

RUSSIA

Russia and the United States are now Oriental neighbors, and not very good neighbors to date. Russia has been an Asiatic nation for centuries. The United States has maintained armed men and ships of war in Asia for a single century, and since the occupation of Japan in September, 1945, has been the leading military force of the Orient.

As a conquered nation occupied and governed not by the UN, but by the US, Japan is being trained as a "democratic" satellite of the United States. Chinese Nationalists fight with American arms. In Korea, American and Russian military forces glare suspiciously at each other across an iron curtain of bayonets. Big American bomber planes are poised within easy range of Vladivostok and Siberia on the airfields of Pacific island bases in whose underground tunnels there may or may not be atomic bombs waiting to be loaded into the big bellies of the B–29s.

How would we feel if as the result of a series of wars we found Red forces holding Mexico and Cuba and Canada and the governments of those countries being bolshevized? Suppose Red planes were based on Bermuda and Honolulu, and the Russian government possessed the atom-bomb secret while we did not. We would be scared stiff.

So is Russia, right now, and with good reason if the agents of Moscow have been listening to some of MacArthur's generals, and to some of our admirals, and to the bloodthirsty guys in Washington and New York and Chicago, and to the newspaper editors who have never seen what an atom bomb can do.

Chapter Twenty-Three

A Blast at Bikini and the Admirals

IT SEEMS INCREDIBLE THAT AFTER DEVELOPING THE most terribly destructive weapon known to man, the United States would turn around and deliberately lull the American people into a false sense of security about this new and deadly explosive. Yet that was the net result of the $70,000,007.00 extravaganza known as the Bikini atom-bomb tests, whose first two acts I witnessed after returning from the Far Eastern world described in the foregoing chapters.

Perhaps it is not generally known, but the Bikini tests were the outcome of the bitter feud between the United States Navy and our Army Air Forces, a feud which blossomed with new vigor after the surrender of Japan. Behind the internecine strife in which no punches were pulled, was a proposal to modernize and streamline our national defense system by creation of a single department under a civilian secretary, and by giving the Air Forces co-equal status with the Navy and the Army ground forces. The air generals argued that the wars against Japan and Germany had proved that no major conflict could be won without air control, and had also demonstrated the necessity for unity of command. Other experts pointed out that in fighting three wars against Japan—the Navy's, MacArthur's, and that of the Army Air Forces—we had indulged in much duplication of effort and matériel at a cost of untold billions, and had undoubtedly wasted many lives.

The Navy opposed the merger. Questioned during the war, Admirals Nimitz and Halsey and nearly every other top commander had been in favor of unification. But as soon as hostilities ended, the Navy's lobby got to work. Nimitz changed his testimony. Halsey changed his mind. As one man, the admirals argued against any change in our antiquated and costly system. Their arguments all had a striking similarity. Merger would "swallow the Navy," and they were against that. To my knowledge, not a single admiral had said, "I oppose merger because it would weaken our national defense." "I am against unification because it would be harmful to our country." They did not contend that merger was not in our national interests. All they said was that they were against unification because it would weaken the Navy's position—and thus their own prestige and power.

The next war might by-pass the Navy. It might be over in a few hours. But the admirals wanted to keep their surface ships. By God, they were going to keep them! They were going to keep Annapolis, with its snobbery and its caste system. Powerful interests were and are backing them in their fight. Front men for the Navy were the chairmen of the Senate and House Naval Affairs Committees, Senator Walsh and Representative Vinson, who would lose their Chairmanships if these committees were eliminated. And behind them is the Navy League, a creature of the big steel interests, and the shipbuilders and ammunition makers, ordnance salesmen, and the men who peddle the oil that runs the ships. Franklin D. Roosevelt, who loved ships, was a strong Navy supporter, too.

The line-up of admirals-naval committees-Navy League-munitions salesmen is a hard one to beat when they insist that we go on squandering our national treasure, our brains and time on monolithic antiquities instead of concentrating on stratospheric warfare. The Navy's spokesmen are smooth and plausible. "We must not give up proven weapons," they say, "in favor of crackpot schemes." They make it sound convincing. But what they do not point out is that those same arguments were used by the Navy in the years between World Wars I and II to prevent the development of long-range, land-based aviation. They were used by the admirals to forestall the growth of carrier aviation advocated by their own far-sighted young naval officers. They were used by the admirals when, in 1936, they brought forward a ten-year building program providing for construction of thirty-two battleships and only eighteen aircraft carriers, and the admirals are still building battleships even though it is a proven fact that we could have beaten Japan without a single battleship.

It was to support their arguments that the Navy must continue to exist *in statu quo* that the admirals' stooges rushed into Japan with the occupation forces and started a propaganda campaign intended to prove to the American taxpayers that the Navy had been the biggest single factor in beating Japan. The Air Forces' drum beaters were right in there beside the Navy men.

As I have said earlier in this book, the Japanese played one side off against the other and told each what it wanted to hear. Both the Army Air Forces and the Navy passed on to the American people as gospel truth the statements of the Japs. You may have seen one of the Navy's propaganda pictures entitled, "Report from Tokyo." With an introduction by Secretary Forrestal, the sound camera recorded in the words of Japanese naval officers how American sea power had forced Japan to surrender. The willing Japs were thoroughly coached in what they had to say. Not one of them—in the picture—had ever heard of B–29s. The Japs paid due tribute (well deserved) to American submarines and one of them stressed the point that American *carrier-based* airplanes had defeated the Japs at Midway in June, 1942.

Mr. Forrestal and his admirals wanted the American people to think that *carrier-based* airplanes have some special properties that enable them to sink ships and which are not possessed by land-based airplanes. This is so much hooey. The fact, of course, is that it didn't matter a hoot in hell whether the ship-sinking airplanes at Midway were land-based or carrier-based. The American sailors who died on ships hit by Japanese carrier-based planes at Midway are no deader than those killed off Guadalcanal by Japanese land-based planes.

The Air Forces had a prompt answer to the Navy's movie. In an effort to discredit the Navy, the Air Forces turned out a statement implying that the B–29 was the only airplane in existence that could carry the atom bomb. The inference was that the Superfortress had some mysterious features not given to other airplanes, and the implication was that the United States thus had a double security inasmuch as even if another nation succeeded in manufacturing the atom bomb it could not drop it. The purpose behind this statement was to discredit Navy aircraft carriers by claiming that they were worthless for atomic bombing. While I agree that carriers are no longer necessary due to the increased range of airplanes, this statement was an outright falsehood. The truth is that almost any military airplane now flying could carry and drop an atomic bomb. The advantage of the B–29 is that its altitude and speed insure a safe getaway for the crew. But even in these aspects, there is at least one British bomber equal to the B–29.

Another Air Forces trick was intended to steal some of the headlines away from the Navy on Navy Day in October, 1945. Three B–29s were dispatched secretly from northern Japan to fly non-stop to Washington where they were to arrive in the midst of Navy Day celebrations and in time to call the public's attention to the fact that the Navy was pretty well washed up as a front-line weapon in modern war. The plan fell short by 700 miles as the planes met headwinds and were forced to land in Chicago. The faces of the air generals fell almost as far.

The payoff, though, was the Air Forces stunt that led to Bikini. In the early days of our occupation of Japan, a publicity man for the Strategic Air Forces fed the American press a rumor that the remnants of the Jap fleet would be towed out to sea and sunk with atomic bombs. The airmen were confident that they could blow a fleet to bits with atom bombs (please note the plural) and thus demonstrate to the people of America that surface ships were obsolete. That would remove the last obstacles to merger, which meant giving the Air Forces an equal place in the sun.

The Navy fought as long as it could against the tests, and then yielded with reasonably good grace after the admirals had done some rapid calculations and come up with the conclusion that instead of meaning the end of surface fleets, the results of the tests could be so manipulated as to confuse the public completely and thus open the way for building bigger and better ships.

Not very much worth while in the interests of world peace or of our national defense came out of Bikini. But the tests did produce one bit of writing which seemed worth preserving. The piece of satire was named "Test Charlie" and referred to the scheduled third experiment, a deep underwater explosion. With the permission of author Stephen White, I reproduce his little work:

Everything was ready for the big explosion.

The most powerful atom bomb in the world was in position 2,500 feet under water. Gathered around it was the guinea pig fleet. It was a scientific experiment. Scientists wanted to know if a big atom bomb could blow hell out of the fleet. The Navy wanted to know. The public wanted to know. They were experimenting.

Thirteen hundred miles away was the electronic button which detonated the bomb. That was the only way to do it. A fuse had been discarded. Impractical.

The critical moment approached. Hushed scientists gathered around the button. Other hushed scientists watched their instruments. Still other hushed scientists rode airplanes over the scene. Never had the world seen so many hushed scientists. It was a new record.

The admiral nodded to his aide. The aide poised his finger over the electronic button. The hushed cabin became even more hushed. The second hand on the clock swept toward the appointed mark. It approached. It neared. It hovered. It met. The aide pressed the electronic button.

Nothing happened.

Again he pressed the button. Still nothing. Again and again. His button finger wearied. Still nothing. He changed fingers. It was no use.

Immediately the admiral swung into action. A crew of scientists was dispatched to the bomb site. They were still hushed. They donned special diving suits and descended 2,500 feet. They entered the bomb caisson.

There the horrid truth became apparent. Their months of preparation had been wasted. They had been hushed to no purpose.

The caisson was empty. The bomb was missing. It had been stolen.

This was serious.

The news was rushed to the admiral. He gasped. It was a natural reaction. When he had finished gasping he rushed to Washington and told the President. The President gasped. Soon all Washington was gasping. Only a few reactionaries refused to gasp. They remained hushed.

The President wasted no time. He called in the Army, the marines, and the FBI. They were ordered to find the bomb at all costs. They stopped gasping and went to work.

They were baffled. The Army sealed all airports. No results. The marines landed in Yucatan and shoved right off again. The FBI found a black sedan with its motor running in Tulsa, Oklahoma. It had nothing to do with the case. The Army, the marines, and the FBI gave up.

But one man refused to give up. He was Dr. Ergo Mutslif, the great physicist. In 1922 he had discovered that electrons whistle. Since then he had done nothing and he was bored. He assumed charge of the case.

He ordered a replica of the electronic button in portable size and slipped it into a satchel. At the President's insistence, the State Department issued him a passport saying he was Earl Browder. With this he could travel anywhere.

Dr. Mutslif had his suspicions. He was a suspicious man. That is what led him to discover that electrons whistle. It was the secret of his success.

He suspected Russia. He wasted no time. He went directly to Russia, entering at Vladivostok. He travelled from Minsk to Pinsk to Dvinsk, and from Tomsk to Omsk. At Omsk he took the railroad to Moscow. Halfway there he slipped off the train.

There, in the middle of Russia, halfway up the steppes, he opened his satchel and took out the portable button. He looked around carefully for NKVD men. There were none in sight. He pressed the button.

It worked. Dr. Mutslif's suspicions had been correct. Somewhere in Russia the delicate bomb responded to the button. It exploded. It was the biggest explosion in history. It destroyed Russia, Poland, Latvia, Estonia, Dr. Mutslif, Yugoslavia, Czechoslovakia, and Sweden.

The mystery was solved. Russia had stolen the bomb. America immediately declared war on Russia. It was futile. Russia could not be found. The marines landed on Yucatan. It was a habit. Otherwise there was no action.

A new bomb is being prepared. This time it will be guarded carefully. With luck the scientists will find out if it will blow hell out of the fleet. It is an important scientific experiment.*

This bit of fiction underlines very effectively the utter absurdity of the Bikini tests. No single atom bomb yet developed will blow up all of Russia and neighboring countries, but the present bomb

---

* When he was shown this story, the Russian correspondent at Bikini—a Red Navy captain—read it with great care. At the end he laughed a little wryly and commented with finality, "It couldn't happen!"

"Why not?" we asked, expecting him to say that Russia wouldn't steal anything, or that the bomb wasn't that powerful.

"It couldn't happen," he repeated. "There's no railway from Omsk to Moscow."

had so thoroughly demonstrated its deadly killing power pre-Bikini that only the skeptics or the misinformed could still doubt that it is capable of destroying our civilization, centered as it is around great cities, ports, and manufacturing centers. After a very detailed, cold-blooded study, a group of top military men in Washington has estimated that fifty per cent of the population of the United States would be killed or wounded in the first few hours of an atomic war in which the blow would fall without warning and would be delivered by supersonic-speed airplanes and by stratospheric, pilotless missiles. If we start now, today, to disperse our cities and bury our industry and transportation underground, then possibly only twenty per cent of our population would die in the first attack.

Yet we had to hold a "scientific experiment" at Bikini to see how many fish the bomb would kill and how many warships it would sink. After its original reluctance, the Navy was quite agreeable to the tests because the admirals had become convinced beforehand that not all the ships would be destroyed.

So the two bombs were set off. The first one was dropped from an airplane at about 30,000 feet, that bit of nonsense being a concession to the airmen who demanded an important part in the show. The bomb could easily have been suspended from an anchored balloon and made to explode exactly at the intended point, but that would have been too simple. At the end of its long drop, the bomb was several hundred yards off its target. Even so, it sank five ships and damaged fifty others in varying degrees. The second, the shallow-water burst, sent to the bottom three of the strongest ships ever built—the U.S.S. "Saratoga," the American battleship "Arkansas," and the Japanese battleship "Nagato." It damaged a number of other ships and charged others with such deadly radioactivity that it would be months before they could be approached in safety.

The tests showed conclusively that an atomic air-burst would destroy all the light ships in its vicinity; and that a miss of as much as 500 yards in an underwater explosion would fatally damage capital ships. It showed that a naval task force would be completely crippled by—say—twenty bombs. It proved that an amphibious landing such as Normandy, Sicily, Iwo Jima, or Okinawa would have been impossible against an atomic-bomb defense. It proved—in the words of General Roy Geiger of the Marine Corps—that war had been "revolutionized."

These results were interesting enough in their way, but the bad feature was that inasmuch as only one bomb was used in each case and not all the ships were sunk, it gave the admirals a new chance to blind the public to the fact that surface ships are the most vulnerable of all targets and never again can be a first-line weapon of offense or defense in warfare.

The costly Bikini show was given the code name CROSSROADS, an inspiration of dramatic nomenclature highly in keeping with the melodramatic aspects of the whole performance. To the public, the name OPERATIONS CROSSROADS suggested that we were actually at the crossroads in thinking about our national defense, and that the experiments would determine whether naval forces were essential in the light of modern weapons and tactics, or whether the money could be better spent on other means of offensive and defensive war.

Not so to the admirals! They entered the tests with the firm determination to go on building ships regardless of the outcome. And they will go on building them—taking money and men and materials from other work—until that fatal day when atomic rockets start plunging onto our cities, and the country, or at least what's left of it, awakes to the fact that it has been betrayed by the admirals.

On A-day minus two, the members of the supposedly impartial Joint Chiefs Evaluation Board came bounding over the blue waters of Bikini lagoon in a small boat and climbed aboard the press ship "Appalachian." The question was put to Vice Admiral John Hoover, whether, if the tests proved the advisability of such a course, the Navy would in the interests of the nation abandon its surface ships.

"Genial John" answered without hesitation, "We will not give up our surface ships!"

And there you have it! Even when enemy parachutists are landing in Chicago and Detroit and New Orleans and Los Angeles, after the radioactivity caused by the storm of atom bombs has finally cleared away from the ruins, the Navy will still be shouting, "We will not give up our surface ships!"

Immediately after the bomb dropped, the admirals cut loose a smoke screen of fast talk about "new construction" and "new formations." This meant, in the first case, the elimination of ship superstructures which were shown to be vulnerable to blast damage even at distances up to a mile; and, in the second, wider dispersal of task forces. There can be no other "new" surface ship construction or "new" formations.

"The results of the test," said one admiral—talking with a straight face about a weapon potentially capable of wiping out civilization—

"indicate the advisability of considering certain changes in naval architecture."

"There is no question," conceded former Congressman Melvin J. Maas, speaking of the bomb that destroyed two cities and killed or injured 320,000 persons, "that the bomb is very destructive. However, my net impression is that it is not very effective against a surface fleet at sea. . . . It has not basically changed naval warfare."

Maas had said before the test, "Even if every ship is sunk, it will simply mean that we must triple or quadruple our present navy." Maas, for eighteen years a member of the House Naval Affairs Committee, is now paid $10,000 a year as a special consultant to that committee.

Vice Admiral W. H. P. Blandy, who conducted the tests with superb efficiency, was deeply impressed by the results and especially by the effects of radioactivity. Admiral Blandy is a man of great intelligence and vision. I suspect that he may be convinced that surface ships are weapons of the past. But if he were to say so publicly, he would immediately become the target of united attacks by the Annapolis hierarchy and perhaps be martyrized as the Navy's Billy Mitchell.

Now, nobody except the "extremists" contends that we should abandon all our ships immediately. The extremists argue that we should give them to Russia in the hope that the Reds would be so diverted by these toys that they would fall behind in their research on atomic bombs and self-propelled, long-range missiles. Of course, this is a foolish hope. There is no provision in the current—1946—Moscow war budget for huge naval expenditures. The Russians are not going to attempt to match our naval might. They are convinced that navies have had their day.

The non-extremists say, "Keep the ships we've got for the next four or five years that it will take us to perfect new airplanes and new missiles. But don't spend a penny more than is necessary on them and don't build any new ones. And most of all do not mislead our public into thinking that surface ships will play a major part in an atomic war. They may serve to carry follow-up forces—but only after the enemy has been defeated in the air."

The storm of controversy and argument that followed the Bikini tests was duck soup for the admirals. It gave them a chance to divert public attention from the lessons of the last war and from the developments in the months since that conflict ended.

269

The most important lesson, as far as navies go, was that airplanes and not surface ships now control sea lanes. Some of the admirals admit that, and they go on to say that therefore we need aircraft carriers. The answer, I believe, is that we did need aircraft carriers. Last war, past tense! What is an aircraft carrier? It is simply a floating base for airplanes that, by reason of its mobility, extends the range of the airplanes it carries. At the beginning of the war against Japan, and indeed nearly until the end, the range of airplanes was so short that we did need carriers. But at the end of the war, airplanes were flying 1,500 miles round-trip to escort the B-29s on bombing missions to Japan. And today, a jet-propelled fighter plane can fly 3,000 miles non-stop from Los Angeles to New York in 4 hours and 19 minutes! We already have big bombers capable of flying to almost any part of the world with loads of atomic bombs. Very soon, these giant planes will be flying at speeds greater than sound.

Look at the map and see the bases we now hold and study the distances to the cities of our prospective enemies. All of them are within range of land-based airplanes which could carry paratroops and landing forces for the follow up after the original bombing. On the other hand, if we attempted a seaborne invasion against strong aerial defenses, plus atomic mines and atom-firing submarines, it is almost a certainty that our ships would be sunk 500 miles from the enemy's coast. We could do that today to any enemy that attempted to invade us by sea, and do it by airplanes alone without sending a single surface ship out of our harbors. The danger to us as a nation in the admirals' line of thinking is that they will get us so involved with antiquated weapons that we will not be ready for the next war, if it comes. That is just what they did in fighting the growth of long-range aviation before the last war.

Now, the United States is a very rich nation. That is why we could afford the luxury of fighting three wars in the Pacific and a couple in Europe while at the same time carrying on nearly normal life at home. Perhaps we can afford to make the admirals happy in their declining years. Why not give them some battleships, and a handful of their toy carriers and toy airplanes, and send them down to hold perpetual maneuvers around Tahiti? That would clear the decks for the forward-looking men in our country's service—Army, Navy, and Air—to go ahead with the plans for unification and to prepare for atomic war. Personally, I don't want the surface-ship admirals to have any part in our national defense in that kind of conflict.

Chapter Twenty-Four

Compliments to Some Generals

IF YOU ACCEPT THE CONTENTION THAT THE "BAT-tleship mentality" that so retarded us before and during our last war still exists in our Navy, you will probably agree that it would not be wise for us to give the admirals control of atomic energy. What some of the admirals would do would be either to outlaw atomic warfare entirely, or limit the use of atomic missles to those fired from warships—preferably battleships—or those dropped by *carrier-based* airplanes. This might not be a bad idea if you could confine the slaughter in war to the killing of professional militarists by other professional militarists, but this is hardly practical. The professionals—as MacArthur remarked—have a habit of going on living.

But in case the preceding pages have given the impression that I am carrying the torch for the Air Forces and the ground generals as opposed to the admirals—or that I think these gentlemen any better equipped than their Annapolis counterparts to control the atom bomb—it is time to set the record straight. To do so will require a brief detour to Europe.

We used to recount a rather grim anecdote during the war in Europe. A group of six or seven GIs of a reserve infantry division are playing cards in a field some ten miles behind the front lines in France. This is a quiet sector which has been in American hands for months. The noise of airplanes is heard, and the soldiers look up anxiously. One of them grabs a pair of binoculars, studies the planes, and announces in a relieved tone, 'Them's Krauts. Messerschmitts." They all resume the game.

A half-hour later, the roar of a new group of low-flying planes is heard. The binocular expert looks at them and shouts in a terrified voice, "Americans!" The doughfoots scatter for foxholes and dive in just as the planes come over with their machine guns spitting. They rake the area thoroughly, setting fire to a half-dozen trucks plainly marked with the big, circled white star that identifies them as American; they do victory rolls in the sky and then pour on the gas and head back to base.

Unfortunately, a tragic grain of truth inspired such tales. More times than has been published, American troops were killed by American planes and the fault was not so much that of the pilots as of the "air men's" credo. The men who are of this faith clung unwaveringly to the belief that the war being fought in the air against Germany and Japan was the main show, and what took place on the ground, on the sea or under the sea was largely incidental to their efforts. De Seversky, with his "Victory Through Air Power," was the loudest spokesman for these air generals.

It was equally unfortunate that a good many American planes were shot down by American anti-aircraft gunners. But in a majority of cases this was not due to the fact that individual gunners were indoctrinated in the idea that any plane was legitimate prey. It was rather the result of inexperience, nervousness, and confusion, the latter frequently being a direct product of recent bombing and strafing by our own planes.

It was the writer's fortune, or misfortune, as a reporter to be either directly on the scene or a near-witness of some of the major snafus of the war both in the Pacific and in Europe:—the Clark Field disaster when our planes were caught on the ground; the first battle of Savo Island on the day after the Guadalcanal landings, when stupidity and timidity cost us four cruisers and hundreds of lives; the torpedoing of the U.S.S. "Saratoga," when the admiral in command did everything but radio to Japanese submarines that he was cruising around day after day in narrow waters—the same waters where the "Wasp" was torpedoed and sunk. I saw the flaming planes plunge into the Mediterranean off the Sicilian Coast on D-day plus one, American planes shot down by American naval guns as they came in low to drop their paratroop reinforcements behind hardpressed Gela. Over four hundred Americans died that night, killed by other Americans.

I was at Anzio on that first fatal day when the hesitation of the high command turned the prospect of a swift, slashing victory into a prolonged and bloody defensive siege. An assignment took me to

General Eisenhower's headquarters in Tunisia at the time Viscount Montgomery very nearly lost us our toehold at Salerno by sitting down with his Eighth Army to hold "practice maneuvers" in the Italian toe while the British-Americans of the Fifth Army fought for their lives a few miles farther north.

I have been bombed by American planes too many times to remember all of them. But there are some that cannot be forgotten. Especially the sustained and vicious attacks made by the U. S. 9th Air Force, ironically dubbed the "9th Luftwaffe" by the survivors, on our front lines near Cherbourg three days before that French port was captured. Nobody was shooting at the 9th's pilots that day. As their commander, Major General "Pete" Quesada, explained from his hedgerow crouch a few feet from me, "The boys just got the wrong hill." So that they attacked us instead of the Germans, and blew hell out of a long line of troops of the 78th Division as they marched up to go into the line. Our artillery was firing frantic identification signals, but plane after plane—P–38s, P–47s—came in to bomb and strafe our hill instead of the one held by the Germans. "Just a little mistake," as Quesada put it.

And then a few days later there was a day in a field behind the St. Lo-Periers road when the air forces gave a demonstration of what Lt. Gen. Walter Bedell Smith, Eisenhower's chief of staff calls close air-ground cooperation. Eisenhower ordered an all-out air attack to blast a hole through which our infantrymen and armor were to pour to break out of the Cotentin peninsula and embark on the liberation of France by a series of swift sweeps. Knowing the propensity of our own air forces to bomb our own troops, the GIs of the 4th, 9th, and 1st Infantry Divisions were drawn back several thousand yards from the easily identifiable St. Lo-Periers highway, which was the natural bomb line and beyond which were the German positions, held by a mixture of youthful and veteran paratroopers, all of them determined soldiers.

So the mediums and heavies came over from England in wave after wave, their wings silver in the bright sunlight. The first planes spotted their targets all right and dropped beyond the highway in German territory. Then smoke and dust from the bombs began to fill the air and the subsequent waves began dumping their bombs closer and closer to our lines. In a short time the St. Lo-Periers highway was hidden from the air, and the newly arrived aviators spotted another parallel road which they mistook for the bomb line—ap-

273

parently not having time to look things over carefully. This second road was well within our lines and down on both sides of it came an earthshaking rain of death. Lt. Gen. Leslie McNair fell, torn apart by American bombs. So did many other Americans, killed by their fellow Americans in the sky. The weather officers had predicted the prevailing winds would blow the smoke toward the German lines, leaving a clearly visible bombing area. When the wind shifted, there seemed to exist no method for informing the pilots that they were bombing their brothers. The fighter escort pilots, circling above the scene, saw it all, but they were powerless to call off the slaughter. No system had been set up to avoid such eventualities.

Such occurrences were no surprise to me because I had heard the airmen's credo from one of the highest of the air-force moguls. Because a good many other airmen share his views, let us identify him simply by the generic name of "Flyboy." When I was covering Eisenhower's headquarters at Sidi Bou Said, Tunisia, after the fall of Sicily, Flyboy took up residence in a nearby palace which had a miniature river running through its splendid, Moslemic halls with their stucco walls and spidery, lattice-work windows. In such surroundings, it was easy to understand how the infantrymen's war seemed remote indeed to the Air Force generals. But some of us had been with infantry and expected to go back with them. In Sicily, I had seen American planes attack on three successive days a town held by Canadian troops. At Brolo, where American forces were holding on by the skin of their teeth after an amphibious endrun around German positions on the north coast of Sicily, American dive bombers had swarmed down on them in a series of deliberate, morale-crushing attacks. Yet at Salerno, Flyboy had thrown in his heavies with surprisingly few casualties to our own side.

I asked Flyboy what means if any were being taken to improve communications between ground and air forces, to establish definite identification before loosing deadly air assaults, to insure that future operations would be conducted as efficiently as those at Salerno. It was already well known that in the Pacific, our Navy fliers had worked out a scheme of close coordination with ground troops. There highly successful tactics were later to be further developed in cooperation with MacArthur's air commander, General George Kenney, who insisted that his airmen fight the enemy and not our own side. To the Navy's credit, it was already far advanced in its work with marine landing forces when the war started.

But in Europe in the fall of 1943, Flyboy wasn't interested. "We have so many tons of bombs to drop," he said bluntly in answer to my question, "and we drop 'em. It is inevitable that we kill some of our men."

I agreed that perhaps an occasional death could not be avoided, but not on any such large scale as the airmen termed "inevitable." In the Pacific, planes worked close up with the ground troops. An air liaison officer was stationed with each infantry battalion major, and he was in direct contact with the planes overhead. The liaison officer would call the pilots: "Hey, there's a Jap machine gun behind that tree one hundred yards from us. We'll toss over a mortar shell." The pilot would spot the smoke and in turn drop a practice smoke bomb. Then, being absolutely sure of the location of the enemy, they would make their bombing and strafing runs. I told Flyboy about it. He answered, "We are not doing anything to improve liaison over here."

Bit by bit, the infantrymen did get a little closer cooperation. But it was a tough fight because Flyboy and many of his buddies didn't give a damn about ground operations except when they won new bases for the heavy bombers. Many airmen resented the idea of air power being used to fight enemy ground troops. They swore that they could beat Germany from the air and by air power alone, and any distraction from what they considered this primary war was most annoying.

Thus at no time did the airmen in Europe throw the entire weight of their strength into the battle for Anzio. In those days we at Anzio wondered why the air forces did not go all out to isolate the beachhead as they had done at Salerno, why they did not make continuous raids on the Germans' few usable communications lines in Italy. We found out later that instead of flying the few miles to Anzio they were flying 1,500 miles to bomb the oil wells of Rumania. That is called "strategic air war."

All this, however, does not make them either traitors or villains. It was their blind conviction that the strategic air war was all-important, and that by fighting it they were hastening the defeat of the enemy.

And so it was that when the "strategic" bombers were diverted to temporary "tactical" support of ground forces, the slaughter of our own troops went on. Our infantry captured the Italian mountain town of Venafro early in November, 1943, and for months afterward our own planes bombed our own troops on the road to Venafro.

275

Even in the widely advertised strategic bombing of Cassino, some twenty miles away, a large number of our B–17s laid their high explosives on Venafro—and this more than four months after it had been captured.

The brightest chapter in air-ground cooperation was the isolation by airplanes of the Normandy beachhead, thus slowing down the Germans' buildup, and the subsequent close working together of planes and tanks in the drive across France. In those operations, the Air Forces did something which for years had seemed perfectly possible and logical, and vitally necessary—to everyone except the air generals. But the "strategic" air men did a lot to spoil such temporarily excellent results by committing such further "inevitable" killings as those at Malmédy, where American troops were bombed by B–17s for seven straight days. During these seven days it was impossible to reach through the chain of command to get the word to our Air Forces that Malmédy was in American hands and had been for some time.

In these days of modern communications, it would not seem too difficult to relay such a message through division, corps, army and army group back to Eisenhower's headquarters and from there through the air liaison generals back to England, where the high priests of air power consulted their maps and turned out their statistics amid the baronial splendors of the huge estates they had appropriated as headquarters. But if the messages did penetrate that far, they never got to the pilots.

Or, in the remote case that the pilots were informed that they were killing their brother Americans, they were, apparently, in too much of a hurry to linger a while over the target area and make correct identification of landmarks. In contrast to the Pacific, where pilots stayed out as long as they had gas, the motto in Europe seemed to be "drop your bombs quick and get home." The American Air Forces didn't believe in having pilots out after dark and throughout the war in Europe the Germans moved on the roads and railroads from dusk to dawn without interference from American airplanes.

A typical example of Air Force megalomania cropped up in a briefing during the Battle of the Bulge in December, 1944. A jubilant Air Force officer announced, "We shot down one hundred thirty-two German planes yesterday for the loss of one-third of that number. It was a marvelous victory."

"But," a reporter interposed, "you didn't stop the German tanks, did you? You didn't even attack them."

"No."

"Let's suppose," said the reporter, "that you played it exactly the way the Germans wanted you to. Let's suppose they wanted to draw you off into air battles while their tanks crashed through and went where they wanted to go. If that is the case, then it was a German victory, too, wasn't it?"

"Why, yes," agreed the nonplussed air man.

A few days later, our planes got to work on the German tank columns, which meanwhile had been stopped by our battered infantry, armor, and artillery forces. Once they got going, the planes did a superb job reminiscent of their finest performances in the early days in France.

The "strategic" air generals in the Pacific shared the same distaste as their counterparts in Europe for turning aside even momentarily from their strategic air war. During the battle of Okinawa, the B–29s were diverted from their fire raids on Japan to attacks on the Japanese bases from which Kamikaze planes were flying to dive into our carriers and other warships supporting the Okinawa fighting. The B–29 commander, Major General Curtis LeMay, and his flying companions were very put out by this diversion. They made it very plain that if all the ships off Okinawa were sunk by Kamikazes, that wouldn't make any great difference. They were sincerely convinced that they were beating Japan from the air, and they resented any diversion from this main endeavor.

Similarly, LeMay and other airmen of the de Seversky school were perturbed by the use of the atom bomb. LeMay would just as soon not have used it, because he believed Japan could be forced into surrender by orthodox bombing with high explosives and incendiaries. It was LeMay who was quoted as saying, after a survey of Bikini lagoon from the air after the first atom bomb test in July, 1946, "This was not a good bomb." All subsequent scientific measurements proved that the bomb was, indeed, a good one, and the evidence is lying still at the bottom of Bikini lagoon in the form of sunken ships.

General Spaatz, in his turn, wasn't too hot about the introduction of such newfangled things as atom bombs and self-propelled missiles. Like the admirals with their battleships, Spaatz likes the idea of a weapon that's a known quantity; in his case, an airplane with men flying it and dropping bombs that contain just ordinary explosives, without any of this confusing radioactivity business. I asked Spaatz on Guam at the time of Japan's surrender what the role of the Air Force would be in a push-button, rocket war.

"Why," he said, "when the rockets come over we'll shoot 'em down with fighter planes."

We protested, "But no fighter plane known can penetrate the sub-stratosphere and reach rocket speeds."

"Nonsense," said the general. "The rockets can't go any three thousand miles an hour. Their speed is determined by the law of gravity."

"But these aren't falling bodies. They are propelled missiles."

"We'll catch 'em just the same," said the general.

Now for a word about some other representatives of the military minds who, if some people have their way, would be given control of the atom bomb and thus control the destiny of man. Since the end of the war, the generals have been riding high in America, a condition of affairs which causes serious concern to many of our citizens. One of the professional soldiers appointed to a key civilian post is our present ambassador to Moscow, Lt. General Walter Bedell Smith, who was Eisenhower's Chief of Staff in Europe. Twice during the war, Bedell Smith ran afoul of American newspaper representatives and was criticized by our press, but these things were overlooked at the time of his appointment to Moscow.

It was Bedell who denied that General Ike had "reprimanded" George Patton for slapping a shell-shocked soldier in Sicily. Literally, Smith was telling at least half the truth, because what Ike had done was to order Patton to apologize, which did not constitute a reprimand in military language. But Bedell Smith's statement was so misleading that Ike was later obliged to reveal the whole truth about the incident and its sequel. It was also Bedell who was held responsible by reporters for the statement that General McNair had been killed "by enemy action" in Normandy, when the general was actually a victim of American bombs.

A good many people, too, disagree with Smith's interpretations of affairs in his current war reminiscences, especially his allegations that there was never any British-American friction at high-command level, that American air-ground teamwork was uniformly excellent throughout the war, and that Ike all but invited the Germans to make their breakthrough in the Ardennes, thereby drawing

278

them into a battle whose results were a foregone conclusion.

My own first meeting with Bedell Smith is still fresh in mind. It was a day or two after Italy had signed the armistice in September, 1943, and the Italian fleet had surrendered. All the principal participants in the highly dramatic armistice negotiations were at Eisenhower's headquarters in Tunisia, and General Ike gave his O.K. for me to talk to them and get the full story for the history books. The Americans involved gave their accounts very readily, but the Italian signatory and chief negotiator, General Castellano, wasn't having any. The Sicilian soldier realized he had a story worth money to any newspaper in the world. He stalled and sideslipped, and then said he would write the story for publication himself in a year or two. When I pointed out that Ike had given instructions for Castellano to talk, the general leaned back in his deckchair on the roof of AFHQ's villa, fingered his green tie, and stared at his red and yellow socks. He refused to tell his story.

Next day I went to Bedell Smith to protest. "General Eisenhower told me to get all the details of the armistice story, sir, but General Castellano won't say anything."

Beetle wasn't very interested. "Well, if he doesn't want to talk there is no way to make him."

"This is a matter of historical importance, sir," I insisted. "The Boss thinks the story should be written."

"I won't have Castellano annoyed in any way."

"The trouble with Castellano," I said, "is that he doesn't realize the role of the press in a democratic country. He is so used to dealing with the corrupt Fascist press . . ."

There followed an argument in which Bedell Smith took the position that Castellano was no Fascist and which was interrupted only when Eisenhower stuck his tanned, friendly face around the partially opened door. "Bedell, can I see you for a moment." Smith went out, and when he came back he was making a visible but only partly successful effort to control himself. He tried changing the subject.

"What do you think of Terry Allen?" he demanded in a tone that left no doubt of his own opinion.

"I don't know him well, but it seems to me he made the First Division one of the best in the Army. He's won every one of his battles." Allen had just been relieved as division commander for unannounced reasons.

279

"Made the First Division!" Smith shouted. "He ruined the First Division. He started out to make it a rough, tough outfit that would win battles. He thought it was enough to win battles, to have battlefield discipline. He didn't realize the importance of discipline when the troops are out of the line."

"He seems to have been able to make enemies," I answered, and on this note our friendly little parley ended.

But, like many another good man, Terry couldn't be kept down. He came back to France and Germany with the 104th Infantry Division which he had trained and made it one of the best fighting outfits of the war.

Among the high-riding generals at war's end was Mark Wayne Clark, and he is still doing okay at this writing despite public demands for an investigation of his conduct of the war in Italy. Clark has been attacked both for timidity and lack of imagination as well as for alleged military ineptitude. In justice to Clark, it should be stated, first of all, that war in the mountains of Italy would have been a murderous affair under any circumstances and we probably would never have fought there except for Churchill's insistence; and, secondly, that Clark never had an overabundance of troops to exploit any of his local successes. Judgment then must be confined to the question of whether he did the best that could have been done with the forces at his command. A good many of the soldiers under him didn't think so. To the GIs, his name of Mark Wayne Clark was twisted into "Mark Time" Clark.

Such incidents as one at San Pietro contributed to the acquisition of his nickname. Three thousand American boys died or were wounded in January, 1944, in capturing this little mountain town which lies a few miles north of the Volturno River and a few miles south of Cassino, the German stronghold where other thousands bled and died. Yet, although this is not generally known, San Pietro had been in American hands exactly three months before the ruined stone houses were finally cleared of the last German defenders and we gained a few more hundred yards on the bloody road to Cassino. On November 7, 1944, Major General Troy Middleton's troops of the 45th Division took the town of Venafro on the Upper Volturno and patrols pushed on over the mountain road and into San Pietro. They found no Germans and were starting to shove on down to encircle the Germans on the hills to their south and rear of them and to take Highway 6, leading to Cassino. They had outflanked the

Germans, driven a salient through their mountain line, and planned to drive on for Cassino before the Germans could get their defenses set up.

Clark heard of the breakthrough and ordered the patrols pulled back. Middleton was subsequently relieved of his command, on the pretext of an injured knee. He was on his way home when General Eisenhower intercepted him in Algiers and assigned the able, mild-mannered Louisianan to his staff. Middleton was promoted to lieutenant general, led the 8th Corps into France, captured Brest, held the line at the Battle of the Bulge, and finished the war deep in the heart of Germany.

Before he went, Middleton gave me a summation of the war in Italy which General George Patton would have wholeheartedly endorsed. "The trouble here," he said, "is that there is too much getting pinned down. Take the case of a patrol attacking up a mountain side under fire by two machine guns. If they keep going, they will take some casualties but they will knock out the guns and gain the dominating high ground. But if, when the machine guns open up, they allow themselves to be pinned down and take shelter behind boulders, it is only a question of time until each one of them is dead or wounded because the Germans have every square foot of the hillside zeroed in with mortar and artillery fire. Multiply that patrol by an army and you have what is happening in Italy. The high command shows no disposition to take its necessary losses at the proper time. Therefore we are getting bled to death without any commensurate gains."

We were attached to Clark's headquarters at the time, and it seemed as if a good many of his staff were more interested in future American politics than in getting on with the war. Reports were circulated that the youngish, tall, and handsome Clark had his heart set on becoming President of the United States, and these rumors were never denied by his highest officers. In fact, they gained substantial support when Clark announced formation of the "Fifth Army Association" whose announced purpose was to perpetuate in postwar life the "ideals and aspirations of the Fifth Army," or words very much to that effect. Failing to see what ideals and aspirations the Fifth Army should have as distinct from those of the United States as a whole, many of us refused to join. Those who did were given glossy cards signed by Mark Wayne Clark and paid for by Lord-knows-who.

If Clark's armies were "pinned down" around Cassino, it is difficult to find a word to describe what happened to them at Anzio.

We landed at Anzio without opposition, taking the enemy completely by surprise and finding the beaches undefended. The road to Rome, only eighteen miles away, was wide open, but to keep it from being slammed against us we faced the obvious necessity of occupying the hills dominating the beachhead and the two principal highways which were the German supply routes for their Cassino stronghold. Once the roads were cut, the Germans at Cassino would be isolated.

Jubilantly, our troops headed for the high ground on the day of the landing. They were moving along fast, their supplies pouring in behind them, when the order came for them to stop and dig in along the Mussolini Canal. So there, perforce, they dug and there they sat for long, bloody weeks while the Germans occupied the high ground and poured tons of shells down on the exposed beachhead. The man who gave the order to stop was Maj. Gen. Lucas, the American in command of all forces at Anzio, but Clark must either have approved it or ordered it and it must have been known likewise to "Jumbo" Wilson, the British general who succeeded Eisenhower in the Mediterranean. What had gone wrong was that Clark (and Wilson) had completely misjudged the reaction of the Germans to the landing in their rear. He had expected them to pull out of Cassino as soon as they learned that we had got ashore at Anzio. He expected his troops to swarm across the Rapido River, break through the demoralized and fleeing Germans, and drive them into the guns of the Anzio forces. But the Germans did nothing of the kind. They slaughtered the troops Clark had ordered into frontal attacks across the Rapido. They kept the trap at Anzio from being closed by stopping us (after we had stopped voluntarily) short of the north-south highways.

General Lucas, the pleasant, white-haired gentleman who had ordered the inland advance at Anzio to be halted, received the press on D-Day plus 3. He was installed in a comfortable villa near the beach, and in itself that was an indication to veteran soldiers and reporters that he didn't intend to go anywhere very fast. Commanders who kept moving didn't take up headquarters in houses. They slept in the field. You seldom caught soldiers like Bradley indoors. But Clark's Fifth Army was headquartered in a palace for much of the war, and Lucas was one of Clark's corps commanders.

We asked General Lucas when he was going to take the commanding high ground and he answered, "My orders are not to take the high ground, but to advance *in the direction* of the high ground." Then he said, "The Hun is a very fine soldier. . . ."

This was likewise a favorite statement of the soldier who was one of the most controversial figures of the war, beloved by the English and anything-but-beloved by countless Americans. He is General Sir Bernard Laws Montgomery, now Viscount of Alamein. Here are some nearly verbatim extracts from General Montgomery's briefing to the correspondents, delivered in London a short time before D-Day in Normandy.

"The Hun is a mighty fine soldier. First-class fighting man the German. Excellent soldier. Hmm. Fine fighter. Takes advantage of terrain. Knows how to hold onto the high ground. Has a fine eye for terrain features. Fine soldier. Hmm. I'm glad to be fighting Rommel again. Know his tactics. Good soldier, Rommel, but I know how he thinks. Happy to be up against him once more. Has a lot of first-class troops, Rommel. Beat him once and can beat him again. Fine soldier, Rommel, Hmm." And so on—all of it as dry as the desert sand on which the British general won his one big victory and as regurgitatively repetitive as a raw onion and cucumber sandwich.

Rommel must have been equally delighted when he learned he was facing Montgomery at one end of the Allied line in Normandy. He knew exactly how Montgomery would fight, because the Briton had exactly one battle in his repertory and he fought that same battle throughout the war. If Montgomery had ever been in over-all command of British and American forces, we would probably have reached Paris sometime in the fall of 1947 and the Rhine in 1960.

A Canadian general whose troops fought under Montgomery explained it this way: "Monty is still fighting the battle of Verdun. Despite his experiences in Africa, he has no concept of a war of movement, of breakthrough and encirclement. At the very outside, he is capable of visualizing an advance of ten miles. He uses paratroops like a scouting patrol."

Montgomery always fought in terms of El Alamein, where he scored his first victory over Rommel's overextended troops, whose supplies across the Mediterranean had been badly cut by the RAF and by the Royal Navy through its grim stand on Malta. At El Alamein, Monty massed 800 artillery guns, all the armor at his command, and all the airplanes. He plastered the German positions with artillery and air bombs and made a mass attack on a three-division front.

He broke through. He went four miles. He sat down. The Germans headed back post-haste across the desert and in due time Monty followed them—his due time having given them the opportunity to prepare their defenses of Tunis. He did make a stab at encirclement at the Mareth Line, but things seem to have gone wrong and it developed into the same old "Montgomery Battle" all over again.

Then came Sicily. Montgomery's forces landed on the southeastern side of the island and Bradley's on the south. Montgomery was to slash out for Catania. But with Montgomery there is no such thing as slashing out. He cannot conceive of a battle as starting in any other way than with two armies lined up against each other in fixed positions. You bring up more than 800 guns, cut loose your barrage, and then order your infantry to advance a couple of miles. Then you sit down again to "reorganize," to "gather your tail under you." That last was Montgomery's favorite expression—except for the line about the Hun being a very fine soldier. By it, Montgomery meant that he would not attack, whatever the enemy situation, unless he had a month's supplies of food and ammunition, unless his guns were all in position, unless everything was all "tidied up"—the maps on the wall of his trailer all neatly marked in red and blue, the staff subjected to innumerable briefings, the soldiers' guns cleaned, their shoes polished.

So Montgomery was a week behind schedule in attacking Catania. He gave the Germans of the Hermann Goering Division time to dig in there, so that they could fight the kind of battle that delighted Montgomery. He fought it—an army against two German regiments, and the regiments held him up so long that most of the three Nazi divisions escaped across the Straits of Messina to face us again in Italy.

Montgomery's Eighth Army followed them across and landed unopposed, and a few days later the American-British Fifth Army went in at Salerno. The plan called for Monty to drive northeastward as rapidly as possible to join forces with the beachhead. Instead, Montgomery sat down to "gather his tail under him," while men of the Fifth Army were fighting desperately for a toehold, and apparently losing. Mark Clark got worried and transferred his headquarters from shore to a ship, ready to slip away to Sicily, if necessary. Meanwhile, Montgomery was "holding maneuvers" a hundred and fifty miles away and making no attempt to go to the rescue of Salerno. He was finally shamed into doing so when a group of correspondents piled into a car at Monty's headquarters and drove up to Salerno, making the first contact with the Fifth Army. They met no Germans on the way. In due course, Monty ordered his troops to follow the route the correspondents had pioneered. Salerno was saved.

The same thing happened at the Sangro River in Italy. I was with the Eighth Army at the time, and when they reached the Sangro there were almost no Germans defending the land beyond it. But Montgomery sat down again, for a long, cold month and when he did attack he found that the Germans had quite naturally set up strong defenses. Hundreds of Canadians died in taking Ortona, which had been undefended a month before. By this time, the "set-piece" battle was an obsession of Montgomery's. He even boasted about it. Having had 800 odd guns at El Alamein, he had added a few more to his pre-attack barrage at the Mareth Line. Then a few more at Catania, and finally an additional few at the Sangro. Thus correspondents could write, and in fact were almost compelled to write, that each successive bombardment was bigger than the previous combination of Alamein-Mareth-Catania-Sangro and so on through Caen-Antwerp and finally the Rhine crossing.

After his battles in the south, Monty's performance at Caen came as no surprise. Here, on the eastern end of the Allied beachhead in France, Montgomery's troops got ashore on D-Day without much trouble and here, once again, he sat down, dug in, and gathered his tail under him. Bradley broke through and captured Cherbourg. Monty stayed at Caen. The First U. S. Army cracked the line at St. Lô and Patton swept through to liberate Brittany. Monty stayed at Caen. The First Army swung around to Argentan. It was now D-Day plus five weeks and Monty's tail was at last under him. He massed his artillery, he attacked, he went a few miles to Falaise. He sat down. The Americans were stopped by orders at Argentan, forbidden to go forward to Falaise and close the gap through which the German Seventh Army was streaming eastward in helter-skelter withdrawal.

Twice more, Monty was to sit down. He sat while the American-British paratroops jumped into Arnheim, and failed to move his forces up to hold that vital bridgehead. Coming to the Rhine, he waited and waited and waited until he could get more guns than Alamein-Mareth-Catania-Sangro-Caen. The First Army grabbed the Remagen bridgehead. Monty waited on the Rhine. Patton made three crossings. Monty waited on the Rhine. At length, with the biggest barrage yet, with a week's-long smokescreen, Monty edged cautiously across. By that time, the outcome of the war had already been decided.

Through it all, Montgomery's well-known conceit was never ruffled. It was even strengthened by such stories as the one told of King George's visit to General Eisenhower. The King asked Ike, "General, what is your opinion of General Montgomery?"

"He is a fine general," Ike replied.

"Yes, yes, General Eisenhower, but what do you really think of him?"

"A first-rate leader of men, Your Majesty."

"I understand now, General Eisenhower, why they call you a diplomat first and a soldier second. But personally, what *is* your real opinion?"

"Well, to tell you the truth, Your Majesty, I think he is after my job."

"Oh, thank God!" said the King, visibly relieved. "I thought he was after mine."

Certainly, I know that we won the war. I know we had many great commanders on land, sea, and air, and know the fighting qualities of our citizen soldiers and sailors. But it took quite a while to separate the good leaders from the bad ones, in the last war, and even some of the bad ones remained in top jobs because of close political connections or by grace of membership in the Annapolis, West Point, or Air Forces fraternities.

The reason for pointing out now, after the war is won and over with, that there were some bad ones at the top is that the next war will be different from the last one. We must eliminate the bad ones now, while there is still time, and get men of brains, determination, and vision. When the rockets start flying—if they do—we won't have time for "Mark Time" tactics, for "gathering one's tail under one," for "tidying up." If our tails aren't under us when the shooting starts, they'll be blown off before we can get going.

Chapter Twenty-Five

A Bloodthirsty Scientist

WELL, IF WE AGREE THAT WE DON'T WANT THE admirals or generals to control atomic energy and through it the destiny of our world, how about selecting some scientists to rule mankind? All right, I give you one of them—an unprepossessing, long-haired, long-faced Englishman who sat around a table with us in the Crossroads Officers' Club on Bikini Island two days before the second act in that lavish and costly drama, "Dirty Work at the Crossroads."

He was about forty-five years old, this learned doctor, in a dirty-ish white shirt open at the neck, and his small-bowled pipe kept going out as for an hour and a half he told us how he would bring peace to the world. He had been allowed to join us over the misgivings of Major Smith, the security officer of CROSSROADS, who had been associated with him at Los Alamos and apparently already knew that this man of science would make some extraordinary statements.

"I don't like newspapers," the Englishman said by way of introduction. "Especially, I hate the *Chicago Tribune*. It is you chaps who cause all the trouble in the world. If I had my way I would close down all radio stations and newspapers for the next one hundred years."

"Well," said one of the five correspondents at the table, "you're not alone in disliking the *Chicago Tribune*. But isn't it rather drastic to propose to eliminate the only means by which the people of the world can get to know each other better and thus, perhaps, end the misunderstanding that causes wars? Do you honestly want to do that?"

We couldn't believe that the doctor was being serious.

"Certainly I would put an end to newspapers and the radio," he said, taking a gulp of beer from a bottle. "They cause all the trouble."

We started to bristle, "Look, you scientists invented the atomic bomb, not newspapermen. You invent all the murderous weapons. We don't do it."

"You start the wars," he said, "and all of you should be suppressed."

"Do you read the newspapers or listen to the radio, doctor?"

"I get all my information from *Time* magazine. There is a good medium of information."

There was a chorus of jeers. *"Time* frequently has been called as inaccurate and misinformed as any widely read publication. . . . It used to be a cocktail of frothy smart-talk shaken up by Yale sophomores."

"That's what I like about it," said the man of learning, sucking his teeth. "I like the smart cracks. They appeal to me. I like it because it hates Russia. But all the rest of you should be suppressed. You shouldn't be allowed to make any more wars."

"We don't make them," we said. "Guys like you do it."

"My life," the scientist said, "has been broken up by two wars. My brother was killed in the first one." He looked as if he were about to weep. "I don't propose under any circumstances to have my cloistered life at Oxford broken up again."

"So you hate the Russians, do you?"

"Ah, the Reds," he said, showing some animation. "I am interested in the Reds."

"I suppose you'd like to drop atom bombs on them."

"Yes," said the doctor, without a moment's hesitation, "I would."

"Right now, do you mean?"

"That's right," he said emphatically. "I'd like to drop a bomb on Moscow tomorrow morning at eight o'clock."

We shook our heads, still not believing our ears, and asked, "Are you kidding, or are you crazy?"

"I want to bomb Moscow tomorrow morning," he said. "I want to kill the ten top Soviet leaders. Then there will be revolt in Russia and I will be sure that my cloistered existence at Oxford will not be disturbed for the rest of my life."

"Then your cloistered life at Oxford is the most important thing in the world?"

"That's right. It was upset by two wars, even though I had fun for two years at Los Alamos in this one."

Somebody turned to Sam Shaeffer, and said, so the Englishman could hear, "This guy is just plain crazy. He should be locked up."

"There's nothing unique about him," said Sam, talking as if he were referring to a specimen. "I worked with scientists for years. They're the most narrow and ignorant men in the world, outside of their own specialties. They are stupid and dangerous."

"So you want the scientists to rule the world?" we asked the Englishman.

"Yes, certainly," he said. "And by the way, I'm getting a bit thirsty."

Somebody went to get a bourbon and soda for him and we studied the scientist closely and asked aloud, "Is the bastard drunk?" The consensus was that he was completely sober. He ignored the "bastard" as he took a pull at his drink and toyed with his pipe. At any minute we expected him to grin and say, "This is all a gag, boys. Have one on me." So we kind of calmed things down and Corney Ryan asked him to write two articles for the London press, summarizing the atomic tests which he had characterized as "a complete farce which will do nothing for mankind."

"Here is your chance," Ryan pointed out, "to give the public the correct and responsible impressions which you say ordinary reporters are incapable of producing. And wouldn't you like to see your byline in the papers?"

The professor declined. "I would be finished professionally. My colleagues would accuse me of seeking publicity." He paused and then went on. "A scientist should be a little man working in a little back room somewhere."

"Not, by any chance, working for the good of mankind?" I asked.

He fumbled with his pipe. "I say! You reporters are a soft-hearted lot. Prattling about the good of mankind." With those words, the battle was joined again.

"And we're finding out," one of the soft-hearted reporters said angrily, "that you scientific bastards are murderers. We understand now that it was you who insisted on dropping the atom bombs on Hiroshima and Nagasaki, when the Japs would have quit anyway without it. You made this atomic toy and you had to set it off."

He made no attempt at denial. "About sixty percent of the scientists at Los Alamos were in favor of dropping the bomb."

"So you killed and wounded three hundred and twenty thousand people to satisfy your scientific curiosity! We don't believe there was ever any justified reason for dropping the bomb."

He looked surprised and this time it was he who said, "You're not serious, are you? I always thought newspapermen were a hard-boiled, realistic lot, but actually you are all idealists and humanitarians. After all, what are three hundred and twenty thousand people?"

"The son of a bitch means it," somebody said. And went on to the Englishman, "So people, human beings, are nothing to you but objects for scientific experiment? I suppose you'd kill three hundred and twenty thousand people again tomorrow."

"Now," he protested, "don't be so soft-hearted. Of course, I would kill them tomorrow. I have already told you that if I had my way, the atom bomb would be dropped on Moscow tomorrow morning. I will do anything so that my cloistered life at Oxford is not disturbed again. Three hundred and twenty thousand people isn't so many in this world. I think you people have killed more with your lies in your newspapers."

"But we didn't kill those people that we saw lying in the hospitals in Hiroshima and Nagasaki, just waiting for death, while your fellow scientists studied them coldly to satisfy their curiosity about this new means of mass murder they had created."

"I say," he lit his pipe, "you *are* sentimentalists. Scientists are curious people. Their curiosity must be satisfied and nothing must get in the way of that satisfaction."

We turned back to the subject of bombing Moscow tomorrow morning at eight o'clock. "What," we asked, "makes you think destroying Moscow would insure your *pax atomica*?"

"It would make peace for my generation, and that is what is important. What happens afterward doesn't matter. There are two ways to have peace. One is to destroy Moscow and the other is to eliminate the little countries of the world. And don't forget that although America alone can make the atom bomb now, England also has atomic piles in Canada and we know how to make the bomb and will be making it soon."

"Intending, no doubt, to use it for the benefit of mankind?"

"Atomic energy," he answered quickly, "can serve no useful purpose for mankind."

We wanted to get all this on the record, word for word. Afterward we all went immediately back to our press ship and wrote down our notes and then compared them, so there could be no mistake in our reports of what we heard. And now we asked the Englishman,

"Isn't the function of science to clarify unknown things and make the world a better place?"

"The function of scientists," he said, "is to have fun. Satisfying our curiosity is where we have our fun."

"You son of a bitch," one reporter said.

Sam Shaeffer, who served in the marines, spoke up, "I have a little girl twenty months old. I hate to think of her with her arms and legs ripped off by an atom bomb to satisfy the curiosity of guys like you. That's what happened to the kids in Hiroshima and Nagasaki. It can happen in Washington, where I live. It would happen to the little children in Moscow which you propose to bomb tomorrow."

"You're a sentimentalist," the doctor answered.

Sam glared over his glasses. "Are you married? Do you have a child?"

"Yes, and I propose to get peace for myself and my family regardless of how many people have to die to insure it."

Shaeffer stood up, "You are ignorant of the world, like most scientists. Now you want political power. God help us, if you get it! You men have made the atomic bomb. You have isolated a toxin of which one ounce, placed in a city reservoir, could kill three hundred and fifty thousand human beings, although human beings mean nothing to you. You are a threat to civilization!"

I had another suggestion, "You know what ought to be done to you, doctor?" I said. "You should be placed up against that coconut tree and shot, not at eight o'clock tomorrow morning but right now."

The loudspeaker squawked, "Last boat for the 'Appalachian'!"

Last boat for hell, if men like the honored English scientist get control of the world. . . .

A trustworthy friend who lived with some of the world's outstanding scientists for more than two years at Los Alamos assures me that the Englishman's views do not represent those of his colleagues as a whole either on the subject of Russia or the question of science's obligations or lack of them to mankind. He agreed, though, that a majority of the scientists was extremely narrow and highly ignorant of matters outside its own highly specialized fields. "For every brilliant and well-rounded man like Compton of M.I.T., you'll find a hundred like your Englishman.

"There are both Russophobes and Russophiles among them," he stated. "Some of the latter are just as violent in their pro-Russian

291

views as the Englishman was anti-Russian. So much so, in fact, that you seriously wonder whether if put to the test they would not turn over atomic secrets to Russia in preference to their own country. Some of them, in Canada and England, have already tried to do this.

"Another group is passionately internationalist and insists that we must have a single, world-wide government of and for all nations, and that the atom bomb must be subjected to international control and supervision.

"Then there are groups within groups, little factions as vicious and malicious in their gossip and plotting and scheming as any thwarted small-town tongue-waggers. They deprecate the work of their rivals. They run down Dr. Vannevar Bush or Dr. Oppenheimer and resent their prominence. They suspect one another of Communistic or Fascistic leanings, or of being too closely allied with big business or having too liberal leanings.

"The cult of pure science is a dangerous thing. It worships 'X' to the ten-millionth power over the Einstein theory. Its icons are the glittering machines of the laboratory; its habiliments the white apron, rubber gloves, and eye shield. Its priests are fanatics of their one, true religion.

"Many such men know neither devotion to country nor to mankind. Thus the German scientists kidnapped by the United States Army (to keep them from falling into Russian hands) and brought to this country after the war to work on rocket-propelled missiles, were perfectly happy to go on with their chores. And not only Germans are like that."

My friend described his "favorite character, a Chicago doctor and one of our leading scientists. He attended the meetings of the Chicago group of Manhattan District, but he refused to be enrolled as 'present' or have his name associated with the work."

What this scientist said was, "For all I know the Germans may still win the war. And they will get a list of those who worked on nuclear fission and developed the atomic bomb. Those will be the ones who will be executed first as war criminals. I'll do everything I can to help make the bomb, but keep my name out of it."

"And that," said my friend, "is an example of a scientist and a real, red-blooded patriot."

"Then you don't want the scientists to get political power?" I asked.

"God spare us that, brother!" he answered feelingly.

292

Well, then, how about letting newspapermen control atomic energy? Not on the basis of their performance at OPERATIONS CROSS-ROADS!

The best-known, scientifically speaking, of all the reporters at Bikini was one William L. Laurence, representative of the *New York Times*. Russian-born and now near his sixties, Laurence has a battered nose and ears that give him the look of a worn-out pugilist of a half-century back and which conceal a sharp brain and a penchant for lurid adjectives. For a long time Laurence had the atom-bomb story all to himself, having been selected by the War Department to cover the Los Alamos developments when the bomb was tested and to ride in the bomber that attacked Nagasaki. Thus the War Department, making available for the exclusive use of Laurence all of the material for the first story on the New Mexico test, placed Laurence in an unchallengeable role as an authority. In that position, Laurence had a serious obligation to his editor and to the public—to report in sober and truthful detail the facts of this portentous development. With man's fate at stake, it was a story that should neither be exaggerated nor underwritten.

Until the "Able" test at Bikini lagoon on the morning of July 1, 1946, no other newsman had seen an atomic explosion and none could question Laurence's word, which was as God's law. On the way out to Bikini on the press ship, he held forth at great length on the terrible sight we were to witness. He scared hell out of us. He put the fear of the atomic god into Dr. Karl Compton, head of M. I. T. and of the presidential Evaluation Board. Compton, even though he was wearing welder's glasses and was in an airplane twenty miles away, covered his eyes with his forearm at the moment of the explosion. One of the science writers on the "Appalachian," after listening to Laurence, was so terrified that he protested against the ship being stationed twenty miles from the lagoon and predicted all aboard would be atomized in a single searing second.

Having prophesied what would happen, Laurence saw on that bright July morning an "awe-inspiring, spine-chilling, blood-curdling spectacle." He told of a glare so bright no human eye could behold it without being blinded. He described a mighty thunder "that seemed to fill all space as if the Gods were angry" at mankind.

Well, "that ain't the way I heer'd it." I checked with the doctors on our ship and they said not a single case was reported of a chilled

293

spine or of curdled blood. Nobody was blinded. Standing within a few feet of Laurence on the "Appalachian" was a sailor from the Bronx who dared to stare straight at this atomic sunburst without the protection of dark goggles. He wasn't affected in the slightest. Laurence heard a "mighty thunder that seemed to fill all the space," but to other listeners it seemed a low, distant rumble that scarcely more than whispered against the eardrums.

Laurence's impressions, of course, did no harm. But some reporters, with their expectations of being blinded, buffeted by high winds, thrown to the deck, and partially deafened, reacted in a bad way. They had been conditioned to expect a stupendous spectacle produced solely for its sensual effect on them. None of this happened and their reaction was childish. Without waiting to find out what the bomb had done, they recorded their petulant resentment at being cheated and wrote the bomb off as a partial dud and the test as a failure. By contrast, they underwrote the atom bomb's results.

Let me say at this point, though, a word about the predictions of possible disaster made by scientists. It was scientists who said that the earth's crust would be cracked, that there would be terrible tidal waves and similar terrifying and damaging phenomena. The newspapermen simply reported what they said and in so doing fell into an error common to newspaper editors and the general public alike. If some religious crackpot predicts that the world will end next Tuesday, the editors either give him no space at all or print a humorous story. But let some bird with a B.Sc. after his name come forth with some similar warning and it is picked up by the Science Editor of the nearest wire service and appears in 1500 newspapers. Post-Bikini, we have a little more data than formerly on which to judge the scientists.

The outcome of the scientific predictions and of some newsmen's copy from Bikini was that many of the public, like the admirals, decided that the reports of atomic-bomb destruction at Hiroshima and Nagasaki had been exaggerated. They agreed with de Seversky and the air generals that the bomb was "just another weapon" and nothing to worry about. This, of course, is the most dangerous possible conclusion that can be reached. The bomb can blow our civilization into ruins. We must remember that and do something about it, before it is too late. . . .

As far as I can see, one of the few persons still eligible to control the bomb is King Juda, formerly of Bikini and now of Rojerik atoll. This sturdy, none-too-bright ruler of the 135 people whose ancestors lived peacefully on remote Bikini for unrecorded centuries is a practicing Christian, a hymn singer, and practicer of the Golden Rule. He is also an unsophisticate in the ways of power politics and nationalisms, so that it was easy for the Navy to talk him into evacuating his pitifully tiny segment of the earth's surface—just barely "surface" at that—to be used in an experiment "for the good of mankind." Of course, there were other uninhabited atolls nearby but the Navy had decided on Bikini and Bikini it had to be.

It was no new experience for the Navy to be fast-talking Pacific Islanders. For decades they have imposed a dictatorial and despotic rule over the natives of Pacific Islands, for instance those of Guam and American Samoa, whose inhabitants are American "nationals" but not citizens and whose king has been an American naval officer. Did you know, for instance, that it was against the law for a Gaumanian to whistle "Yankee Doodle Dandy" or "The Star-Spangled Banner?" Or any other tune, for that matter, because some years ago an American commander was annoyed by the whistling of the cheerful Chamorros and decreed that henceforth they would not be allowed to whistle.

So the Navy asked Juda, "Will you help mankind?"

Certainly, said Juda. Unlike the people of Connecticut who did not want to give up a few square miles of their state for the United Nations, he and his tribe gave up all they owned—a few palm-bedecked spots of sand that man needed for his most awesome experiment. If you asked Juda through his interpreter what the world should do with the atom bomb, he would probably say:

"What is the purpose of the bomb?"

"To kill people, to set them on fire, to burn down their cities, to maim them, to poison them by unseen rays."

"And what good can it do for mankind?"

"None whatever. No bomb does any good for mankind."

"Then," Juda would rule, "let us make no more bombs."

That's damn good advice, and if we are smart, we will take it.

12/1/47